Blockchain and Crypto Assets

Investment Guide

by HashKey Capital

The Commercial Press

Blockchain and Crypto Assets Investment Guide

Author: HashKey Capital

Editor: Chris Cheung

Cover design: Cathy Chiu

Publisher: The Commercial Press (H.K.) Ltd.
8/F, Eastern Central Plaza, 3 Yiu Hing Road, Shaukeiwan, Hong Kong

Distributor: SUP Publishing Logistics (HK) Limited
16/F, Tsuen Wan Industrial Centre, 220-248 Texaco Road, Tsuen Wan, N.T., Hong Kong

Printer: Elegance Printing and Book Binding Co. Ltd.
Block A, 4th Floor, Hoi Bun Industrial Building
6 Wing Yip Street, Kwun Tong, Kowloon, Hong Kong

©2022 The Commercial Press (H.K.) Ltd.
First edition, Second printing, Oct 2022

ISBN: 978 962 07 6689 3
Printed in Hong Kong, China

Contents

PART 2   EMERGING INDUSTRY AND NEW PARTICIPANTS – THE COMPOSITION OF BLOCKCHAIN'S ECOSYSTEM

CRYPTO ASSET INVESTMENT: FROM THE FRINGES TO THE MAINSTREAM

David Swenson, who was back to the Investment Office of Yale University in 1985, grew Yale's endowment fund from US$1 billion to the current US$31 billion in approximately three decades. Swenson's death in May 2021 has prompted an outpouring of tributes from investment professionals globally. He is considered the "godfather" of the institutional investment, who pioneered the "Yale model" that has been massively adopted by the investment circles.

Typically, university endowment funds are considered to adopt the most conservative investment style worldwide. However, David Swenson has reformed the set rules and introduced three new initiatives in the fund's allocation and portfolio: first, allocation of capital into alternative investments such as venture capital, private equity, and hedge funds into the portfolio; second, embracing physical assets such as commodities and even forest land into fund allocation; and third, expanding the investment horizon into emerging markets. Swenson's foresight and wisdom are at the core of why the Yale Endowment stands out for its long-term steady returns.

Alternative assets and alternative investment strategies are always an evolving methodology. There is no best, only better. Since Bitcoin was introduced in 2009, a new asset class – crypto assets – has begun to attract the attention of investors. We can still recall that in 2010, someone paid 10,000 Bitcoins for two pizzas. As of early 2022, one

Bitcoin is worth around US$40,000. Not to mention the overall market capitalization of crypto assets is close to US$2 trillion.

This is the right time! As professional investment institutions or qualified investors, we can no longer afford the opportunity cost of ignoring crypto assets as an alternative asset. We should seriously explore whether and how we can include crypto assets into our portfolio and develop alternative strategies for crypto asset investment with an optimistic attitude towards new technologies, new trends, and new worlds. On August 6, 1991, Tim Berbers-Lee publicly introduced the World Wide Web (WWW) on the internet. By around 2000, just ten years later, when the current internet giant market had largely taken shape, the stocks of these internet companies were arguably the best-performing assets in the past 20 years. It has been just over a decade since the Bitcoin blockchain was born in 2009, and today blockchain technology is starting to mature and early blockchain use cases are starting to emerge. It is probably time for crypto assets to take over internet stocks, and contribute with the best returns in the next two decades.

Eric Beinhocker, the Executive Director of the Institute for New Economic Thinking at the Oxford Martin School, in his book *The Origin of Wealth* tells an interesting story: when he went to Kenya to do fieldwork, the local Maasai asked about Beinhocker's wealth, and when they learned that the professor's family did not even have a single cow, they wondered how someone so "poor" could afford to travel such long distances to Kenya and take a camera appeared to be quite expensive. For a Maasai tribesman, wealth is measured in cattle. For people in modern society, it is measured by a string of characters in a bank account. In the future, people's wealth will be measured in crypto assets inside their digital wallets.

According to Beinhocker, "wealth is created through an evolutionary process". He noted that the explosion in wealth in human history began in 1750, and that "over 97 percent of total wealth was created in the just last 0.01 percent period of time of human history." The professor believes that the underlying logic lies in the technological revolution represented by Newton's theory and the social revolution led by Britain and the United States, which greatly accelerated the speed of wealth creation. Crypto assets, on the other hand, are the new form of wealth evolution – the digital form of wealth, under the general historical trend of the digital revolution of human society following the industrial revolution and the information revolution.

Starting from 2021, global crypto asset investment and trading have started to move from the fringes to the mainstream: major banks in Europe and the United States have launched custody services for crypto assets; the SEC has approved Bitcoin ETFs; various crypto asset private investment funds have exceeded a total of US$50 billion in AUM; many private banks or wealth management institutions have started to provide crypto asset trading and custody services for eligible clients; Visa, PayPal and even Apple Pay have integrated Bitcoin payments and transactions; Coinbase, the world's largest digital currency exchange, has been listed on Nasdaq.

With the growing interest in crypto-asset investment, there is a real need for a comprehensive and in-depth guidebook on crypto-asset investment. HashKey Capital team has compiled the book, *Blockchain and crypto assets investment guide*, collecting years of pioneering investment experience in crypto-assets, in response to the demand of clients and the market. This book comes just at the right time and will benefit all in the crypto community.

Here I would like to wish this book a great success!

Feng Xiao
Vice Chairman, China Wanxiang Holdings Co., Ltd.
Founder, Wanxiang Blockchain Labs

BLOCKCHAIN AND CRYPTO ASSET INVESTMENT – THE START OF A NEW REVOLUTION

It has been over a decade since the birth of blockchain as an revolutionary technology which transformed pieces of computer code into a new asset class worth US$2 trillion. While blockchain as an industry is still in the early stages, we are thrilled to see blockchain starting to make its mark in the next generation of technology and business, such as cross-border payments, supply chain, IoT, and central bank digital currencies. There is no doubt that investment institutions have played a vital role in the mainstream adoption of blockchain and crypto assets. If blockchain technology and crypto assets are a bold experiment being made to the traditional financial system, investment institutions can be considered as the catalysts of this great adventure, which is a perfect match to this emerging industry. Professor Tom Nicholas of Harvard University described, in his book, *VC, An American History*, venture capital as a state of mind that manifests a great desire for innovation, risk-taking, and pursuit for reward.

Since 2008, the world has seen advances in technology innovation, as well as human and societal, with the birth of technology giants like the FAANG in the U.S. and Tencent and Ali in China, reflecting huge opportunities for investment institutions. The internet, built two economic cycles ago, has grown fruits for investors over the last decade. Blockchain and crypto assets were created during the Global Financial Crisis, and are likely to yield outperforming results in the next economic cycle. Nowadays at least 100 crypto projects have reached the threshold of the traditional definition of unicorn. The huge opportunities that lie in this emerging industry have already been eyed by mainstream institutions other than the native crypto communities. Diem, a global payment and financial network developed by Facebook (Meta) and acquired by Silvergate is building a set of infrastructures for global users; Coinbase, the world's largest compliant exchange, has already been listed on Nasdaq in 2021 with a relatively high market capitalization of over US$90 billion, and many other crypto projects have started preparing for their public listing. Conservative estimates suggest that the total valuation of crypto assets and blockchain projects could reach at least US$10 trillion in the next two to three industry cycles.

HashKey Capital, as an early VC manager engaged in blockchain and crypto asset investment boasts an experienced team that has been investing in blockchain projects since 2014. In 2018, HashKey Capital started planning its investments to cover all the subsectors in the industry in an institutional operation model. Bearing in mind the philosophy of long-term investment and value investing, HashKey Capital, together with its affiliates have invested in more than 400 projects in total, and has been deeply involved in many well-known projects such as Ethereum, Polkadot, Dfinity, Cosmos, and so on in the early days to contribute to the blockchain and crypto asset world. By engaging deeply in the ecosystem construction and supporting the developers of different projects while making investments, our dream of growing together with the crypto community has gradually turned into reality. Going through peaks and valleys, we have gained many experiences and lessons throughout crypto asset investment journey, at the same time elevating our knowledge towards the entire crypto world.

It is our long-held methodology to leverage traditional finance experience into blockchain and crypto assets investment activities.

The methodology that we can draw from traditional finance lies in the framework for evaluating assets and teams, the tools for fund management and the ways to articulate our vision and mission to investors who intend to enter the space. The development of the blockchain industry is not only in the technology part, but also in the portfolio management of these new alternative assets. The essence behind this is the rival between public chains and consortium chains, where consortium chains can be the compliant solutions adopted by the mainstream institutions, while crypto assets generated from public chains will be the first to be accepted by investment institutions. In addition, the open infrastructure of public chains will reshape the entire financial system in a long-term perspective.

Crypto assets' uniqueness lies in that there is not a befitting traditional valuation framework that can be applied here. Most crypto assets derive their value from consensus, and to measure the value of consensus is more of an art, not a science. With the emergence of decentralized finance (DeFi), we have further found that applying the experience of the traditional finance industry is the right path to take, and the DeFi industry has proven to generate considerable cashflows for which traditional methods are perfectly applicable. This is the biggest change in crypto assets we have seen since 2020. The increasing applicability of the methodology means that more traditional institutions can understand this industry, and there we will finally going to have a group of crypto unicorns that can stand alongside that of the traditional internet and consumer industries.

The role of crypto investment institutions is to precisely identify opportunities and manage risks, making investments that can cover different subsectors after iterative and careful thinking. Like the classic Chinese book on Weiqi – *The Book of Go* says: "When it comes to choosing strategies for a Go game, it is important to be connected to each move throughout the whole game. From the beginning to the end, each move seeks to take the initiative." By participating in ecosystem building, we are looking for the strategic/key sectors that can lead us to the future, driving the development of the ecosystem with investment, which in turn, brings investment opportunities. Through this way, we can ensure the first-mover advantage, thus forming a closed loop of investment and ecosystem construction.

We are publishing this book to sum up our years of experience and thoughts on investment from an institutional perspective. On the other hand, with the entry of mainstream institutions and maturity of the crypto world, we hope to provide some insights on the crypto industry for our peers who are about to or have already started their crypto journey. The structure of this book reflected our cognition, where the first part provides a vertical analysis on the evolution of blockchain and crypto history, the second part horizontally scanning the industry and ecosystem, and the third part, the strategies and practices of the investment management framework, is the essence of the whole book. With such a concise structure, we hope to bring the most intuitive feeling and experience to readers.

The journey of investment in the emerging industry of blockchain and crypto assets can be said to be the paradise of the most adventurous individuals in the new world. We are excited about the picturesque landscapes of the new world, where words cannot describe everything. However, with the mindset of openness, transparency, and inclusiveness of crypto culture, we dare not enjoy it exclusively, therefore writing them down in this book for the benefit of the readers.

PART 1

BRIEF HISTORY OF BLOCKCHAIN AND ENCRYPTED ASSETS

CHAPTER 1

THE AGE OF GEEKS: WHEN ENCRYPTED ASSETS WERE STILL UNCONVENTIONAL TOYS

The Bitcoin Genesis can always be traced back to the cyberpunk community, being literally a combination of cyber and punk. It is a science fiction story that depicts the social collapse and reorganization in the high-tech future. The Declaration of the Independence of Cyberspace (1996) stated that "The cyberspace is an independent world", a proposition with a potentially strong connotation to crypto. From cyberpunk, there came the cyberpunk culture, which is a collection of rock music, hippies, religion, utopian ideas, cyberpunk, freedom and rebellion. 1,400 geeks, including many influential figures in the internet community, discussed their visions of the future freely through the Cypherpunks mailing list. Among them was an epoch-making name – Satoshi Nakamoto. Later in the story, Bitcoin came into being with the emergence of blockchain technology, and an unprecedented trend swept the globe.

Today, we can still find the cyberpunk philosophy in the blockchain field, such as advocating technology, privacy protection, personal heroism and pursuing institutional evolution and transcendence of individual values. Nowadays we see that the blockchain has moved towards an extremely inclusive attitude, which is in line with the cyberpunk spirit. The Bitcoin seeds and their germination are not affected by the mainstreaming blockchain adoption, without which, these seeds would not grow into the exceptional products that we have the privilege to deal with. Every Bitcoin characteristic still influences each of its participants. Let's uncover the story of this great era from its very beginning.

The term cyberpunk was first proposed by Eric Hughes in his *A Cypherpunk's Manifesto* published in 1993. However, "cyberpunk" was quietly emerging in the San Francisco Bay area as a technology trend before that. The group of cyberpunks was composed of some "genius geeks" and IT elites, including Tim May, a scientist from Intel, Julian Assange the founder of WikiLeaks, Tim Berners Lee, the inventor of the World Wide Web, Sean Parker, one of the co-founders of

Facebook, and, of course, Satoshi Nakamoto, the father of Bitcoin. Their purpose was clear: pursuing the ultimate freedom and privacy, with robust cryptographic algorithms to protect personal information and privacy from attacks on the internet, rather than relying on large organizations such as governments and enterprises to protect individual privacy. In the 1990s, blind signature, PGP, HashCash, B-money and peer-to-peer technology were created in succession, laying a foundation for the birth of blockchain. However, these technologies were too novel and ahead of time to be used widely. As time went on, the group of cyberpunks disbanded. In October 2008, an anonymous person named Satoshi Nakamoto released a White Paper – "Bitcoin: P2P E-cash System" – to the cyberpunk mailing list, which directly drew on the models of B-money and HashCash while overcoming their limitations. As a result, the concept of blockchain became widely known for the first time.

1.1 Genesis: Bitcoin was born from the economic crisis

Since its birth, the internet has expanded and developed, gradually forming a virtual world parallel to the physical world. While having many intersections, the two worlds are distinctive from each other. However, the internet serves only as of the technologies and tools for the traditional financial industry, whereas its original intention at its birth has been forgotten with decades of development. The borderless internet is disintegrating, and it is increasingly accepted that the internet has borders, and countries are tightening their regulation of the internet. However, early cyberpunks have been trying to build a financial and monetary system on the internet to enable real-time money transfers around the world. On November 1, 2008, Nakamoto published the Bitcoin white paper on the internet, which integrated and optimized previous attempts to create "electronic money" by other cyberpunks. On January 4, 2009, Nakamoto created the first Bitcoin block – the GenesisBlock – from a small server in Helsinki, Finland, and won the block reward of 50 Bitcoins. That was the start of his legendary career. Brief yet clear, the Bitcoin white paper explains the necessity of the decentralized cash system and clarifies the blockchain technology adopted, including the Proof of Work consensus mechanism, the BTC incentive/economic model, transaction signatures and verification based on asymmetric cryptography. The Bitcoin network is immune to attack by any individual as long as there are enough users maintaining it. Also, the consensus and unity of the network can be achieved, thus solving the Byzantine Generals problem, as long as the majority of users are honest.

Bitcoin was born during the financial crisis. In 2008, the United States suffered a severe subprime mortgage crisis. To cope with this situation, the United States launched a quantitative easing policy, kept printing money, and even channeled public resources into saving the domestic real estate market. What happened in America also caused a global financial tsunami, with stock markets plunging as investors stampeded out, exchange rates fluctuating dramatically, and assets in everyone's hands depreciating. Against this backdrop, Bitcoin, which has limited supply, could offer an alternative to withstand inflation in economic development without centralized control.

1.2   The disappearance of Satoshi Nakamoto

In December 2010, Satoshi Nakamoto published his last article in the Bitcoin forum, mentioning some issues in the latest version of the software, and then stopped appearing publicly, only keeping in touch with only a few people from the core Bitcoin development team via email. Satoshi Nakamoto's disappearance added into Bitcoin a legendary element, which also cleared the way for its development. Bitcoin became more decentralized, where everyone could access it with no one in a dominant position. Perhaps Satoshi Nakamoto foresaw the obstacles he might bring to Bitcoin's development. He learned from the failures of his predecessors and left silently when Bitcoin went on track.

In 2017, Mike Hearn, an early Bitcoin developer, disclosed all his email correspondence with Nakamoto between 2009 and 2011. In an email on April 12, 2009, Satoshi Nakamoto predicted that Bitcoin could become a worldwide payment system like Visa. On December 1, 2018, Satoshi Nakamoto's P2P Foundation account (where Bitcoin was first published and the code open sourced) was suddenly updated with only one word: nour, after he added Wagner Tamanaha, a marketing expert, as a friend. The account was hacked in 2014, making it uncertain whether the update was done by himself.

1.3　Transactions: Early Bitcoin payment

As an electronic currency, Bitcoin can be transferred and support physical transactions. On January 12, 2009, Nakamoto moved 10 of the 50 Bitcoins he mined to Hal Finney, an early Bitcoin developer, making it the very first Bitcoin transfer. On May 22, 2010, a programmer named Laszlo Hanyecz bought two pizzas (about US$40) with 10,000 Bitcoins, which marked the first real-life transaction using Bitcoin. On February 25, 2018, Laszlo Hanyecz again paid for two pizzas (about US$62) with Bitcoins. Yet, he spent only 0.00649 Bitcoin this time.

1.4 Bitcoin was given a new role – A store of value

In the ten-plus years since the birth of Bitcoin, the price has undergone multiple violent fluctuations, ten-fold increases, and 50% falls. Still, it is going upward generally, gaining millions of times in just over ten years, more than any asset in human history. In 2020, institutional investors joined the game and drove Bitcoin to a record-high of US$40,000. Mainstream institutions have gradually recognized Bitcoin.

Despite the considerable success, Bitcoin has not become a mainstream means of payment, which essentially deviates from the original vision set in the white paper. A typical BTC transfer needs to be confirmed by six blocks (for one hour), and even longer for large-amount transfers. It is too inefficient to be used for everyday transactions. However, Bitcoin provides a pseudonymous alternative for online transfer. This is the first time in human history to use technical means to guarantee the sanctity of private property. Without the control of centralized banks, capital can flow more freely. Meanwhile, the risks become higher as it offers a way for some illegal transactions.

Today, the significance of Bitcoin lies more in the storage of value and the free global circulation of assets. Investors tend to take it as an alternative to withstand inflation due to its limited supply. It serves as a safe haven asset in countries with political instability and frequent wars.

1.5 Community: The cyberpunks' utopia

In the early days, there were three Bitcoin forums: Bitcointalk.

org founded by Satoshi Nakamoto, Bitcoin.org by Bitcoin developer Matti Malmi and the Bitcoin subreddit section on Reddit. They all have administrators, opinion leaders and important participants and involve a certain degree of community governance. The early Bitcoin Foundation was established in 2012 in response to the questions from the U.S. government about the legitimacy of Bitcoin. Over the next couple of years, the Foundation played a role in the development and community governance before disappearing from the scene after 2015.

Hal Finney, Gavin Andresen and Cobra, the early promoters of Bitcoin we are familiar with, have many connections with the early community.

Hal Finney and Phil Zimmermann jointly created the earliest anonymous remailer PGP in the early 1990s and created the first reusable proof of work system in 2004. He is also an active member of the Extropians movement, trying to address the problems of Transhumanism and the extension of life expectancy. The first transaction in Bitcoin's history took place between Satoshi Nakamoto and Hal Finney. As early as a decade ago, he was one of the first to join the Bitcoin open-source coding and developer community. In 2009, Finney got his first bitcoin from Nakamoto. Then, he was diagnosed with Amyotrophic Lateral Sclerosis (ALS) and passed away on August 28, 2014, with his body kept at a low temperature of minus 196 degrees Celsius in anticipation of future thawing once medical technology is advanced enough. He was one of the first adopters of human body freezing technology.

Satoshi Nakamoto invited Gavin Andresen to join the Bitcoin community in 2010 and has been building a software development team ever since. He was one of the five developers who could change the Bitcoin codes and process Bitcoin transactions. In 2010, he built the Bitcoin Faucet website to give each visitor 5 Bitcoins for free, aiming to accelerate the circulation of Bitcoin around the world as soon as possible. In 2012, he founded the Bitcoin Foundation, the top tier of Bitcoin advocacy. After the Bitcoin Cash – BCH – fork, he became one of the most important proponents of Bitcoin Cash (BCH), which, in Gavin's view, is the closest thing to the Bitcoin chain initially envisioned by Satoshi Nakamoto.

Cobra was an early supporter of Bitcoin and shared administrative privileges with other administrators of the three Bitcoin community sites, Bitcoin.org, r/Bitcoin and Bitcointalk.org, but Cobra himself, like Satoshi Nakamoto, has remained anonymous.

In the community, cyberpunks worked together to discuss governance options, guide Bitcoin's development properly, and maximize its use cases. Since the beginning, participants regarded Bitcoin more as a social practice and did not run it as a company. Many of them did not recognize the potentially high value of Bitcoin.

1.6   Blockchain and Bitcoin

Bitcoin is generally believed to be a decentralized peer-to-peer and payment network based on blockchain technology. However, we cannot find the concept of "blockchain" in the Bitcoin white paper but rather find the concept of blocks in the form of ledgers and the chain structure connecting the blocks together. Therefore, in the early days, the term was block chain instead of blockchain that we currently use. Today, most people start to know this decentralized peer-to-peer network with Bitcoin and then move into blockchain technology. Bitcoin was born out of the cyberpunk spirit in the context of the financial crisis, taking on the hope of cyberpunks to change the current situation.

Eric Hughes shows how cyberpunks value privacy protection and information freedom in his *A Cypherpunk's Manifesto* published in 1993.

- *Privacy is necessary for an open society in the electronic age.*
- *The freedom of speech, even more than privacy, is fundamental to an open society.*
- *Each party to a transaction have knowledge only of that which is directly necessary for that transaction.*
- *Privacy in an open society requires an anonymous transaction system.*
- *Privacy in an open society also requires cryptography.*
- *To encrypt is to indicate the desire for privacy.*
- *Electronic technologies allow for anonymous privacy.*
- *Cypherpunks are dedicated to building anonymous systems.*
- *Cypherpunks deplore regulations on cryptography, for encryption is fundamentally a private act.*
- *The Cypherpunks are actively engaged in making the networks safer for privacy. Let us proceed together apace.*

We have realized that all pursuits and ambitions of the cyberpunks can be found in Bitcoin. It is fair to say that Bitcoin carries cyberpunks' dream and brings it into reality. Bitcoin technology integrates the pioneers' e-cash, B-money and P2P, and creatively adopts a chain-based structure for data, which is arguably the masterpiece of the geek era.

There is no way to find out why the ceiling of Bitcoin is 21 million coins, for which the creator Satoshi Nakamoto's choice is the only explanation. Of course, even if other quantities were chosen as the upper limit, they would also be questioned. Therefore, it might be more appropriate to attribute it to personal preferences. A more accepted assumption is that the number comes from the movie, *The Hitchhiker's Guide to the Galaxy* that mentions "the Answer to Life, the

Universe and Everything is 42", of which 21 is half. Others believe this figure points to nothingness as 42 does not carry any meaning and is more like a scientist's creation.

1.7   Bitcoin copycats

Two years after the birth of Bitcoin, two new cryptocurrencies emerged in 2011. One was Namecoin, and the other was Litecoin which is still active on the stage of cryptocurrencies. Many characteristics of Bitcoin can be found in these two copycats.

Built on the domain name system, Namecoin is a Bitcoin fork. It is based on Bitcoin's code, with the same upper ceiling of 21 million coins. In September 2010, a discussion began on BitcoinTalk over a hypothetical system called BitDNS and Bitcoin universality. Gavin Andresen and Satoshi Nakamoto, who joined the discussion, supported the idea of BitDNS and announced the award for BitDNS on BitcoinTalk in December 2010. In June 2011, Wikileaks mentioned the project on Twitter. In block 19,200, Namecoin activated merged mining upgrade, allowing miners to mine Bitcoin and Namecoin simultaneously rather than having to choose between one and the other. The upgrade corrected the problem that miners jump from one blockchain to another when the previous one becomes more profitable.

Namecoin has an interesting slogan: Bitcoin frees money – Namecoin frees DNS, identities, and other technologies. Like Bitcoin, Namecoin also adopts the SHA-256d algorithm.

Litecoin was also released in 2011, six months after Namecoin, by Charlie Lee, a former Google engineer, with a cap of 84 million. Its withdrawal takes 2.5 min, 1/4 of Bitcoin's block time. However,

Litecoin has no intention of overtaking Bitcoin. The argument that "Bitcoin is gold while Litecoin is silver" still rings true. Litecoin is dedicated to improving the transaction performance of Bitcoin. It offers faster processing, lower fees, a more decentralized mining network and less scarcity. Today, Litecoin is still active on the stage of cryptocurrencies, remaining among the top 20.

DOGECOIN

Dogecoin was created for fun by the engineers Billy Markus and Jackson Palmer. It is special because of its unlimited issuance, whose logo is the famous Japanese Shiba Inu meme. Dogecoin has gained popularity as a meme. The name Doge came from a dog's name in an anime that was later associated with the Shiba meme. The emoji went viral on social networks and was rated the meme of the year.

Jackson Palmer, one of the co-founders of Dogecoin, decided to use Doge as the logo of the cryptocurrency he created for payments to attract a wider audience. He bought Dogecoin.com and used it as the main image for Dogecoin. When Markus saw it, he decided to join Palmer in its development.

Dogecoin is the result of a series of forks. Litecoin was forked into Junkcoin, which was further forked into Luckycoin, and Dogecoin was created from a Luckycoin fork. Adopting the same hashing algorithm as Litecoin, Dogecoin can also be mined with a Litecoin miner.

Dogecoin was created in December 2013, and in January 2014, its trading volume once exceeded that of Bitcoin. In 2015, its founder Palmer completely exited from the project and liquidated all his Dogecoins.

It was not until 2019 that Dogecoin seemed to come back to life again. Among the CEO candidates elected by the Dogecoin community in 2019, Elon Musk, Tesla CEO, got the most votes. Subsequently, Musk expressed his love for Dogecoin and began to release Dogecoin related content on Twitter from time to time. In May 2021, Dogecoin became the fourth largest digital asset in the world, trailing only Bitcoin, Ethereum and BNB.

Dogecoin has spread widely for many reasons. The first one is Elon Musk's strong advocacy. Second, meme culture is very much prevalent in the crypto world, and Doge's image also has a solid cultural base and continues to generate more memes on social networks. While the third is that, Dogecoin is easy to understand, with only the payment function. It is easier to be accepted by both insiders and outsiders than the complex functions of other crypto assets.

Therefore, the popularity of Dogecoin is more of a cultural and communication factor than the value of the currency. Although it could be seen as a joke cryptocurrency at the beginning, its evolution is driven by public adoption. In other words, the connotation of crypto assets is not determined by their creators. Instead, it is given more life by the community and culture surrounding it.

References

"Cypherpunk", https://www.jianshu.com/p/1fd307914104.

"Exploring the most mysterious community in cryptocurrency", https://bihu.com/article/1248260442.

CHAPTER 2

EARLY COMMERCIALIZATION: THE EMERGENCE OF THE CRYPTO ASSET INFRASTRUCTURE

The birth of Bitcoin in 2009 was followed by the continual construction of supporting financial infrastructure. Because of the financial attributes of Bitcoin, early entrepreneurs focused mainly on exchanges, wallets and miners. As these infrastructures keep upgrading, the investment value of the Bitcoin ecosystem is coming to light.

With all the major events in the Bitcoin development, the increasing trading volume and continuous innovation of exchanges support the sustainable development of which the endogenous demand is the basis. The number of cryptocurrency exchanges is increasing, so are players in the Bitcoin ecosystem. Repeated thefts and risk incidents happening at exchanges have increased the awareness of Bitcoin holders about the risks of trading and reminded exchanges of the paramount importance of keeping users' assets secure.

In terms of Bitcoin wallets, the technical threshold for a regular user was too high at the beginning, allowing very few to access and understand the wallets, which gave wallet service providers the time window for commercialization. Wallet service providers have gradually transitioned from a centralized trading model to independent operations and then to decentralization, where protecting user privacy and security is the primary goal. The Bitcoin bull market has stimulated miners' enthusiasm for mining. The continuous increase of computing power and difficulty of the whole network is the overall trend, and the mining methods are also constantly being updated. Such an ecosystem has given birth to many mining pool service providers and miner equipment manufacturers, and the continuous upgrading and iteration of mining pools and miners have further increased the chance of getting Bitcoin. Instead of selling Bitcoin for profits instantly, more and more miners choose to accumulate them and wait for appreciation.

Some early VCs also saw the investment value of the Bitcoin ecosystem — a high-risk and high-yield asset class that fits quite well with venture capital's investment strategy and risk appetite. VCs are at the forefront of the institutional investment in crypto assets. They helped start-up teams with financing to build new blockchain projects. Just like in the 1990s when enormous funds were poured into internet enterprises, these commercial projects have opened the door to wealth for VCs in future.

2.1　The emergence of commercial infrastructure

After the birth of Bitcoin, a group of early entrepreneurs saw the commercial value of this new type of currency. To drive its commercial value and make it more widely accepted, these intelligent value discoverers started to build the commercial infrastructure such as exchanges, wallets and mining pools, laying a foundation for the later market boom.

2.1.1　The first generation of exchanges

(1) The first BTC exchange in the world: Bitcoinmarket.com

March 2010 saw the emergence of the Bitcoin Market, the world's first Bitcoin exchange. On January 15, 2010, DWDollar, a user on the Bitcointalk forum, first proposed the idea of a Bitcoin exchange in an attempt to create a free marketplace in which people could buy and sell Bitcoin. In this marketplace, Bitcoin was regarded as a commodity that could be traded and valued in U.S. dollars. The Bitcoinmarket.com platform went live two months later, supporting automatic custody transactions and PayPal for payments. Initially, the platform did not have much trading volume, with a Reddit post on March 17 that had this to say: "Now there are nine registered users, but only three deposited. Of the nine users, four were handled by me. We just had our first real transaction today at noon." In addition, as Bitcoinmarket.com was the first of its kind, it had many loopholes. The platform was buggy when running, and the developers had to keep fixing it. As the price of Bitcoin soared, the number of fraudsters also increased. On June 4, 2010, the platform eventually removed the PayPal payment option due to a user's fraud. The trading volumes began to shrink rapidly, resulting in the shutdown of Bitcoinmarket. com later that month. Bitcoin Market was a flash in the pan. There is still no way to know the exact date when it was closed until today. Despite the closure of Bitcoin Market, the emergence of the exchange is a milestone in the history of Bitcoin.

(2) MT. Gox, a giant of a generation

In July 2010, Jed McCaleb, an American entrepreneur and a big fan of Bitcoin who later co-founded Ripple, launched MT. Gox, which became the successor of Bitcoin Market. By 2014, the Bitcoin trading volume on the exchange reached 70% of the world's total. MT. Gox was much more advanced technologically than Bitcoinmarket.com, which could better the security of the assets under its custody. Since MT. Gox ran 24×7 and was fast in handling transactions, it has reached a trading volume exceeding US$100 in a single day within its first week and became the world's largest Bitcoin exchange in less than a month. On February 9, 2011, the price of Bitcoin hit over US$1 on MT. Gox, making it the top trading platform.

There is also an interesting episode behind the creation of MT. Gox. In Jed's words, MT. Gox came at a quite convenient time. The founder, Jed McCaleb, is a legendary entrepreneur – he created the file transfer network eDonkey in 2000, which was one of the largest file-sharing networks in the world at that time. Therefore, Jed was honored as the "father of eDonkey" by fans of the application. After eDonkey was closed, Jed was introduced to Bitcoin in 2010, and realized that there was a very important link – a trading mechanism – missing in the Bitcoin industry. There was no technical difficulty in creating such a trading platform for Jed, and he filled the gap in the industry in July 2011. However, as he did not take Bitcoin exchange as his lifelong pursuit, six months later, he sold the website to Mark Karpelès, a French developer, and moved on to his next project, Ripple (an open payment network based on distributed financial technology). Mark Karpelès was a French developer living in Japan, known as "Fat French" because of his body figure. After taking over MT. Gox, he gained quite much prominence in the Bitcoin community, who was not only selected to the board of the Bitcoin Foundation but also became the most powerful man in the Bitcoin community.

While MT. Gox became a giant, a crisis was coming. In February 2014, the exchange got hacked, with more than 850,000 Bitcoins worth US$7 billion being stolen, which shook the cryptocurrency community and sent Bitcoin price plummeting. MT. Gox declared bankruptcy, while Mark Karpelès was sentenced to jail. The whereabouts of the stolen Bitcoin remains a mystery to this day. This incident has always been a reminder to exchanges that the security of user assets is paramount.

2.1.2   The emergence of Chinese Bitcoin exchanges

Bitcoin has more than 13 years of history since its birth. China was one of the first countries to widely adopt Bitcoin. Driven by overseas Bitcoin exchanges, an increasing number of Chinese investors had a demand for Bitcoin trading. Entrepreneurs started to think about building a platform that would enable Chinese investors to buy and sell Bitcoin in RMB. BTC China (BTCC) was the dominant player in Bitcoin trading, while Gate.io focused on altcoin trading. Over time, the cryptocurrency trading platforms have evolved from the dominance of BTC China to the triumvirate of Binance, Huobi and OKCoin, with medium and small names blooming together.

(1) China's first Bitcoin exchange – BTC China (BTCC)

Launched on June 9, 2011, "BTC China" (BTCC), China's first exchange, once occupied 80% of the global market's trading volume, with Bitcoin price reaching as high as 150 RMB on the first day of its launch. BTCC provided a trusted platform for users to trade Bitcoin, where Chinese users could buy Bitcoin in RMB directly. BTCC led the way for digital currency exchange in China at the time, with almost all players choosing to trade Bitcoin on this platform.

At that time, Bitcoin was not as appealing for most investors as it is now. Yang Linke, the founder of BTCC, did not give up his sauna business while pioneering the digital currency industry and did not have much hope for Bitcoin. However, Bitcoin saw its first surge in 2013, with the price climbing over US$1,000. It was then that some Chinese players began to understand and buy digital currency to make money. Yang Linke became the first to test the water in China's virtual currency exchange space, and the exchange brought him a considerable fortune. On November 4, 2013, BTCC exceeded Mt. Gox and Bitstamp in terms of daily trading volume, making it the world's largest exchange in the world, with the highest single-day trading volume reaching over 80,000 Bitcoins and the highest daily trading volume exceeding RMB 200 million. Wallstreetcn.com also reported that BTCC sits firmly at the top in terms of the trading volume, with half of the market's Bitcoin trading volume coming from Chinese investors. The average Bitcoin price for the day was US$253. On September 4, 2017, the central bank banned ICOs and did not allow the issuance and trading of virtual currency. This ban ultimately ended the environment for exchanges to grow abruptly in China. On September 30, 2017, BTCC ceased its operations.

(2) Altcoin exchange – Gate.io

In April 2013, Bter, the emerging exchange that predecessed

Gate.io, was born. Its slogan on the official website was "Come with us to change the world". Unlike the other three of China's major exchanges, BTC China, Huobi and OkCoin that provided the trading of only Bitcoin and Litecoin, Gate.io also offered trading of altcoins. At that time, there were also other platforms focusing on altcoins, including Yuanbao and Bitcoin Age. It is said that any currency could be found at the exchange. Gate.io established its position by meeting the demand of targeted altcoin players. Different from large exchanges focusing on mainstream currencies, Gate.io decided to choose the altcoin niche market. However, the exchange was hacked many times because a good variety of altcoins were traded. Due to the lack of security awareness and cybersecurity practices during its early days, the trading system was frequently invaded by hackers, causing tremendous loss to the exchange and users. Coincidentally, beyond China and all around the world, exchanges were a common hacking attack target. In addition to Mt. Gox. mentioned before, Bitfinex, for example, lost 120,000 Bitcoins to a hacker in 2016, which were worth 72 million U.S. dollars. Bter also got hacked back in 2015. Under tremendous pressure, the hacked Bter bore all losses, promising that they would make up for users' losses. That was high-regarded in the crypto community. However, just like BTC China, as mentioned above, Bter was also subject to regulation by the central bank. On October 12, 2017, Bter declared ceasing all transactions. In the meantime, Gate.io was officially registered in the Cayman Islands, and it is still one of the most prominent exchanges in the world.

(3) Rising stars – Huobi, OKCoin

In September 2013, Li Lin founded huobi.com, a digital currency trading website. Dissatisfied with the trading experience in BTC China, Li Lin laid his eyes on the secondary market of Bitcoin. As a founder of "Renren Discount", he knew users' sensitivity to price well, and boldly proposed to exempt transaction fees just four months after its launch, which attracted a large number of users in a short time. Huobi thus became the first digital currency exchange in China that did not charge fees (resumed later in 2017), making it a rising star in the field of digital currency exchanges. In December 2013, the platform became the world's largest digital asset trading platform with a cumulative trading volume of RMB 30 billion, accounting for more than half of the crypto asset trading around the world. VCs were also very optimistic about the rise of Huobi. In November 2013, Huobi received investment from Zhen Fund and Dai Zhikang, an angel investor. Wang Qiang, a co-founder of Zhen Fund, said: "Huobi, must flourish!" In April 2014, huobi.com got another Series A funding of tens of millions of RMB from Sequoia Capital. Today, Huobi is not only a digital currency exchange but also engaged in blockchain technology research, project investment and ecosystem development, such as Huobi Research Institute and Huobi Eco-chain, which have an important position in the development of blockchain in China.

A few months after Huobi, OKCoin was launched in October 2013. The founder Xu Mingxing, having two unsuccessful business before made his third trial, started OKCoin, which reached a monthly transaction record of RMB 2.6 billion three months after its launch. In December, the volume reached RMB 4 billion a day. Now, OKCoin's monthly transaction volume remains around tens of billions, and the system can easily handle such a high transaction volume.

In addition to Bitcoin, seeing the market demand of Litecoin, OKCoin took the lead in opening Litecoin transactions and became the leading platform for Litecoin transactions in China. That was a brilliant and first-mover advantage for OKCoin as it was the only exchange available for Litecoin trading in China. Yang Linke from BTC China reluctantly said that OKCoin took their users away. Litecoin was initially priced between 1 RMB and 6 RMB, but later soared over 80 times to 380 RMB. This led to a rapid rise of OKCoin. Three months after its launch, the number of users exceeded 100,000. By the end of 2013, it completed Series A funding of tens of million RMB, becoming a major competitor of BTC China. Similarly, OKCoin suspended its RMB/Bitcoin trading from October 31, affected by the September 4th regulation, 2017, and gradually transformed into a brand for blockchain technology application and development. In June 2020, OKCoin was ruled by the court to be rebranded into OKEx and be associated with Beijing Lekuda Company.

2013 was the Warring States period of China's digital currency exchanges. There were five major exchanges offering mainstream coins such as Bitcoin, including BTC China, OKCoin, Huobi, China Bitcoin and BTCTrade. In addition, there were also exchanges focusing on altcoins, including Bter and Bitcoin Age. By then, the exchange sector in China was led by the five major exchanges and the other two altcoin exchanges. However, the September 4th regulation was a sword falling on China's exchanges. It was the darkest moment in China's cryptocurrency industry, with some exchanges closing their business, some going abroad, and some taking this opportunity to spring up.

2.1.3   Crypto wallets in the early days

Blockchain, in its essence, is a network of value via which crypto assets are transferred. Crypto assets are presented in a string of data, and this string of immutable data cannot be in our physical wallets. It is stored in high-tech wallets instead. That is how blockchain wallets came into being.

(1) The oldest Bitcoin wallet (client): Bitcoin-Qt (later renamed as Bitcoin Core)

Bitcoin Core is the first wallet software released by Satoshi Nakamoto in 2009, also known as the Bitcoin official wallet. This

Bitcoin client follows the principle of complete decentralization without the participation of servers. Payment and collection can be conducted on any computer. To use Bitcoin Core, users have to download full nodes on the chain and synchronize all data before using the wallet. Therefore, it is known as a full node wallet and is considered a strategy to increase blockchain redundancy in the early days when there were only a few nodes. At the same time, Bitcoin Core also supports mining, which means it is an implementation of the Bitcoin protocol. Additionally, it has absolute dominance in the market in terms of the number of users. Data is kept locally and cannot be hacked when disconnected from the internet. This means the highest degree of security and privacy. However, with the increase of Bitcoin network data, the shortcomings of the full node wallet are gradually exposed. These wallets require users to independently store data of the whole blockchain and download full nodes. Data on Bitcoin Core are updated slowly and take too much disk space and memory, where the storage space required to operate a node can even fill up a home PC. The wallet needs a backup every time it generates a new receiving address. If the backup fails, the private key of the new address cannot be recovered if it is lost. Consequently, Bitcoin Core is more suitable for high-end Bitcoin users. In addition, the files generated by Bitcoin Core are on the PC desktop and are easier to be stolen by malware. But the fact that the software is open source is respectable, which means no individual can manipulate its development. Therefore, it is also the best software among the Bitcoin protocol implementations.

(2) Independent wallets

In 2009, Bitcoin's main network was launched, and the blockchain was in its infancy. As a huge distributed ledger, Bitcoin only had simple functions of transfer and bookkeeping. Restricted by the development of blockchain technology, wallets back then were only used to store Bitcoin, i.e., a single-asset wallet. These wallets supported only one cryptocurrency, which is also known as the wallet 1.0 period (from 2009 to 2013). Since 2011, some blockchain agnostic wallets have gradually emerged in the Bitcoin wallet market, driving the construction of Bitcoin wallet facilities into a boom. The pioneers of these wallets include Blockchain.info and BitPay.

》　　@BitPay wallet

BitPay is arguably one of the most successful applications among wallets. On June 29, 2011, BitPay, a Bitcoin payment processor, launched the first Bitcoin e-wallet for smartphones. Thus, it is called the PayPal of digital currency, providing a payment solution for merchants that use Bitcoin for transactions. Merchants can convert the received Bitcoin into fiat via BitPay, with a 0.99% fee for each transaction. The initial business of BitPay included wallet and payments for customers, which was quite straightforward for users to create wallets and transactions with a high transfer efficiency. BitPay wallet has been trendy since it was launched, with a daily transaction of up to US$1 million. In addition, the software used by BitPay is 100% open source and have been tested and audited by the Bitcoin community. Users have absolute control over their private keys and digital assets. No third party can freeze or steal the digital assets in the wallet. Generally speaking, BitPay has a high degree of security and transparency. So far, there have been no major security scandals with BitPay, a fact enough to prove its superiority in security. BitPay offers additional functions in addition to the basic functions of receiving and payment. The wallet has launched a number of cryptocurrency debit cards on the platform, combining cryptocurrency with the consumer market. With these cards, users can buy products or services in any merchants that accept them. The prices of these offerings denoted in fiat currency are converted into cryptocurrency. However, the merchants do not receive cryptocurrency directly, but the fiat sent from BitPay instead. Therefore, the BitPay wallet essentially acts as an intermediary and contributes to the popularity of cryptocurrency in the consumer market. Overall, the BitPay wallet is easy to use with high security. At the same time, it tries to explore the application of cryptocurrency in the consumer market. All these features make it an attractive wallet. Nowadays, it stands out in the wallet market and has developed into the world's largest Bitcoin payment service provider.

» @Blockchain wallet

Founded in Luxembourg in 2011, Blockchain wallet (formerly blockchain.info) mainly provides latest transaction data, Bitcoin-oriented financial data, block output and other on-chain data. Blockchain wallet is one of the pioneers in the field of wallet encryption. Like BitPay, users can receive crypto assets via mobile phone and web page. Initially, it only supported Bitcoin (BTC) handling. Later, Ethereum (ETH) and Bitcoin Cash (BCH) were also added. The Blockchain wallet is also a centralized wallet, i.e., custodial wallet, storing the keys on behalf of the users. All data is managed by a centralized platform with excellent ease of use. Besides, all the codes are completely open-source. The security center of the platform backups funds in users' wallets and protects them from any unauthorized access, thus ensuring security. After years of development, Blockchain.info has become one of the most mature companies in the cryptocurrency and blockchain industry, the leader on-chain wallet and the largest wallet software supplier of the Bitcoin network. So far, more than 30 million users have invested in and stored cryptocurrencies with the wallet, with a transaction amount of over US$200 billion. It is one of the most trusted platforms by cryptocurrency fans. In addition, users can also analyze the crypto market via the market page of the website and expand API services to facilitate developers' building on the blockchain.

2.1.4 Miners and pools

What really marks the commercialization of Bitcoin is the

emergence of a large number of miners and pools. As mentioned above, the value of Bitcoin has been accepted by more and more people after creating a range of commercial facilities, and Bitcoin has witnessed bull markets many times. Mining, the most direct and relatively low-cost way to acquire Bitcoins, has begun to undergo a dramatic change from hobbyist miners to highly professional miners.

Mining is the process of exploring and generating new Bitcoins. It works similarly to minerals mining, hence the ones who are mining Bitcoins are called miners. In the Bitcoin network, nodes constantly verify the blockchain, and miners package on-chain transactions into blocks and attach them to the blockchain. Miners who take the lead in successfully finishing packaging a new block get Bitcoins as rewards. The process of packaging transactions into new blocks is called mining. Miners are incentivized to support the Bitcoin network without a central issuing agency. It also adds the new Bitcoins into the currency circulation system.

Bitcoin mining adopts the PoW – Proof of Work consensus mechanism. Nodes in the network compete with each other to solve a mathematical problem. Once finding the answer to this mathematical problem, miners broadcast it to the entire network for other miners to verify the correctness. Although PoW is criticized for consuming large quantities of electrical power and creating mathematical problems with no practical value, it was still the consensus mechanism of many blockchain 1.0 networks and remains so in many important blockchains such as Ethereum 1.0.

With the increasing computing power of the whole network, the mining difficulty is growing, indicating more mining activity on the Bitcoin network. This is also reflected by the rising hash rate, a figure that illustrates the computing power used to solve the Proof of Work cryptographic equation. Gradually, the enormous computing power on the network makes it more and more difficult for individual miners to have enough computing power to make any meaningful rewards from mining. Therefore, the income of many independent miners is hard to guarantee. The concept of a mining pool is proposed to enhance mining stability. A mining pool connects miners around the globe and groups their computing power. The total computing power is used to achieve a higher speed in processing and mining blocks, greatly enhancing the chance of getting rewards, which are to be allocated based on the computing power contributed by each machine.

At the end of 2010, Slushpool, the world's first Bitcoin mining pool, emerged. In the beginning, it ranked among the Top three in terms of computing power. Slushpool is still active today as a firm supporter of Bitcoin. As of 2022 only Bitcoin and Zcash can be mined on this platform. Subsequently, many large mining pools began to be intensively launched. In May 2013, F2Pool was launched. It was the earliest Bitcoin pool in China and a global leading digital currency mining pool that supports Bitcoin, Litecoin, Ethereum and others. Its computing power occupied up to 50% of China's total. In May 2014, the GHash.IO mining pool emerged as a dark horse in the community. It did not charge a commission, and in July 2014, the computing power corresponded to over 51% of the entire network. For the first time, the mining community expressed concern about the possibility of a 51% attack. If a node has more than 51% of the computing power of the whole network, it can leverage this advantage to tamper with the records on the blockchain. Later, Ghash lowered it to 42%. In October 2014, AntPool was launched, and the BTCC Pool was launched shortly after in the same month. The year 2014 is arguably the year of China's mining pool boom. The advantages in resources and production are one of the main reasons for the development of the mining industry. In addition to F2Pool, AntPool and BTCC Pool also quickly squeezed into the top ten of China's mining pools. According to the data in December 2014, F2Pool accounted for 22.59%, AntPool 11.03% and BTCC Pool 6.20%. The leading pools almost had a monopoly position. After 2017, BTC.com and AntPool, backed by Bitmain, overtook F2Pool as the "Mining Giant".

In terms of miners, Bitcoin mining in 2010 was done only through CPU, the so-called first-generation miners. That was the initial stage of Bitcoin when mining was not so hard, and most PCs consumed less energy than they earned mining Bitcoin. As the computing power of the whole network increased, the computing speed of ordinary CPU could not adapt to mining the increasingly difficult algorithms. Second generation miners started to use GPUs – mining with one or more high-end graphics cards. Soon enough, the graphics card market was in short supply, and GPU failed to meet Bitcoin's exponentially rising computing power. At this time, some technology enthusiasts came up with the idea of creating a mining device specially created to calculate the Bitcoin algorithm. Still, these machines turned out not so effective. Until January 2013, the ASIC chip miner "Avalon" developed by Zhang Nanqian significantly increased the mining efficiency and computing power while reducing the energy consumption. This was mainly because of its chip configuration. In the following year, the power consumption of Avalon miners decreased from 5,000J/T of the first generation to 1,250J/T of the third generation, with an energy efficiency ratio up by four times. Such mining equipment kept its leading position for one year and a half after its birth. At the end of 2013, Bitmain, a technology company focusing on designing and developing high-speed and low-power customized chips, developed Ant miner S1. Due to its sharp technological advantage, S1's power consumption was far lower than other products. Bitmain quickly got a large market share. By that time, Bitcoin soared to US$1,200. During the bull market in 2017, Bitmain accounted for 75% of the market share and was the number one player of the encryption miner.

Seeing the success of Bitmain, many technology companies

swarmed in, including KNC, Pigeon, TMR and Bter. However, constrained by both R&D capacity and financing, they quit before making a profit because chips had an extremely high requirement on R&D capacity and needed to race with computing power and be upgraded in time. At the beginning of 2015, Bitmain launched the fifth generation Ant miner S5, which adopts the chip BM1384 independently developed by Bitmain. With compactness, high heat dissipation, low power consumption and large computing power, S5 had dominated the mining market. Bitmain used to own the biggest Bitcoin mining farm in the Ordos, Inner Mongolia, the center of Bitcoin mining. The farm has more than 20,000 miners that consume almost US$40,000 of electricity per day. Bitmain miners have an overwhelming advantage over its competitors in terms of technology, price and market share.

2.2 Early investors

Since Bitcoin started to be adopted by more people, VCs began to participate in the ecosystem. In particular, due to the peer-to-peer nature of Bitcoin, middleman is unnecessary, the interaction between investors and entrepreneurs is very efficient. Many commercial projects have created enormous wealth for VCs.

2.2.1 The first blockchain funds in China – Zhen Fund and Sequoia Capital China

(1) Zhen Fund

Zhen Fund is arguably the most active traditional VC in the blockchain field, an angel fund managing over US$1 billion. It was jointly established by Xu Xiaoping and Wang Qiang in Beijing in early 2012, New Oriental and Sequoia Capital co-founders. Xu, the founder of Zhen Fund, ranked 10th in China's top venture investors list in 2017. Ranked first was Shen Nanpeng, founder of Sequoia Capital China. Its investment scope mainly includes education, e-commerce, entertainment, culture, artificial intelligence, big data. The total AUM – Assets under Management – is over US$1 billion.

On January 9, 2018, Xu talked about the promising future of blockchain in a 500 group from Zhen Fund, and stressed the confidentiality of the message. He essentially said that the blockchain era was coming and asked everyone to embrace the change actively. He called on all entrepreneurs and investors to accept blockchain technology while focusing on developing practical technologies and products. Blockchain projects invested by Zhen Fund include Huobi, one of China's three major digital currency exchanges, blockchain-based Ecom Chain, decentralized exchange DDEX and virtual currency management service provider MobileCoin.

(2) Sequoia Capital China

Another VC actively investing in Huobi together with Zhen Fund is Sequoia Capital, which is also the largest institutional shareholder of Huobi that participated in Huobi's multi-million-dollar Series A round of financing in 2014. Established in the United States in 1972, Sequoia Capital manages nearly 30 funds involving more than US$10 billion. It has investments in Apple, Yahoo, Google, Oracle and YouTube, which have become the pacesetter in their industries. Sequoia Capital has always been a leading VC with its unique vision and forward-looking audacity. Sequoia China currently has a total of eight funds with assets of approximately US$2.5 billion and over RMB 4 billion under management. Sequoia has always been passionate about blockchain and is skilled at identifying the trend, and has invested in multiple blockchain projects, with a token issuance ratio of 55.56%. Each project yielded a good return in its following investments in blockchain projects. These projects include the leading

crypto miner manufacturer Bitmain, the leading crypto exchange
Huobi, public chain network Nervos Network, 2B protocol AERGO,
and many other projects. Shen Nanpeng, the global executive partner
of Sequoia Capital, believes that blockchain is an irreversible trend
that must be learned and adapted to.

2.2.2 A giant in the cryptocurrency world – Digital Currency Group (DCG)

Located on Wall Street, New York, Digital Currency Group is
a financial institution investing in blockchain. DCG's investment
strategy is relatively aggressive and open, covering a wide range of
areas, especially popular segments. As one of the most active investors
in the industry, DCG has more than 50 investments in 15 countries,
including BitGo, BitPay, BitPagos, BitPesa, Chain, Circle, Coinbase,
Gyft, Kraken, Ripple Labs, TradeBlock, Unocoin and Xapo. What is
more impressive is that the strongest players of each crypto segment
are in their portfolio.

The success of Digital Currency Group could not have been
achieved without its founder, Barry Silbert, who obtained his initial
capital by holding Bitcoin in 2011. In 2012, he founded Bitcoin
Opportunity Corp, also a VC in cryptocurrency space. In 2013, as
an angel investor, he invested in Coinbase, the largest cryptocurrency
exchange in the United States, BitPay, a crypto asset payment tool
and Ripple, a payment service provider. Now they are all leading
enterprises in their respective segments. When people had doubts
and were pessimistic about blockchain, Barry Silbert proposed to the
board of directors of his start-up to use US$3 million of the company
funds to buy Bitcoin, which led to the birth of Digital Currency
Group.

Since its establishment, Digital Currency Group has focused on
cryptocurrency investments. Unlike other investment funds, DCG
has become an incubator for many blockchain startups by focusing

on supporting the growth of startups in addition to its investment business. Now, DCG has the largest share in the global cryptocurrency market, with hundreds of millions of dollar worth of digital currencies controlled by its headquarters in New York, and Grayscale, one of the largest cryptocurrency funds, being its wholly-owned subsidiary.

References

"The Legendary Life of Jed McCaleb, Founder of E-donkey", Wanyun BaaS, https://my.oschina.net/u/3620978/blog/1605756.

"The First Bitcoin Exchange with Free Lunch", Jinse Finance, https://www.jinse.com/blockchain/441262.html.

Wu Fengyu, "China's largest Bitcoin exchange will stop trading at the end of September", Taiwan Academy of Banking and Finance, http://www.tabf.org.tw/BECommon/Doc/FormEdit/1940.pdf.

"Li Lin's Huobi Siege", Zhang Shaohua, All Weather TMT, https://awtmt.com/articles/3258818?from=wscn.

"History of cryptocurrency exchange: Gate.io's seven years of rebirth", Sina, https://finance.sina.com.cn/blockchain/roll/2020-04-21/doc-iirczymi7547231.shtml.

Hai Bin, "History of domestic cryptocurrency exchanges, a fight for the iron throne", Chainnews, https://www.chainnews.com/articles/454471828816.htm.

"A review of the top ten traditional financial institutions investing on blockchain", Sohu, https://www.sohu.com/a/248611405_100160504.

"Xu Xiaoping, founder of Zhen Fund, calls for embracing blockchain", Xinshang, https://baijiahao.baidu.com/s?id=1589197109998723345&wfr=spider&for=pc.

"A review of the blockchain wallet's evolution", Chainnews, https://www.chainnews.com/articles/680901039310.htm.

"Seven-year history of mining pools", Lieyun Finance, https://www.lieyuncj.com/p/12169.

CHAPTER 3

TWISTED MASS ADOPTION:
THE ICO BOOM

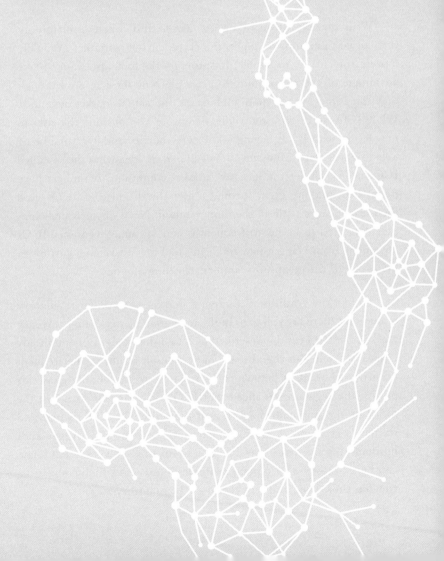

The concept of ICO is a reproduction of the IPO in the stock market. As the development of blockchain smart contract technology has dramatically reduced the financing cost of crypto startups, fundraising with tokens is more convenient and cost-saving for blockchain projects. In the past few years, such a financing method has been booming rapidly, with ICOs raising more than US$1 billion a year at the height of the frenzy, greatly exceeding the amount of money raised via traditional venture capital.

With the explosion of crypto assets and tokens multiplying their price thousands of times, the cryptocurrency market gradually moved from reality to bubble. Investors on the look also want to take advantage of the opportunity to get a piece of the pie, even though they sometimes do not quite understand the actual market dynamics. While ICOs were growing wildly, they were also pushing the risks to new levels, with ICOs having a low entry barrier and everyone being able to participate. Many investors still had no idea what the so-called ICO means. Under the lucrative market conditions, scammers have flocked in, making great fortune under the disguise of ICOs, and then disappeared with all the money raised. News on such malicious incidents used to be heard frequently, and on some occasions, ICOs have gone from being a new financing tool for blockchain startups to being one of the means of scammers cheating money.

Unlike the traditional financial market with many regulatory limitations, there are still gaps in the regulation of the virtual currency market. An ICO can be described as a tool that does not commit any crimes by itself. But the absence of regulation results in the frequent occurrences of illicit behaviors. In response to the blindly chase for profits, the regulators realized that ICO had seriously disturbed the order of the financial market, and therefore, they intervened and started to crack down on illegitimate projects. The ICO frenzy ends up shattering the many "get rich quick" dreams. The crazy ICO days can be described as a typical example of excessive financialization, which is short-lived and reduced to a relic in history.

3.1   ICO – A product of the blockchain gold rush

ICO (Initial Coin Offering), referring to the initial public offering of digital currencies, aims to raise funds from the public through the issuance of tokens with the support of blockchain and smart contract technology.

Compared to IPO, the object to be issued by the project behind the ICO is a token rather than stock. Unlike Bitcoin, where miners earn tokens through their computing power, the project founder can directly mint tokens, creating a token sale under the ICO model. The tokens minted are used only in the decentralized application built on the platform. The funds raised by the ICO go directly to an entity controlled by the founders, supposedly to pay for research and development and to reward the team and their backers and take on the risks of the project's development process.

Ethereum is arguably the most typical example of an ICO. In 2014, Vitalik Buterin, the founder of Ethereum, raised over US$18.4 million with the public token sale of ETH. Today, that number may have been multiplied by 150 times and continues to increase. Investors were buying ETH partly for use on the Ethereum blockchain and smart contract platform and partially to benefit from the upside. Other early blockchain projects have tried this approach too. ERC20, the smart contract standard for tokens developed in late 2016, has led to a surge in ICO projects. This standardized set of smart contract instructions on Ethereum provides a universal and consistent mechanism for ICO token transactions, relieving the tokens from the need to have their native blockchain or the maintenance of their independent computing capabilities. Ethereum's computer network performs these processes for them, and its ease of use simplifies the issuance of tokens on Ethereum.

Figure 3.1 shows the overview of ICO funding in the market from January 2017 to March 2019, with $1.5 billion raised through ICOs in the first seven and a half months of 2017, far more than these companies could get through traditional VCs. Even after the SEC issued a warning in August that these tokens are considered securities and should be regulated, the enthusiasm did not seem to have waned. This chart naturally raises the question of whether ICO could become a widespread form of funding that could become an alternative to traditional venture capital.

Figure 3.1: ICO funding overview from January 2017 to March 2019

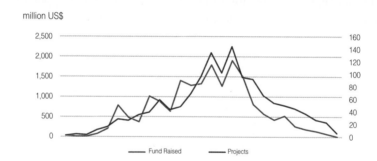

Source: ICO Rating website

What is the difference between ICO fundraising and traditional VC? First, in terms of legal rights, VC investors can obtain the shares of the entity representing the right to vote on the execution of the project as well as the seats in the board of directors, which means that investors get the rights to supervise the company or project and have their interests guaranteed. In contrast, shareholders' voting rights are automatically distributed and secured through the smart contracts in an ICO, which is hard to achieve due to the technical challenge and practical obstacles. All the equity constraints currently depend on government policies and laws in the real world.

The second is the investment threshold. In the VC investment process, there are usually professional investment analysts who decide on the investment direction. They know the relevant industry background well, thus reasonably predicting the industry's future development prospects. In addition, VC will assist the target company in choosing a diversified portfolio and investing only in the best teams in the best markets. Therefore, the VC assistance for the company cannot be neglected. The retail investors in ICO investments are often newbies who have not assessed the risks of the projects just to invest for a quick profit. In the investment process of traditional venture capital, VCs will perform due diligence on the entrepreneurs, who, in turn, are also asked to provide a full report to ensure that their projects do have potential, including explanations on what problems the project will solve, who are the team members, what are the prospects, and how much revenue will be generated. Some ICO projects also have white papers, which may look flawless, but the team may not have the execution capacity. And due to the lack of regulation and the anonymity of the ICO, fake ICO projects can get as much investment, but challenging to be held accountable, ended up with the investors losing their money.

Last but not least, there are regulatory issues. The inability of ICO investors to acquire equity will bring another problem: the regulability of the projects. Suppose the project owner runs away after receiving money from investors. In that case, investors will not be able to get back their funds in the absence of relevant legal constraints and regulations by regulators such as the SEC. In the case that an investor buys a token, the project owner will give the token to the investor through a smart contract or manual distribution. And that will be the end of the whole investment process. There is no way to know the flow of funds afterwards. While in a traditional VC investment, the VC will decide who will be on the board of directors to manage the company and the next step of the company's operation and will even bring in a professional CEO to lead the company when it grows too fast and needs additional professional management.

ICOs are a low-cost funding solution that allows token issuers to find an easy way to reach the global investment community. A large number of end-investors are entering the early rounds of investment that would have previously been reserved for VCs and professionals. Token issuers no longer need to negotiate heavily with VCs over equity dilution and board control, nor do they need to please investment banks for customers and get the SEC's approval in advance. All they need is to find their audience/community and promote their tokens to them. This is a straightforward and low-cost way to lower the barrier to entrepreneurship and give dreamers more opportunities to try out new ideas. But at the same time, many scammers are also attracted. Some projects simply reorganize or wrap up the features of blockchain to raise money illegally under the banner of "disrupting traditional industries". After a few months of ICO market frenzy, some projects using blockchain as gimmicks to cheat money out of investors are exposed, which is a good education for the market. In short, ICOs can be seen as a product of the blockchain gold rush, which avoids regulation to provide a seemingly viable model for investors to participate in early investment in projects or companies. Behind the huge gains lie huge risks.

3.2　　Ethereum – The world computer

As a cryptocurrency second only to Bitcoin in terms of market capitalization, Ethereum has received attention as much as Bitcoin recently. Ethereum is an infrastructure network and an open-source public blockchain platform with smart contract functionality that enables everyone to build various blockchain applications on top of it. ETH is the native cryptocurrency of the platform. The project was conceived by Vitalik Buterin, a Russian-Canadian young genius. He described his idea in a newspaper at the end of 2013, which attracted about 30 people to discuss the concept with him. Later, in 2014, the 20-year-old Vitalik published the Ethereum Whitepaper. Today, he has taken the blockchain to a new peak with Ethereum, opening up the era of Blockchain 2.0.

Ethereum did not cause a stir when it was born. After all, Bitcoin was the focus of attention at that time. Ethereum, as a latecomer and naturally, did not attract much attention. Some even thought that Ethereum was purely a money grab. Many people did not anticipate that the blueprint drawn by the 20-year-old Vitalik could make waves in the cryptocurrency world. In May 2014, Vitalik Buterin came to China for the first time, which was seen as a way to promote Ethereum and open up paths for the subsequent ETH pre-sale. Vitalik wrote in his blog: "When I first came to China in May 2014, I only saw miners and exchanges. They were already strong, with over 70 people working at Huobi and OKCoin. But there wasn't a lot of interesting stuff outside of those companies." Then, Vitalik met with the crypto community in China and gave an hour-long speech on the topic of "The Opportunity for Altcoins and Digital Cryptocurrencies". However, most attendees were skeptical about Ethereum and the "young genius" in front of them, which was directly reflected in the ETH pre-sale afterwards. In June 2014, the Ethereum ICO started with the ETH pre-sale raising more than 30,000 Bitcoins in 42 days, equivalent to over US$18 million at 2014 prices. This caused quite a sensation, and Ethereum was criticized as "a money-grabbing scheme". However, an industry insider described in an article analyzing Ethereum in 2016 – "99% in the crypto community have missed this opportunity".

In May 2015, Vitalik Buterin came to China with his Ethereum investment pitch. Unfortunately, the financing process did not go well, and many people thought it was a scam like any other crypto projects. Vitalik travelled around China and finally got critical early support from Xiao Feng, chairman of Wanxiang Blockchain, who invested in ETH and sponsored the Ethereum Foundation. Also, in 2015, Wanxiang Blockchain Lab was established with Vitalik joining as the Chief Scientist.

2016 was an important year that marked the flourishing of blockchain technology and many new startups, projects and stories. People gradually shifted from studying only the blockchain and Bitcoin theory and started focusing on its use cases and real-life application value, i.e., what kind of problems can be solved with blockchain. At that point, many large organizations showed strong interest in this emerging technology.

Ethereum smart contract has dramatically advanced the development of blockchain applications. In this context, Wanxiang Blockchain Lab and the Ethereum Foundation jointly organized the second Blockchain Global Summit 2016, titled "Blockchain New Economy – Horizon". The Ethereum Developer Conference Demo Day provided a showcase for blockchain startups. Both Developer Conference Demo Day and the second Summit were held during the Blockchain Week, where Vitalik was also invited as a speaker to share his insights on the industry and where guests also presented new technical theories such as cross-chains and sidechains. These ideas have all made in the meantime significant progress. In addition, Qtum, imToken, VeChain, Cosmos and other projects have made presentations at the Demo Day during that Blockchain Week. Nowadays, all these startups have become major projects in their respective fields. After that, Wanxiang Blockchain Lab and Ethereum development team co-organized multiple hackathon events and provided technical guidance to participants to support the emergence of new ideas and projects.

Bitcoin, which has a relatively single monetary function, cannot be applied to non-monetary scenarios. Vitalik drew upon the most crucial idea of decentralization from Bitcoin. Instead of defining its own blockchain protocols, which can only support a few incompatible applications, Ethereum allows developers to build applications efficiently and quickly in a defined programming language called Solidity. Because of Solidity's flexibility as the programming language, Ethereum now has unlimited possibilities to build complex smart contracts so that they can be used to build decentralized autonomous organizations (DAO) and run decentralized autonomous applications (dApps). Computers running on Ethereum compete to execute the code instructions on dApps. The winners are rewarded with ETH for providing the best computing results judged based on the hashing algorithm. These dApps can run in a completely autonomous way, and users can trust that the results will be consistent and deterministic with the provisions of the smart contract. Ethereum is like a world computer that is constantly operating, where anyone can upload and execute applications. On Ethereum, you can write code to manage digital assets and run programs, and more importantly, it is all free from any middleman. In the words of Vitalik: "Ethereum is a decentralized and absolutely equal world, full of efficiency and trust".

In fact, after the launch of Ethereum, people remained at the level of theoretical discussion without any practical experience regarding a smart contract, its specific use, and the role of ETH. It was only after the emergence of the ERC20 token standard on Ethereum (which allows anyone to issue tokens) when the industry accidentally discovered that the efficiency and cost of using ERC20 for ICO fundraising seemed to be better than the traditional investment and funding methods, people began to realize the value of Ethereum. Because of the key role played by the smart contract system, Ethereum was able to achieve improved efficiency and reduced cost in ICOs.

.

Since then, cryptocurrency has gone through bull markets. The ERC20 token standard was followed by the release of the ERC721 token standard, with *CryptoKitties* being the representative project. *CryptoKitties* set off a frenzy among players as soon as it was released. If ICO showed investors the power of Ethereum, *CryptoKitties* showed the power of Ethereum to gamers outside the field who were not too concerned about blockchain technology. It was essentially unlocking the power of smart contracts. The success of smart contracts on ICO and *CryptoKitties* has shown everyone a crypto digital world that is able to disrupt the traditional world. Once all the rules are set, they are automatically enforced in an open, fair, and irreversible way, with no external interference or tampering. By this point, the whole industry seemed optimistic about the performance of smart contracts and their disruptive nature. As a result, a large number of digital currencies supporting smart contract functionality have since emerged. These new projects, despite great momentum, can hardly end up with good results in the industry.

Since the Ethereum ecosystem is the most compatible and widely adopted blockchain platform, various tokens and applications are developed based on it, resulting in ETH being one of the most recognized and commonly circulated virtual currencies. The subsequent ICOs have increased the variety of altcoins and the demand for Ethereum, pushing up the overall value of all virtual currencies. Looking at the overall virtual currency market capitalization share, Ethereum ranks continually in the second position under Bitcoin. Since 2013, it saw the highest record in market share of over 30 per cent in July 2017, with only seven per cent lower than Bitcoin before falling back again.

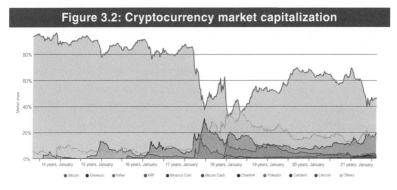

Figure 3.2: Cryptocurrency market capitalization

Source: coinmarketcap.com

The cryptocurrency entered a bull market in 2017, followed by Ethereum welcoming a crazy year after a hard fork on the network. The bull market started due to the entry of new funds, a large part of which is credited to ICOs. The easy-to-use and Turing Complete features of Ethereum smart contracts made the issuance of digital currencies an easy job. The expansion of the ERC20 token standard and the considerable influence brought by The DAO crowdfunding have attracted more projects to use Ethereum for ICO funding. In fact, many ICO projects began to sprout quietly in 2016, leading to the mushrooming of ICOs in 2017. Data from ICOData.io shows that in 2016, there were only 29 ICO projects with a fundraising amount of more than US$90,000, while in 2017, those two figures grew to 876 and US$6.2 billion, respectively. It can be said that Ethereum was pushed to the forefront of the crypto fundraising scene by the ICOs. Not only blockchain startups issued tokens, but also listed companies, traditional internet companies, and even scammers and pyramid schemes have taken the path of issuing tokens. In addition, the rise of ICOs also attracted more people to participate in the Ethereum ecosystem. There has been an explosive growth in the number of people using Ethereum and the volume of Ethereum transactions, with the number of Ethereum addresses increasing nearly 20 times. At the end of May 2017, Ethereum was listed on OKCoin and Huobi.

Since then, the ETH price has been climbing, reaching an all-time high of US$4,812 in October 2021.

Although Ethereum had a dazzling year in 2017, it faces various problems, such as asset security issues and a long-standing Ethereum's scalability problem exposed from the booming of CryptoKitties – the low TPS (transactions per second). Ethereum is now in its sixth year, but security and congestion are the main issues that need to be addressed even today.

3.3   The penalty from the SEC

In the ICO space, there were inevitably companies raising money illegitimately under the ICO umbrella, which brings risks or losses to investors. In this regard, the U.S. Securities and Exchange Commission (SEC) has also increased its efforts to investigate and regulate ICO projects. Once the token issued through an ICO is deemed by the SEC as a security, it means that the token is subject to the same strict regulation as a security. If the token issued does not meet the regulatory requirements, it will also face a fine from the SEC. Projects investigated and punished by the SEC generally have two outcomes: either settling and paying the fine, or if they insist on not settling, the most probable outcome is the end of the project.

The Howey Test is a test created to determine whether an asset (including tokens) should be classified as a security. The test was established in a court case in the United States in 1946. It provides that a sale is considered a security offering if it: 1) is an investment in a common enterprise; 2) is entirely dependent on the efforts of others; and 3) with the expectations of producing a profit. This is done by scoring a blockchain project against the test, where the higher the score, the closer the nature of the project's token is to a security.

If a token is identified as a security, it would be subject to SEC regulation, where a detailed prospectus must be prepared prior to issuance. The issuer must comply with U.S. federal securities laws by registering its transactions with the government. In addition, it is obligated to disclose important information to allow investors to make investment decisions. The SEC also emphasizes that regardless of the technology used, whether a particular transaction involves the issuance and sale of securities depends on the actual scenario and circumstances, i.e., an issuer cannot evade the federal securities laws by simply labelling its product as a cryptocurrency. We will further introduce three cases of SEC investigations in this chapter, covering an overview of the events, the SEC's view, and the responses of the penalized companies.

3.3.1 The illegal token offering of Telegram

On October 11, 2019, the SEC announced that it had initiated an emergency action and obtained a temporary restraining order from the U.S. Supreme Court against the Telegram Group offshore entity and its wholly-owned subsidiary TON Issuer Inc. for their ongoing digital token offerings inside and outside the U.S., which had raised more than US$1.7 billion from investors (the second-largest fundraising case in ICO history). At that time, it was less than 20 days from TON's mainnet launch. After eight months of litigation, the sides settled, with Telegram returning US$1.224 billion (72% of the US$1.7 billion raised) to investors. At the same time, Telegram was also convicted of paying a US $18.5 million fine to the SEC, and notifying the SEC in advance in case the company wanted to reissue tokens, or any digital assets with distributed ledger technology (DLT), over the next three years.

After the shutdown of blockchain project Telegram Open Network (TON), Telegram has been fighting a lawsuit against the SEC since October 2019. The SEC alleged that the TON network token did not pass the Howey Test, arguing that its token, Gram, constituted an investment contract and was a security, therefore halted alleged unregistered securities offering by Telegram. Stephanie Avakian, co-director of the SEC's Division of Enforcement, said in a statement: "Our emergency action today is intended to prevent Telegram from flooding the U.S. markets with digital tokens that we allege were unlawfully sold. We allege that the defendants have failed to provide investors with information regarding Grams and Telegram's business operations, financial condition, risk factors, and management that the securities laws require." Telegram, for its part, said they were selling rights in the form of Gram, which will be distributed when the network goes live. Telegram had not yet issued tokens when they sold the rights, but the SEC disagreed with this assertion, and Telegram's tokens themselves were still securities. As a result, the SEC stopped the network from going live, saying there was a substantial likelihood that Telegram's plan to distribute Gram was an issuance of securities that fell within the SEC's jurisdiction. The SEC argued that Telegram failed to disclose relevant information, failed to respect investors' right to know, attempted to issue bonds publicly, and received proceeds.

3.3.2 Block.one accused of unregistered token sale

On September 30, 2019, the SEC announced a US$24 million penalty to Block.one, who started the EOS blockchain due to unauthorized token sales. EOS is undoubtedly the most successful ICO case to date, with a fundraising period of 355 days starting on June 26, 2017, and ending on June 1, 2018, raising a whopping US$4.1 billion. The SEC claims that Block.one issued tokens to raise funds without registration, and its fundraising plan states that the funds will be used by Block.one for general expenses, to develop and promote the EOS blockchain, which has met the Howey Test and the SEC's definition of securities. The SEC also emphasized that although the company's token offering was made before the SEC issued its DAO report, it was made over a one-year period, which means the token offering continued after the release of the DAO report. Block. one did not register its ICO with the SEC as a security offering under the U.S. federal securities laws, nor did it request an exemption from securities registration. Therefore, it was found to have violated the federal securities laws. In the DAO report, the SEC stated that "the Commission has determined that DAO tokens are securities under the Securities Act of 1933 ("Securities Act") and the Securities Exchange Act of 1934 ("Exchange Act")." The SEC additionally provided three criteria: 1) the principles of the securities laws apply to the token offering; 2) the investor purchases the token with the expectation of a profit; and 3) the profit is derived from running a particular company.

The SEC stated that a number of U.S. investors participated in Block.one's ICO, and companies that offer or sell securities to U.S. investors must comply with the securities laws, irrespective of the industry they operate in or the labels they place on the investment products they offer. Steven Peikin, Co-director of the SEC's Division of Enforcement, said, "The SEC remains committed to bringing enforcement cases when investors are deprived of material information they need to make informed investment decisions." However, Block.one disagreed with the SEC's view and stated that the token released in the ICO made before the launch of its mainnet was an ERC 20 token, which is no longer in circulation today, so there was no need to register the tokens as securities with the SEC. In the end, Block.one chose to settle the case, and after coordination, Block.one paid a one-time fine of US$24 million to the SEC.

3.3.3 SEC sues Kik for conducting US$100 million token offering

The SEC sued Kik Interactive Inc. on June 4, 2019, for conducting an illegal US$100 million securities offering of digital tokens, alleging that the company sold the security tokens to U.S. investors without registering their offer and sale as required by the

U.S. securities laws. Kik had lost money for years on its sole product, an online messaging application, and the company's management predicted that it would run out of money in 2017. In early 2017, the company sought to be financed through the sale of one trillion digital tokens. Kik sold its Kin tokens to the public, raising more than US$55 million from U.S. investors.

The SEC further alleges that Kik marketed the Kin tokens as an investment opportunity. Kik allegedly told investors that rising demand would drive up the value of Kin and that Kik would undertake crucial work to spur that demand, including incorporating the tokens into its messaging app, creating a new Kin transaction service. When Kik offered and sold the tokens, the SEC alleged these services and systems did not exist, and there was nothing to purchase using Kin. The Kin offering involved securities transactions, and Kik was required to comply with the registration requirements of the U.S. securities laws.

The SEC stated that Kik sold US$100 million securities without registering them and that Kik failed to disclose important information relevant to investors' decisions, and that they had claimed that the company would profit alongside investors from the increased demand that it would foster. Reaping future profits based on the efforts of others is one of the hallmarks of issuing securities and therefore would need to comply with U.S. federal securities laws. On the other hand, Kik argued that the assumptions of the SEC's complaint against Kik went far beyond the definition of the Howey Test and insisted on not settling with the SEC, resulting in the termination of the project.

From the above cases, it can be concluded that as long as the tokens meet SEC's definition of securities, they must be regulated by the SEC, unless qualified for any SEC's exemption from registration requirements (e.g., Reg D). Reg D is a regulation governing private placement exemptions, which allows an issuer to raise capital without needing to register the securities with the SEC but must file the "Form D" disclosure document within 15 days after the first securities are sold. There is no cap on fundraising through Reg D, but it does require a one-year lock-up period and is limited to a maximum of 2,000 investors. Under CFR §230.504(a)(1), Reg D is not available to startups that either has no specific business plan or purpose or has indicated that its business plan is to engage in a merger or acquisition of unidentified companies; private sale under Reg D include no public promotion; and the scope and requirements for corporate disclosure under Reg D are higher.

Blockstack is the first ICO project approved by the SEC in history, which spent US$2 million to settle with the SEC. Blockstack's token sale approval by the SEC marks a big step for cryptocurrencies on the road to legality showcasing, especially on the legalization of ICOs. It points the way for startups to raise money. As for the future of token issuance through ICO, those who meet the definition of security but do not register the offering and disclose the information to investors must either be penalized by the SEC or do it legally as required.

3.3.4   Misbehavior due to lack of regulation

It can be said that ICO resembles an IPO. Cryptocurrency is the necessary part for most blockchain projects, which sometimes coincides with the nature of IPO shares. However, unlike IPOs, ICOs use blockchain technology to raise virtual currency automatically through smart contracts instead of the manual process. The pre-written computer program automatically raises virtual currencies, bypassing the traditional IPO procedures and regulatory requirements for fundraisers, who can carry out fundraising activities with a very low threshold. The lack of written laws for this new means of funding based on smart contracts has led to the inadequate disclosure of information about ICO projects to investors, thus resulting in questioning ICOs legitimacy. Such an unregulated fundraising method undoubtedly exposes investors and the entire financial market to substantial legal risks.

Since it is not mandatory for ICO projects to disclose information, investors are unable to know the operating status of ICO companies and sometimes have no knowledge of the use of funds raised through ICO. It is challenging to protect investors' rights and interests. Tokens that potentially represent equity in a company are likely to be at risk of illegal fundraising or fraud, and this risk can easily affect the trading platform that helped them complete the ICO. When issuing tokens via ICO, investors base their investment on basic information such as the project's white paper. The risk of such an investment without any due diligence is huge.

In November 2017, Modern Tech, a Vietnamese cryptocurrency company that conducted two ICO offerings, ran off with US$660 million raised from approximately 32,000 investors, making it the largest ICO scam in the world. The company was founded by seven Vietnamese in Ho Chi Minh City, and the project was mainly promoted through KOLs and referral rewards, which is quite the same as a pyramid scheme. The project team disappeared immediately after the scam came to light, leaving the investors nowhere to safeguard their legal rights. It is in the same tricks as most projects that ran off with the money: the project itself has no substant contents, nor do they have an operating team, except for a website and the so-called white paper. They are ghost projects relying on KOL's false propaganda to mislead investors. Modern Tech had held a number of promotional meetups in Vietnam to mislead the public with monthly interest rates of up to 50% and the ability to recover the principal after only a few months of investment. In addition, like the ICO scams in China, the Vietnamese team also recruit members through referrals, who could be rewarded with an 8% commission for each new member they introduced. The property management of the building where the company was located said that the company had long since left and cleared the rent, and there was no way to know where they were going. Investors can only express their discontent and anger by demonstrating in front of the building.

In addition to mixed trading platforms and illegal fundraising, there are also money laundering problems, tax evasion, and information leakage. Currently, virtual currency trading platforms, such as Huobi, OKCoin, and Binance, provide direct transactions between fiat currencies and virtual currencies. As virtual currency accounts do not need to be registered, personal assets can be converted into virtual assets to be hidden for money laundering and tax evasion. There are no clear regulations from the tax authorities in various countries, including the IRS, on whether and how the profits or capital gains from the sale of ICO tokens are subject to taxation. On the other hand, the issuance of ICO projects is global, and investors can circumvent the regulation of local governments and regulators to participate in offshore ICO projects, which leaves room for criminals utilizing ICOs for money laundering. Finally, the customer privacy and data security of the ICO issuance platform is also crucial, and it is necessary to ensure that the platform has no information security vulnerabilities and sufficient ability to resist the risk of hacking.

ICO projects are in conflict with securities regulation, and when the bubble bursts, it can leave innocent investors vulnerable. This get-rich-quickly "gold rush" driven by ICOs, a blockchain-based crowdfunding tool for startup teams, has all the hallmarks of the dot-com bubble in the late 1990s. ICOs can be seen as a product of the blockchain gold rush, which avoided legal regulation, lacked restraint, grew wildly, and eventually became a relic of history.

References

"Central bankers first talk about ICO: Regulators cannot judge the good or bad of the projects", http://finance.sina.com.cn/roll/2017-07-07/doc-ifyhwehx5299251. shtml.

"Hong Kong SFC: ICO scams are flooding, investors should be aware of the risks", https://www.jinse.com/news/bitcoin/184657.html.

Song Di, "The crazy ICO investment intermediaries: Raised standards at different levels and false advertising", http://finance.sina.com.cn/roll/2018-03-25/doc-ifysnevm7677100.shtml.

"Telegram facing $10 million penalty from SEC for its illegal token sale", https://www.panewslab.com/zh_hk/articledetails/2682.html.

"Telegram to return $1.2 Billion to investors and pay $18.5 million penalty to settle SEC charges", https://www.sec.gov/news/press-release/2020-146.

"SEC sues Kik for conducting $100 million token offering", https://www.chaindd.com/3203237.html.

"Block.one to pay $24 million penalty as EOS settles with SEC", http://www.btcinst.com/bitcoin/news/1128.html.

Chen Roudi and Chu Kang, "What you must know about STO issuance rules – Secrets of Reg D, Reg A, Reg S", https://www.odaily.com/post/5134501.

"Application for exemptions from fundraising registration", http://www.mascapital.group/?p=591.

"5 ICO projects with the largest fraudulent amounts in history", https://36kr.com/p/1722494140417.

"Details of the world's largest ICO scam revealed", https://finance.sina.com.cn/blockchain/coin/2018-04-17/doc-ifzihnen8102788.shtml.

CHAPTER 4

THE BOOM AND BUST THAT DIDN'T HINDER TECHNOLOGICAL PROGRESS – THE INTERGENERATIONAL DEVELOPMENT OF BLOCKCHAIN TECHNOLOGY

People gradually returned to a rational and more consolidated understanding of blockchain after the ICO boom, driving it into a trough of disillusionment after the peak of inflated expectations of the Gartner hype cycle. Nevertheless, technological development did not stop because of the bubble burst. The technical iteration of blockchain can be roughly divided into three stages: blockchain 1.0, 2.0 and 3.0. Blockchain 1.0 was marked by the birth of Bitcoin. Blockchain technology at this stage served mainly for cryptocurrencies used for transactions. Blockchain 2.0 was represented by the emergence of Ethereum and smart contracts. It builds a financial infrastructure for crypto assets, enabling tokens to be used in a wider range of use cases, other than simple value transfers. For Blockchain 3.0, there has not been a capitulation yet. Web 3.0 is generally regarded as the most suitable direction considering the market needs.

Compared with Web 2.0, Web 3.0 enables content autonomy, open protocols, identity autonomy and trustless exchange of digital assets. In addition, blockchain has developed rapidly in recent years with a wide range of use cases. Individual chains such as Ethereum and Bitcoin are unable to meet the increasing demand in transaction volume. Thus, multi-chain and cross-chain technologies such as Cosmos and Polkadot have come into being. In addition to multi-chain and cross-chain, distributed applications are also among the most important technological innovations in the blockchain. Distributed applications refer to applications distributed on a number of servers or nodes. The decentralized network mechanism of blockchain gives a natural ground for dApps' development. The two hottest sub dApp industries are the decentralized finance – DeFi, which counters conventional centralized finance, and the NFT, which develops the creator economy.

4.1 Constant technological iteration, blockchain 1.0-2.0-3.0

4.1.1 Blockchain 1.0 – Cryptocurrency

Blockchain technology was born many years ago, but it was not until the birth of Bitcoin in 2008 that the era of blockchain 1.0 was truly declared. At that time, Bitcoin was the cryptocurrency used for transactions, and consequently, blockchain technology was used to record simple transactions only.

The representative currencies in the 1.0 era were BTC and LTC, both of which were applied in similar scenarios. In the blockchain 1.0 era, there were miners, currency holders and investors/speculators. Miners were responsible for new BTC issuance through mining, using mining-specific computers, for validating the transactions and securing the network. Currency holders participated in the circulation of Bitcoin, and investors/speculators traded Bitcoin in the market via exchanges or OTC. As the Bitcoin blocks are small (1MB) and take some time to be settled on the blockchain (on average ten minutes to have a transaction confirmation), coins such as LTC, BCH and BSV emerged as Bitcoin forks. Most of them have made optimizations in block size and block generation time. At the same time, some anonymous coins focusing on improving transfer privacy, such as XMR, ZEC and DASH, were also born, in order to hide the transaction information on the chain.

In the case of Bitcoin, a representative of the 1.0 era, the blueprint depicted in the white paper was a payment system. At that time, Satoshi Nakamoto intended to build a peer-to-peer cash system that was not controlled by the government or financial institutions. Since Bitcoins had little value in the beginning, they were mined without any financial benefits. Those involved in maintaining the network back then did so out of faith. Bitcoin experienced many crises even in its infancy, but it managed to survive.

As the first cryptocurrency, Bitcoin could not become a mainstream payment currency because the price fluctuated violently, making it hard for pricing in an actual transaction of a product. As the Bitcoin network is slow in the production of blocks, Bitcoin's price may have dramatic fluctuations during the process of settling the transactions. The final settlement may sometimes take time (sometimes over 30 minutes), meaning that the Bitcoin price can change before a transaction is settled. At the same time, the total transaction volume supported by the Bitcoin network could not meet the daily transaction needs. Although limited for transactional purposes, Bitcoin was in the meantime regarded as an alternative inflation hedge asset. Considering that Bitcoin has a fixed limited supply, Bitcoin is also considered digital gold, but its volatile price makes it difficult for most people to accept it, and the expectation of holding BTC as an inflation hedge was sometimes broken by violent price fluctuations. Despite that, after several cycles of bull and bear markets, it was found that the overall market value and recognition were increasing year by year. After some time and the entry of mainstream institutions, the Bitcoin volatility began to decrease gradually, and some institutions started to increase their Bitcoin exposure. Despite the need to hedge against inflation, institutions and individuals invested in Bitcoin more as a part of their portfolio. Gradually, they were used to storing some idle/free-floating funds in the form of Bitcoin. Because of its pseudo-anonymity, scarcity and high liquidity, Bitcoin became a good store of value.

Cryptocurrencies in the blockchain 1.0 era could only be used to exchange value. Their main economic value lies in their functions of a store of value and inflation hedge. After 13 years of development, Bitcoin has achieved decentralized consensus, with more institutions and individuals willing to invest in Bitcoin as a part of the portfolio and store of value. The blockchain 1.0 era began with the Bitcoin white paper in 2008 and ended with the inception of Ethereum in 2014. Nowadays, we can consider the Bitcoin market as consolidated.

4.1.2   Blockchain 2.0 – Programmable asset

The main differences between blockchain 2.0 and 1.0 are the smart contract and the use of Turing Complete programming languages. The concept of the smart contract was proposed by Nick Szabo, a computer scientist and cryptologist, as early as 1994. However, a consensus mechanism was needed to ensure that the contracts were open, transparent and immutable. Ethereum finally achieved this by the end of 2013. If blockchain 1.0 reached the sanctity of private property and protection against inflation, then 2.0 built a financial infrastructure for private property on the basis of 1.0, expanding the use cases of tokens. In blockchain 2.0, tokens are no longer used only for settlement, circulation and value storage. They now have multiple functions, such as complex financial product transactions, game development, asset tokenization, digital IDs and social networking.

Ethereum was the pioneer of the 2.0 era. As the first public chain integrated smart contracts, many developers and projects have moved onto Ethereum to develop their products compared to the user ecosystem of the 1.0 era, which also allows these developers to build open-source dApps under a completely decentralized consensus. Anyone can participate in the development of a project and make suggestions.

In Ethereum, ETH does not have a fixed supply like BTC. A slight inflation was kept as this economic model could best reflect the socioeconomic development and encourage holders to invest their ETH, forming a circular economy. Under the constraints of the Ethereum smart contracts, a large number of decentralized applications were developed. Not only is ETH a decentralized crypto asset, but it has also enabled more projects and protocols to become decentralized. In decentralized applications (also known as dApps), the interactions between users are made through codes based on the smart contract that was agreed in advance, keeping the assets in the control of users, which allows for improved security. Privacy is protected, and these protocols do not require KYC. With the rapid development of the Ethereum ecosystem, a large number of copycats emerged. They tried to overcome the weaknesses of Ethereum or reshape the blockchain network according to Ethereum's vision.

Nowadays, figures show that the total number of Ethereum addresses far exceeds that of Bitcoin. Blockchain 2.0 indeed allowed public adoption.

4.1.3   Blockchain 3.0 – Web3 vision

Blockchain 3.0 is still under development. Web 3.0 has developed rapidly in recent years, and it is considered the most likely future direction of blockchain. Web 3.0 is proposed based on Web 2.0. In Web 2.0, internet corporations had issues related to data-sharing, a difficult relationship with its users, privacy and security risks, which set significant obstacles to users who wanted to complete all operations with a single account as there was no interoperability and users' ownership of the data. The vision proposed in the 3.0 era is that the information on an application can interact directly with the relevant information on other applications. The information of multiple applications can be integrated through a third-party information platform. This is also in line with the underlying idea of blockchain, for decentralized applications do not require the collection of massive user data. The openness of transaction information and protocol code makes it easy for other projects to interact and cooperate. Users need only one wallet address to shuttle freely through the blockchain ecosystem without leaking their privacy.

In this sense, blockchain 3.0 is no longer a simple public chain system, where developers can continue developing on Ethereum, breaking away from Ethereum due to its inefficiency, or developing in cross-chain networks. Moreover, the ecosystem is limited to finance and trading, but it starts covering media, games, chatting applications and many more. The Web3 vision is a convergence between the blockchain world and the internet world, which allows a borderless internet with the help of blockchain. When that happens, the value of the internet will belong to users, and our lives will be more convenient and more accessible.

4.2 Entering the multi-chain and cross-chain era

4.2.1 Multi-chain and cross-chain brought by the development of the blockchain industry

As the blockchain industry has been evolving, many blockchains with different consensus mechanisms, cryptographic algorithms and support for smart contracts have emerged. Therefore, in some blockchains, the information on one chain cannot easily interact with that on another, and even some blockchains are closed. Multi-chain refers to these parallel blockchains, which are like parallel universes. Because each is different in data and mechanisms and has its own ecosystem, often any interactions can only be achieved via centralized institutions (exchanges, for example). Accepting the model of multi-chain coexistence means replacing the traditional model of "one chain for all" with a new one – "one chain for one contract" to redesign a public chain that ensures the proper operation of each contract.

The efforts to bridge such blockchains in a decentralized way and thus enable information exchange and money transfer have given birth to cross-chain technology. Centralized institutions can also achieve the cross-chain model, but it goes against the vision of a decentralized blockchain network. Each blockchain keeps its independent consensus mechanism, encryption algorithm, and smart contract language under the cross-chain network, which is a one-connect-all scheme. The cross-chain network is responsible for connecting different networks in a standardized way, and the data and assets on each chain can interact in the cross-chain network. The connection between the cross-chain network and individual blockchains is like an interface via which data and transfers on each blockchain enter the cross-chain network, enabling integrated contract interaction in the cross-chain network.

4.2.2   Development of multi-chain in recent years

Multi-chain networks are essentially an improvement on Bitcoin and Ethereum chains. The limitations in the efficiency and functions of these two chains led to the emergence of many other public chains.

Bitcoin improvement alternatives are:

- Confirmation speed (Litecoin – LTC – modifies the total supply limited to 84 million, and blocks are confirmed on average every 2.5 minutes)

- Block size (Bitcoin Cash – BCH – expands the block size of Bitcoin from 1MB to 32MB while BSV expands it to 128MB)

- Anonymity (Monero – XMR – ring signature technology, DASH mixed currency technology and Zcash's zero-knowledge proof and hidden address transfer functions all strengthen the anonymity and non-traceability of a cryptocurrency)

- Encryption algorithm (both Litecoin and Dogecoin adopt the Scrypt encryption algorithm, making it easier to mine on ordinary laptops)   .

Many other Bitcoin forks have not made a big difference.

Bitcoin still dominates the whole crypto market with its irreplaceable consensus. Among these improvements, Ethereum, which adds the smart contract feature, has officially brought the blockchain into the 2.0 era.

Taking Ethereum as the benchmark, other public chains that came later have improved their efficiency in the following ways:

- Changing the consensus mechanism (QTUM adopts PoS – Proof of Stake – and returns to the Bitcoin's UTXO model; EOS and TRON adopts DPoS – Delegated Proof of Stake and a proxy system, which further improve the efficiency of blockchain and yet weaken decentralization; Filecoin – FIL – proposes a new system of Proof of Spacetime – POST that can be used for blockchain data storage)

- Applying sharding technology (both Harmony and ZIL use sharding technology to expand the block size and increase the confirmation speed of the block and respective transactions)

- Other Ethereum inspire blockchains (Binance Smart Chain – BSC – and HECO chain are exchange platform chains, and forking Ethereum code is the most appropriate way to establish their own DeFi ecosystem)

Like Bitcoin, Ethereum is still the dominator of the 2.0 era in terms of adoption, and all clones are only sharing dividends thanks to Ethereum congestion.

4.2.3   Development of cross-chain in recent years

With a growing number of public chains also comes the growing demand for cross-chain networks. There are centralized and decentralized cross-chain solutions. A centralized cross-chain solution is easy to be implemented. For example, swapping BTC on Bitcoin blockchain to WBTC and renBTC on the Ethereum blockchain is a simple cross-chain practice of assets transfer under a centralized institutional custodian. Such institutions receive users' BTCs and issue cross-chain BTC tokens with a 1:1 bridging loan on Ethereum. The same is true for centralized exchanges. Users can complete the swap between BTC and ETH in a centralized exchange, so as to achieve a cross-chain asset transfer.

This book mainly discusses the cases of decentralized cross-chain of public chains. The two main cross-chain projects in recent years are Cosmos and Polkadot, which have similarities and yet fundamental differences.

(1) Cosmos

Cosmos, which means a parallel universe, had its ICO in April 2017 and supported transactions between different blockchains. Cosmos is written in Golang language, which facilitates smart contract and dApps development. Cosmos supports cross-chain transactions and the migration of existing blockchains such as Ethereum's overall ledger to the Cosmos network. By taking full advantage of its scalability, Cosmos completely eliminates the current inefficient blockchain and facilitates projects that wish to re-deploy on the Cosmos network.

The two infrastructures used to build the Cosmos network are the Tendermint consensus protocol and IBC cross-chain communication. The Tendermint consensus protocol is essentially a voting system, based on the Byzantine consensus algorithm, which guarantees that the final voting result is in consensus as long as more than 2/3 of the nodes are honest nodes, and thus realizes real-time final consensus. IBC cross-chain communication is the communication protocol between Tendermint blockchains, and is also the basis for interoperability. IBC makes use of its instant finality to allow heterogeneous blockchains to exchange tokens with each other.

According to the white paper, the voting node in Cosmos is called a validator, responsible for block generation. When the Cosmos main network was formally launched, 100 validators were selected.

The economic model of the ATOM token (the Cosmos currency) is quite similar to that of other DPoS coins. There is no upper limit for the total supply. Instead, additional issuance and transaction rewards are obtained through staking.

In the Cosmos network, the integration point of each blockchain is a hub. The Cosmos team is only responsible for the security of the Cosmos Hub. When more and more blockchains are integrated into the Cosmos network, the consensus and value of the whole network are improved with the increasing number of nodes. However, the security of all hubs cannot be guaranteed from the underlying architecture. Once a node is attacked, it may cause the collapse of the whole network. Over the last three years of development, the number of blockchains integrated with the network has increased, but the ecosystem has progressed slowly. The relatively large blockchains accessed include Binance DEX and IRIS, and ecosystem projects include Kava, Band and Terra.

(2) Polkadot

Polkadot had its ICO in October 2017. The substrate and concurrent runtime modules used in the development are written based on Rust, which is suitable for blockchain development. However, the development threshold of Rust is too high for developers who are used to Ethereum and new developers. The NPoS (Nominated Proof of Stake) consensus mechanism is adopted to improve the PoS mechanism, and the concept of the nominee is introduced. The DOT holders can choose the validator it trusts to stake DOT and then share the rewards of the validator. To become a validator, one needs to become a candidate first and run for election. This is fairer and more decentralized than the DPoS proxy model. However, to ensure the efficiency of the blockchain network, the number of validators is fixed by the system, which also prevents Polkadot from reaching as high a level of decentralization as BTC and ETH.

Polkadot contains many parachains, each of which has its own independent business and mechanism. Transactions can occur on or between parachains. The whole Polkadot blockchain ensures that each parachain is secure and trustworthy, while parachains can interact with each other.

Figure 4.1: Schematic diagram of Polkadot

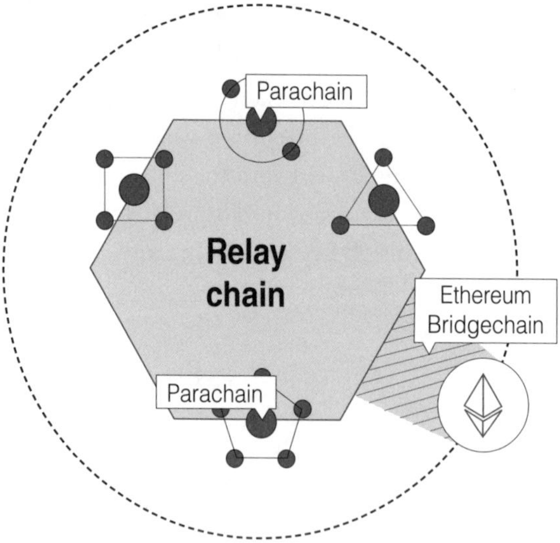

Source: Polkadot website

As shown in the diagram, Polkadot consists of the following parts:

The relay chain: the center of Polkadot, coordinating consensus and transactions between parachains;

The parachain: collecting and processing transactions;

The bridge: the bridge to connect ETH, BTC and other blockchains.

Unlike Cosmos, parachains are connected more closely in Polkadot. Each parachain is connected to the relay chain through the slot interface, which regulates the overall service and security. However, since parachains are connected through slot auctions by locking DOTs, those who have a greater amount of DOTs may manipulate the ownership of the slots, making it virtually impossible for the entire blockchain network to achieve a high degree of decentralization in the early stage. As time goes on, a more decentralized holding of DOTs can increase the consensus value of the network.

Polkadot's main network was officially put into operation in 2020, and a formal slot auction was kick started in November 2021. Polkadot ecosystem projects are developing rapidly and will be launched successively after the slot auctions, covering infrastructure, DeFi, NFT, games, DID, social networking, Oracles, and other fields. Many teams and projects want to gain early dividends in this new ecosystem. Whether real cross-chain interactive communication can be realized in the future remains to be seen.

The efficiency and decentralization have always been a dilemma for blockchain. The birth of cross-chain solutions may realize the unified interaction of blockchain information, enabling projects on highly decentralized blockchains such as Ethereum, Bitcoin and other public chains to be migrated to sidechains or other chains through cross-chain solutions to meet the requirements of high-performance.

4.3   The emergence of distributed applications

Distributed applications refer to applications distributed on different servers, with user interaction and data storage also in multiple regions. For some applications, users can also participate in the provision of storage and services, such as the BitTorrent BT download that supports P2P download and storage. Resources are downloaded and stored in a server and in the users' computers. Distributed applications can reduce the pressure of servers and provide services to many regions around the world. The failure of a single server does not affect the regular operation of applications, but there are trade-offs that result in a slow or unstable speed.

4.3.1   The emergence of dApps

The poor user experience of traditional distributed applications is mainly due to the need for a lot of money to purchase a large number of servers, and the lack of incentives for users to provide services for the system, which makes many distributed applications difficult to be implemented for all the good ideas and visions.

With the blockchain network, dApps seem to have found their proper direction. The decentralized nature of the blockchain network offers dApp a ground for development, and token incentives can also encourage users to use these dApps and provide related services spontaneously. Developers only need to deploy a smart contract on Ethereum to have the business logic of the dApp running on the blockchain, the costs of which are negligible compared with the traditional centralized applications. Users bear the cost of using the network and need to pay for gas to call/execute dApp's smart contract, so that dApp developers do not have to spend time on server construction and programming, saving energy to focus on contract security and front-end development.

4.3.2   NFT carries on the momentum

NFT stands for non-fungible token. The most common NFTs are issued using the ERC-721 standard, which is different from the tokens issued with the ERC-20 token standard. Each NFT is unique, meeting the needs of virtual items such as collectibles and games. Therefore, NFT was mainly designed to serve this end.

In 2017, *CryptoKitties*, a blockchain pet game, became popular on the Ethereum network and even once caused network congestion. Each pet in the game is an independent NFT, and the rules of the game are easy and coded on smart contracts. It allows pet breeding and creating into newborn *CryptoKitties*. Each pet has different attributes, and they can be traded just like any other ERC721 token. Collectors who like the game are willing to buy pets with unique attributes or high rarity in the market. However, as blockchain entered the 2018 crypto winter, this game has gradually faded out during the bear market.

Though losing its popularity, *CryptoKitties* has given a standard for more teams that want to play games and collect unique items on the blockchain. At present, NFT covers a wide range of use cases such as crypto-art, games, marketplaces and virtual world items.

Games and virtual world assets are the earliest use cases for NFTs. The generated game metadata exist on the chain as individual NFTs without contact with the real world. In-game data cannot be changed at will. This makes it difficult for game developers to modify game parameters, change directions and reduce the value of virtual assets in games, thus protecting the rights and interests of players.

Crypto and digital art is the big new NFT trend that has been evolving over the last two years. NFT platforms cooperate with artists to issue digital art directly on the chain to meet the growing demand from collectors. Exchanges also evolve by charging transaction fees and a percentage of artists' income. Both SuperRare and Origin are crypto-art platforms recently developed. This field has high requirements for IP. The platform needs to be bound with well-known artists, sports events and stars. Digital artworks created by them have a high collection value, with which more users can be attracted to the platform.

Marketplaces such as OpenSea can trade a variety of NFTs, including game items, NFT souvenirs and various artworks. Transactions on the platform are also recorded on the Ethereum blockchain for more transparency. The platform charges a commission for every transaction.

4.3.3   DeFi boom

2020 was a year that witnessed DeFi's booming. DeFi has achieved explosive growth, increasing TVL – Total Locked Value by more than 30 times. This leads to a bull market of blockchain and the development of DeFi protocols, giving DeFi the capability of being a challenger to compete with centralized finance.

As early as 2017, during the bull market, ETHlend, Synthetix, 0x, Maker and many other DeFi projects completed their ICOs. Several of them depicted a visionary DeFi blueprint and realized the most basic functions of lending and trading in finance. However, as a result of the high gas fee and low execution efficiency, DeFi had never exerted much influence in the blockchain world. People thought of it as merely a vision. Finance is considered a highly time-sensitive and data-explosive industry. The speed of the blockchain network has no way to match the financial market. It seemed unimaginable to wait 15 seconds to complete a transaction in the financial world where milliseconds count. With the advent of the bear market in 2018, tokens LEND, and SNX fell below the issue price by over 90% since their all-time high.

By the end of 2018, Uniswap was launched. The unique AMM – Automated Market Maker – trading mechanism made transactions timely and efficient on the blockchain. However, the disadvantages of this mechanism were also apparent, including the high gas fees, users' inability to control the prices they want to trade, the need to lock in many tokens to provide liquidity, and many others.

After a quiet year in 2019, the DeFi market finally ushered in an explosion. At the beginning of 2020, the strong market and institutions' support brought a surge in lockups. Uniswap lockups, the number of DAI generated by Maker, the number of wBTC for cross-chain and LEND lockups and lending were all boosted exponentially, creating conditions for DeFi's development. On March 12, 2020, Bitcoin and Ethereum fell by more than 50%. Many DeFi protocols suffered a huge impact as a result. Soaring gas and untimely liquidation caused some users under huge losses. However, after the crisis, DeFi quickly recovered its vitality. This huge market fluctuation turned into a touchstone. Some participants decided to leave because of the losses, but more began to recognize the DeFi's potential.

In June 2020, the use of liquidity mining and farming once again ignited market enthusiasm, as funds flocked in to be locked up in the DeFi market to get governance tokens for ultra-high annualized returns. That was a win-win attempt for the DeFi protocols and its participant liquidity providers. Many DeFi protocols completed token distribution while capturing the necessary liquidity to develop their DeFi ecosystems. Several projects represented by Balancer, Curve and Sushi captured a lot of liquidity in a short time and became a frontline DeFi protocol, with Sushi once surpassing Uniswap as the largest decentralized exchange in terms of lockup volume. Some smart money with high-risk appetites also started to mine on DeFi for profit, thus giving birth to a number of DeFi whales.

With the development of DeFi, a prosperous DeFi ecosystem

has been shaped, covering lending, trading, aggregator, Oracle, derivatives, synthetic assets, stablecoins, insurance and so on. Dozens of well-known DeFi protocols have emerged. In the foreseeable future, DeFi will still maintain fast growth. With the growth of layer2 solutions and high-performance blockchains, DeFi may undergo further transformation. We will introduce the development of DeFi in detail in Chapter 7.

References

"What are the characteristics of blockchain 1.0, 2.0 and 3.0?", 528btc, https://www.528btc.com/ask/160370670855279.html.

"What is web 3.0?", Coinmarketcap, https://coinmarketcap.com/alexandria/article/what-is-web-3-0#:~:text=Definition%3A%20What%20Is%20Web%20 3.0,learning%20(ML)%2C%20Big%20Data.

Charles Silver, "What is web 3.0?", Forbes, https://www.forbes.com/sites/forbestechcouncil/2020/01/06/what-is-web-3-0/?sh=390d4d5b58df.

The Ontology Team, "Blockchain 101: What is cross chain?", Medium, https://medium.com/ontologynetwork/blockchain-101-what-is-cross-chain-b16c5b4cda8a.

Jingdata, "Parachain and Cross-Chain Research Report", JINGDATA, https://www.jingdata.com/article/31.html.

Gavin Wood, "Polkadot White Paper", Polkadot Network, https://polkadot.network/PolkaDotPaper.pdf.

"Polkadot Structure", Polkadot Wiki, https://wiki.polkadot.network/en/.

"Cosmos White Paper", Cosmos Network, https://v1.cosmos.network/resources/whitepaper.

CHAPTER 5

THE BEGINNING OF MASS ADOPTION

The adoption of blockchain technology has been snowballing in recent years, and people have gradually moved from blindly speculating on digital currency and thinking that "blockchain" is just a word to make money by merely implementing some blockchain technology. More and more developers have been joining the blockchain and crypto ecosystem. Once the development focus started to shift from speculation on digital currency to the industry use cases, the blockchain industry took an essential step towards maturity. When any new technology emerges, it is always accompanied by a bubble, which is helpful for the industry's growth in some way. Every time the bubble bursts, the true technology believers stay. In the end, winners are the companies that can deliver the technology and workable products. Those who can survive will be highly rewarded after severe competition.

The deep integration of blockchain technology in different industries is fundamentally an important sign that blockchain technology has started to mature. As the business value that can be achieved by using blockchain technology becomes more meaningful, blockchain technology becomes closer to maturity. It can be implemented and adopted on a large scale only when technology has developed well-established patterns and maturity and provide a stronger use case. This chapter will focus on how blockchain can make use of its unique advantages in different areas to integrate with and empower various industries.

Meanwhile, the mass adoption of blockchain requires strict regulatory standards and strong regulatory instruments to prevent regulatory "darkness under the lights". It is important to strengthen regulation effectively. A global regulatory view on blockchain technology is also one of the focuses of this chapter.

5.1   Historical similarities between blockchain and the internet

Firstly, let's take a look at the internet. The internet was born in 1969, starting by connecting two computers for communications. However, the symbolic event that really brought the internet into public eyes was the World Wide Web in 1989, of which the turning point was the emergence of the Mosaic web browser in 1993. From 1995 to 2000, the internet business ecosystem was crowded. With the emergence of blockchain technology, mankind is once again standing at a crossroads of potentially giant efficiency leaps. The frenzy for blockchain today is quite much the same as that for the speculation on internet back in the day – capital from around the world flooded into the internet space, just as wealthy people worldwide are investing in blockchain today.

At the end of the 20th century, people's understanding of the internet was very similar to the general public's knowledge of blockchain today. When someone mentioned the concept of sending files by email, people said, "Why would we need such a thing? A phone call is enough." The ICO boom in 2018 is similar to what happened in 1995 when the IPO of the browser pioneer Netscape sent everyone into a hysteria. The blockchain industry is now similar to the internet in 1996, when people were still crazy about the technology and expecting extraordinary products from the industry, just like they expect the emergence of a superb, groundbreaking application in the blockchain space.

Of course, the comparison between blockchain and the internet is not so linear. Nevertheless, the future development of blockchain can draw many valuable lessons from the history of the internet. While internet technology can be appropriately understood as a decentralized system of information transmission and is primarily applied to enable the rapid sending and receiving of information,

Bitcoin technology is a decentralized system of value transfer. For example, by doing a Bitcoin transfer, you are transmitting a share of ownership value because your Bitcoin becomes someone else's. This is achieved because blockchain technology is immutable and traceable. Based on the rapid development of the network, the value transfer system of blockchains is also slowly being integrated into our lives soon.

Blockchain does not seem to solve any practical problems for the general public. Only a breakthrough application can promote the acceptance of blockchain by the public. The internet was also once a bubble and called a Ponzi scheme. From 1995 to 2000, the internet industry's primary business model was IPO offerings and increasing stock prices through partnerships with other internet startups. But today, we all benefit from this great innovation. Most of the core technology and developer knowledge we use today came from the investments of the dot-com enthusiasts back then.

In 2000, JAVA, MySQL and many other large internet companies that focused on solving real problems emerged. That's when people realized that this was revolutionary and could make a difference. In contrast to the status of the crypto world today, Bitcoin has not yet reached mass adoption except for payments, and Ethereum is providing a more groundbreaking technology as the "world computer". Many Ethereum ICOs are as crazy as investing in the dot-com in the 90s was. But at the same time, these investments are being made in a variety of important infrastructures, tools, and core technologies to attract developers and entrepreneurs to establish the knowledge base and experience together. Compared to the history of the internet, the blockchain is at the same stage the internet was in 1996.

There are many similarities between blockchain at the current stage and the early days of the internet. Currently, there are still areas in blockchain technology that have not yet matured, and some projects or products that once attracted great attention may end up being unsustainable or unsuccessful. As the internet is not limited to use cases like emails and forums, blockchain technology is also subject to constant upgrades, improvements and new use cases. Blockchain technology has grown a lot in just a decade, with new applications taking shape, but there is still a long way to go to have a mass adopted killer app. Like the rise of the internet, the blockchain space has made considerable achievements in attracting investment and talents. A large number of high-level talents such as developers and financial specialists have flocked to the industry, helping and promoting the rapid development of the industry. Looking back at the history of the internet, we can find that every technological revolution goes through this process of excitement, hype, depression, questioning, and reshuffling. However, this process does not mean that the technology and products are problematic, but rather a necessary path for maturity. Even today, the internet cannot solve all practical issues, but it cannot be denied that it has greatly improved productivity. The same is true for blockchain. Blockchain technology will also experience similar doubts, troughs and reshuffles, but the development of blockchain technology is irreversible. Rome was not built in one day, so does the current internet empire, which is also applicable to the development of blockchain technology, which is still in its infancy.

5.2   A new step forward in global regulations

In terms of regulation, countries worldwide generally hold a technology-neutral attitude, which means they do not object to the blockchain as a technology. The concerns are mainly in implementing use cases and regulations on digital asset transactions as well as the financial market. Regulations are being formulated around the use cases and digital currencies, but the attitude of countries around the world towards the regulation of the digital asset market varies according to their national restrictions.

Looking at the current situation of global digital asset regulation, a small number of countries have a positive attitude towards digital assets, with specific bills for digital currencies and relatively relaxed policies for blockchain startups or virtual currencies, including countries such as Singapore, Japan, Canada, Australia, Germany, Thailand, Sweden, Norway, and others. The vast majority of countries tend to be more cautious towards virtual currencies, where have not formulated any bills specifically for virtual currencies and digital assets, mostly applying the same existing regulations on financial assets for digital assets with a cautious and strict attitude, including countries/regions of the United States, the United Kingdom, India, Malaysia, Italy, Turkey, the Netherlands, Spain, New Zealand, Russia, Hong Kong, China, and Taiwan, China. Still, some countries hold a conservative wait-and-see attitude towards blockchain from their national circumstances or environment, where there are almost no regulations on digital assets, and any trading and issuance of digital assets are illegal, including countries such as China, Bangladesh, Iran and Pakistan. In this book, five countries and regions, namely the United States, Hong Kong, China, Singapore, Japan, and mainland China, holding different attitudes were selected to illustrate the current state of digital asset regulation.

5.2.1　The United States

First, most states in the U.S. recognize the legitimacy of blockchain technology, despite concerns from U.S. academics about its "immutable" nature. Regulators in the U.S. include the SEC, CFTC, IRS, FinCEN, who use the Howey Test as a standard to determine whether a digital asset is a security asset when it is first publicly offered and traded.

The Howey Test includes explicitly three aspects: first, the form in which virtual assets are issued and sold; second, whether crypto-asset holders can profit in the real world outside the blockchain; and third, the operational status of the blockchain network when digital assets are issued. Security assets are subject to U.S. securities laws and regulated by the SEC, which requires filing an application report and registration to disclose the necessary information about the issuance to the public. With traditional securities regulations applied, this type of asset issuance becomes an STO (Security Token Offering). Issuers can also make private offerings of tokens through exemptions under Reg D, Reg S, Reg A+, etc. Exempted tokens do not need to be registered with the SEC but are still subject to securities laws.

Trading platforms are required to apply for registration and, along with a federal license, trading platforms opened in certain states must also be licensed by that state. Assets deemed as non-securities are not regulated by federal law and are consequently exposed to lower policy risk. Still, multiple regulatory agencies work together to prevent the risk of possible violations. In addition, the regulations on blockchain vary from federal to individual states. Each state will make further legislation to regulate digital assets based on their social conditions to ensure financial stability. Federal legislation mainly includes the Securities Exchange Act of 1934, U.S. Securities Act of 1933, Bank Secrecy Act, etc. Regulations are more friendly in states such as Colorado, Wyoming (where in July 2021 the DAO Law was passed), Texas, California, Ohio. In terms of the tax system, the U.S. has the Notice 2014-21 as guidance on tax for digital assets, which requires cryptocurrencies to follow the tax regulations for physical assets. Overall, the U.S. has a straightforward approach to regulating projects in the blockchain area and a more robust legal regime. Compliance projects that have been approved include Coinbase, the largest digital currency exchange in the U.S. that was listed on Nasdaq on April 14, 2021, with a market capitalization of US$85 billion on its first day of trading.

5.2.2   Hong Kong, China

Hong Kong is very cautious towards blockchain, and its regulators focus on the issuance and trading of digital assets. In addition to the Hong Kong Securities and Futures Commission (SFC) as the primary regulator, there are also bureaus such as HKMA (Hong Kong Monetary Authority) and HKEX (Hong Kong Exchanges and Clearing Limited) that assist the SFC in creating regulatory frameworks.

The SFC Statement on the regulatory framework for virtual asset portfolios managers, fund distributors and trading platform operators and the Circular to intermediaries on the distribution of virtual asset funds issued by SFC on November 1, 2018, sets out the framework for the regulation of virtual asset trading platforms, with virtual asset portfolio managers and fund distributors being the first to be included in the scope of supervision. SFC assesses the business content and risks of the managers and exchanges to issue licenses if they meet the requirements.

In November 2019, the SFC issued the *Warning on Virtual Asset Futures Contracts* and *Position Paper: Regulation of Virtual Asset Trading Platforms*, which empowers the SFC to issue licenses to persons or institutions for regulated activities as defined in the Securities and Futures Ordinance, signaling a significant step forward in the regulation of blockchain crypto asset trading in Hong Kong. Security tokens (i.e., tokens that can be deemed as equity, unsecured bonds and collective investment schemes) are subject to regulation by the SFC under the Securities and Futures Ordinance. Security tokens and their initial token offerings, or providing advice or services for, managing or promoting such tokens, are "regulated activities", where individuals or institutions involved are required to register and obtain a license from the SFC. The SFC is temporarily applying the current license for digital asset investment institutions in terms of licensing.

In terms of trading platforms, Hong Kong has mainly adopted a "sandbox mechanism" for initial regulation, issuing licenses to eligible platforms based on their performance and moving on to the next sandbox stage. After a review period of at least 12 months, the regulator will thoroughly understand before formulating a reasonable regulatory approach. The Position Paper clearly states that compliant trading platforms must meet the SFC's regulations and conditions, including anti-money laundering, anti-terrorism, and fiat deposit. It is worth noting that it voluntarily joins the licensing system proposed in the Position Paper and voluntarily licensed digital asset trading platforms are included in the regulatory regime, excluding non-securities-based virtual assets. However, the trading volume of digital assets has increased significantly in recent years.

Due to some of the anonymity features of digital assets, there are risks of money laundering, terrorism, fraud, market manipulation and other financial system risks. In response, the Financial Services and the Treasury Bureau proposes establishing a mandatory licensing system to replace the original voluntary licensing system, under which all digital asset companies must be licensed and fully regulated before they can operate. It also makes further requirements on the previous Position Paper in terms of anti-money laundering, anti-terrorist financing and risk control.

On November 3, 2020, the Financial Services and the Treasury Bureau released the *Consultation on Legislative Proposals to Enhance Anti-Money Laundering and Counter-Terrorist Financing Regulation*, which was to launch a public consultation on the proposed regulation of money laundering and terrorist financing. The proposal in the consultation paper is that any institution engaging in the business of trading platforms for digital assets in Hong Kong will need to obtain a license from the SFC and must comply with the Anti-Money Laundering and Counter-Terrorist Financing Ordinance. While it is a voluntarily participated licensing system in the Position Paper, the consultation paper proposes mandatory licensing with the aim of bringing all digital currencies into the regulatory regime to protect the interests of investors. In general, in Hong Kong, all institutions or individuals engaged in the digital currency must hold a license issued by the SFC and be subject to its supervision.

5.2.3   Singapore

Singapore is the residence choice of many blockchain projects, whose regulatory stance on the blockchain is very clear with a friendly policy and relatively simple registrations process for projects. The Singapore government tends to view digital assets as "commodities" rather than "currencies" and encourages academic research on blockchain technology. The Intellectual Property Office of Singapore is accelerating the process of granting blockchain patents. The issuance and trading of digital assets are mainly regulated by the Monetary Authority of Singapore (MAS), with reference to the Securities and Futures Act and the Fintech Regulatory Sandbox Guidelines. Among them, the Securities and Futures Act defines digital virtual assets as commodities.

Singapore is relatively loose on regulating initial public offerings and the trading of digital assets. The MAS released *A Guide to Digital Token Offerings* in November 2017, which sets out the specific rules on issuing tokens. At present, MAS will classify tokens into three major categories according to the nature of the tokens: utility tokens, payment tokens and securities tokens, among which utility tokens are not subject to regulation as long as they do not involve money laundering and terrorist financing and other illegal and criminal acts, securities tokens issued through STO are regulated by the Securities and Futures Article Act unless exempted by the relevant provisions, while the Payment Services Act applies to the regulation of payment tokens.

Similar to Hong Kong, China, MAS requires institutions engaged in virtual asset trading and services to be licensed and comply with anti-money laundering and anti-terrorism regulations. In terms of trading platforms, it is divided into licensed traditional trading platforms (approved exchange) and specialized digital currency trading platforms (recognized market operator) without a license. Like Hong Kong, China and some European countries, Singapore also adopts a sandbox regulatory model. The licenses and sandbox model adopted by Singapore are conducive to the development of blockchain technology but also requires projects to comply with anti-money laundering and anti-terrorist principles. In a nutshell, Singapore's approach to virtual assets enables an appropriate balance between changes and risks.

5.2.4   Japan

Japan holds an inclusive and supportive attitude towards the development of various blockchain projects. The main regulatory body in Japan is the Japanese FSA – Financial Services Agency, with major regulations including the Payment Services Act, the Enforcement Decree of the Act on the Consumer Protection, and the Financial Instruments and Exchange Act, which requires the registration of institutions engaged in virtual currencies to operate, and other provisions regarding the taxation of cryptocurrencies.

Regarding the initial token offering and trading of digital assets, Japan's Financial Services Agency does not prohibit but regulate them under the Payment Services Act. It stipulates that blockchain application scenarios for commercial use must be registered with and regulated by the regulator. While the token offerings of different projects are regulated by different acts, such as the Investment Act and the Settlement Act, as the cases of the projects may be. In terms of taxation, income from crypto assets in Japan is also included in gross personal income but is not counted in capital gains.

Although Japan made it available for exchange license

applications early, the commercialization process has been slow. Japan was the first country to legalize digital currency trading and initiate the exchange license. It has been accepting applications from its domestic and overseas exchanges for digital currency exchange licenses recognized by the FSA since April 2017. However, the FSA's approval of cryptocurrency exchanges has become very strict since 2018 due to the hack on Coincheck, and few licenses have been issued subsequently, with some cases including OKCoin, which had a two-year-long application process.

5.2.5　Mainland China

Currently, there are almost no regulations on digital assets in mainland China. From the perspective of digital asset market regulation, mainland China has a conservative attitude, and it is illegal to engage in any virtual currency transactions in mainland China. Still, China confers great importance to the blockchain as a technology.

On December 5, 2013, the People's Bank of China, the Ministry of Industry and Information Technology, the China Banking Regulatory Commission, the China Securities Regulatory Commission and the China Insurance Regulatory Commission jointly issued the *Notice on Preventing the Risks of Bitcoin*, clearly stating that Bitcoin does not have the same legal status as fiat and cannot be circulated as a currency in the market. On September 4, 2017, the People's Bank of China, and seven ministries and commissions, jointly issued the *Notice on Preventing the Risks of Token Offering and Fundraising*. It stipulated that no organization or individual shall engage in financing activities of token offering, and virtual currency activities in mainland China have been almost completely banned since September 4. In June 2021, Xinjiang, Inner Mongolia, Qinghai, Sichuan and Yunnan also announced the shutdown of cryptocurrency mining activity.

As for blockchain technology, on October 24, 2019, in the

18th collective learning on the status and trends of blockchain technology development, General Secretary Xi Jinping emphasized that blockchain is a breakthrough technological innovation and plays an important role in promoting industry transformation and that the development of blockchain technology and industry should be accelerated. This study clarified China's supportive attitude toward blockchain technology. On August 10, 2019, Mu Changchun, deputy director of the Department of Payment and Settlement of the People's Bank of China, introduced the DCEP, the central bank's legal digital currency, at the 3rd China Finance 40 Forum in Yichun, where the central bank's digital currency has now made great progress in China and has been applied in several cities on a pilot basis.

In general, mainland China is conservative in terms of trading and offering digital currencies, without any law or bill in place for digital currency trading and offerings. However, at the technological level, the Chinese government is very supportive of the development of blockchain technology and believes that blockchain technology can better serve the real economy in the future, where the DCEP will have broader application scenarios. General Secretary Xi Jinping also pointed out some specific application scenarios of blockchain in finance, people's livelihood, and government affairs, such as building smart cities, improving the efficiency of capital utilization, solving problems related to risk control and so on.

5.2.6   Outlook on future global regulatory trends

At present, countries around the world generally have a neutral attitude towards blockchain technology. However, there are global efforts to promote digital asset regulation on the regulatory level, with regulation mainly focused on the issuance and trading of tokens and licenses being the primary regulatory approach. Currently, at least 14 countries or regions around the world have launched regulatory licenses related to crypto digital currencies, including the United States, Canada, Switzerland, Australia, Cayman, Japan, Malaysia, the

Philippines, Thailand, Hong Kong, China, Gibraltar, the United Arab Emirates, Malta and Estonia. The licenses are mainly used to regulate companies that trade and invest in digital currencies, and they include requirements for anti-money laundering and anti-terrorist financing, with activities such as the issuance and trading of virtual assets being regulated.

As for the development of future regulations on digital assets, first, countries worldwide will strengthen their support for blockchain technology in the future. In addition, bills specifically for digital will be improved, and the process of joint regulation will be accelerated. In order to actively promote the development of global blockchain technology and the process of digital currency regulation, some international organizations have set up separate blockchain departments, such as the International Monetary Fund's Fintech Advisory Group and the World Bank's Blockchain Lab, among others. In addition, there are also organizations like the Financial Action Task Force (FATF) that call on countries around the world to establish mandatory anti-money laundering and anti-terrorist financing policies to strengthen risk control of digital assets and crack down on criminal activities. FATF launched a year-long worldwide anti-money laundering and anti-terrorist financing review of digital assets starting in June 2020.

5.3   Diversified use cases

5.3.1   Opportunities on-chain – Consortium blockchain

Blockchains can be divided into public, private and consortium chains according to the degree of openness. A consortium blockchain is different from public and private chains. It is a semi-public and semi-centralized blockchain, which only serves the members of the consortium. The development cost of a consortium chain is generally higher, and the time required for implementation is longer, which is better for leading enterprises in the same industry to jointly build. Unlike public chains, such as Ethereum, consortium chains are partially centralized, and the data and assets within the consortium chain can only be recorded, traded and transmitted among permission members. Compared with public chains, the data value of the leading enterprises in the industry can be circulated efficiently due to the lower degree of decentralization, better transaction speed, higher efficiency and lower operation cost, thus achieving the purpose of promoting the development of the whole industry. In this section, we will analyze the application scenarios, use cases and value of the consortium chain by introducing two classic cases in this field, AntChain and IBM Hyperledger, and look into the future of the consortium chain.

(1) AntChain

AntChain, is an industry-specific consortium chain for large enterprises. Launched in 2019 with typical use cases including traceability, cross-border remittance, electronic bills, and on-chain services, it brings high-efficiency services to enterprises. The service targets of this industry consortium chain are limited to large leading enterprises, which are required to build their own blockchain systems and then access the blockchain through the AntChain interface. This is often a high threshold for SMEs, and the application value of the industry consortium chain is limited due to the lack of SMEs participation and resource integration.

In March 2020, after the launch of AntChain, an industry consortium chain called OpenChain, created as a consortium chain created for SMEs, was launched. It was then opened for public testing on November 8, 2019, and went commercially live on March 31, 2020. The difference between the open consortium chain and the industry consortium chain is that the development threshold is greatly reduced. The time to launch an application live on-chain was shortened, bringing convenience for SMEs to develop blockchain applications and realize the value flow between enterprises. The development cost for SMEs is basically less than 10,000 RMB, and the deployment can be completed within minutes. OpenChain provides SMEs with the interface to access AntChain so that they can enjoy the AntChain services even if they do not have the ability to build a blockchain on their own. The operational mode of AntChain is relatively similar to that of a public chain, which also uses gas fees for transactions, and the transaction volume can reach 100 transactions per second. In addition, the privacy capabilities on the chain are strong.

In addition to the underlying technology, the AntChain use cases are also very diverse, including the following six types:

- **Entertainment and games:** OpenChain can provide functions such as in-game asset retrieval and protection for mini gaming programs, and help them acquire users.

- **Charity traceability:** Using blockchain technology to empower the internet of Things (IoT), the source/destination of donations and the flow of all the goods and materials can be traced on the chain to achieve openness, transparency, and traceability.

- **Copyright and contract:** OpenChain can provide services such as auditing, query and data monitoring to solve the problem of identification and collaboration.

- **Social organization:** Consortium chains can facilitate the formation and maintenance of various types of organizations.

- **Financial instruments:** Finance is the earliest use case that was widely applied to the consortium chain. With the consortium chain, financial instruments can help SMEs achieve low-cost information flow, improve efficiency and maintain a high degree of transparency.

- **On-chain collaboration:** AntChain can provide on-chain services for enterprises and connect enterprises within the Ant ecosystem to achieve collaboration.

At present, a considerable number of enterprises have integrated with the OpenChain of Ant Financial and accessed to Alibaba's traffic. The AntChain ecosystem is booming with main customers including ChainIDE, Mima Technology, Zhejiang Zhuo Ke, CCMusic and many others. OpenChain provides a new infrastructure for enterprises to develop blockchain applications.

(2) IBM Hyperledger

Another primary application of the consortium chain model is the Hyperledger Fabric, a Linux Foundation-hosted open-source project launched in 2016. Hyperledger made the most outstanding progress among the 70 open-source organizations initiated by Linux. It aims to create an enterprise-level distributed ledger to advance business transactions between enterprises while hoping to build an open-source technology community, set up a distributed ledger testing network, and work together to advance the distributed process around the globe and promote digitalization. It is a global collaboration of industry leaders covering a wide range of areas such as the financial industry, supply chain services, internet of Things and manufacturing.

The current members of the Hyperledger ecosystem are mainly banks, internet companies and Fintech companies worldwide. Members in China include those well-known internet giant companies of Alibaba, Tencent and Baidu, who joined the Hyperledger ecosystem in 2018. Globally, IBM, the multinational technology company and consulting firm, and Intel, the world's largest semiconductor company, are the most critical ecosystem members. To date, there are close to 20 enterprise blockchain application projects on Hyperledger, and the chart below shows the composition of Hyperledger's ecosystem. One of the featured projects is Fabric by IBM, an open-source platform with a better scalable architecture to meet enterprise-level service demand. According to IBM, Fabric currently has more than 200 customers, among which there are big customers such as Alibaba, Dell, Google and Microsoft. From the ecosystem point of view, Hyperledger is now the world's largest blockchain consortium, whose members increased at the fastest pace among all Linux organizations, with 20 members from China and a quarter from the Asia-Pacific region.

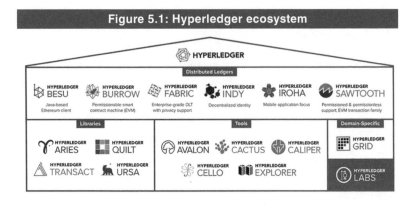

Figure 5.1: Hyperledger ecosystem

Source: Hyperledger website

The Hyperledger consortium chain has encountered bottlenecks in its development while growing rapidly, with the most critical one being the development of basic guidelines within the consortium. The rapid growth of Hyperledger members and projects in recent years leads to the need for a unified standard within the consortium to achieve maximum integration of internal resources. In order to develop the basic principles for the consortium to follow, IBM, the leading company within the consortium, promotes the principle of openness to avoid excessive centralization within the blockchain, specifically including the three principles of open code, open standards and open governance, intending to lower the barriers to communication between enterprises, provide an open environment, achieving common governance and effective integration of resources, and thus promoting the development of the consortium as a whole.

(3) Outlook on consortium chain

The consortium chain is generally more efficient and commercially sound, making it the best choice for enterprise-level applications by referring to the operation model and concepts of public chains such as gas fee enabled transactions and distributed governance. The current global environment is ideal for implementing and developing consortium chain projects. More enterprises are starting to change the way they look at blockchain and trying to deploy consortium chains. We expect that in the future, the degree of connectivity between different consortium chains and between consortium chains and public chains, as well as the integration of resources, will be better. The ecosystem will be more prosperous with more SMEs joining. As the transaction volume and content on the subsequent consortium chains deepen and the value rises, incentives and supporting regulatory mechanisms will gradually introduce a more harmonious ecosystem environment. In terms of application scenarios and the existing established applications in the financial sector, more scenarios will emerge in the fields related to the people's livelihood, such as smart cities, education, healthcare and culture.

5.3.2 Blockchain as a service (BaaS)

Blockchain as a service (BaaS) refers to empowering the blockchain ecosystem and the development platform and dApps by taking advantage of cloud technology infrastructure. The benefit of the combination of blockchain and cloud computing is that it effectively reduces the deployment cost of enterprise blockchain applications. BaaS nodes can quickly establish a developer-friendly development environment and provide from scratch various services based on blockchain technology. In the development of blockchain decentralized applications, the consensus mechanism of public chains such as Ethereum may lead to lower transaction efficiency and higher gas fee. In comparison, the BaaS platform is more suitable for a large enterprise to deploy as it has a lower technical threshold and higher deployment efficiency than deploying on public chains.

BSN is a typical BaaS platform whose initiators are central government-owned enterprises in China. It is a blockchain service network that connects all data centers by creating a blockchain environment. The underlying data centers include Tencent Cloud, Ali Cloud and other service providers, which use their bandwidth or storage space to BSN for sale. The upper layer network integrates the consortium chain and public chain framework to create the blockchain operational environment. The current consortium chain framework integrated by BSN includes Fabric, FISCO BCOS and Xuper Chain. The public chain includes Ethereum and EOS, as the infrastructure

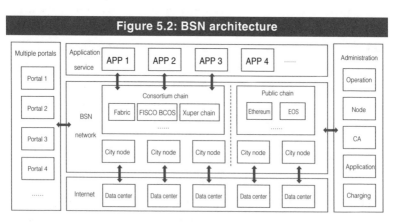

Figure 5.2: BSN architecture

Source: PANews website

for developers to use. In April 2020, BSC was incorporated in New Infrastructure and officially started to be used for commercial purpose in China. As of November 2020, BSN has more than 130 nodes worldwide, located in six continents.

The advantages of the BSN network lie in the following three main aspects:

- **Easy to use:** BSN network provides all kinds of blockchain management services for developers, including node management, operation and maintenance, application management and change management, all of which are automated, so it is convenient for developers to operate in the network.

- **High security:** BSN network provides various security services such as C.A. management, identity authentication, data security management and permission management to ensure the security of applications and funds.

- **Flexible and open:** The three levels of participants in the BSN network are cloud service providers, consortium and public chains, and BSN portals who are free to join or exit. It is flexible and open for participation as long as they meet the protocol criteria.

5.3.3 Crypto finance

The financial sector is the one that developed at an early stage and is most diversified with a more established application of blockchain among multiple use cases. With the application of blockchain in the financial industry, it gradually develops from a single application to a more diversified one. Based on numerous financial application scenarios, we have selected four more important scenarios, namely insurance services, supply chain and trade finance, cross-border payment, and trust services, to analyze the application value of blockchain technology in the financial field.

(1) Insurance services

The consensus mechanism of blockchain technology and the concept of joint governance have something in common with the idea of the moral choice of insurance. Insurance services are considered a crucial development direction of blockchain in finance in the future, and digital policy is the future trend. At present, the pain points of the traditional insurance industry mainly include: first, high trust cost due to the less communication between customers and insurance companies, resulting in non-transparent policy information; second, great difficulty in moral assessment of decision making and a high degree of centralization; third, risk of default in payment, claim and settlement, and the phenomenon of "insurance fraud", due to the imperfect regulation on the insurance market.

The benefits for the traditional insurance industry through blockchain technology include:

- **Improving efficiency and reducing cost:** With blockchain technology, each insurance policy can be put on-chain as an NFT. All information, transactions and flow data are recorded on the chain to ensure the authenticity and transparency of the transactions, including personal information of the policyholders, insurance categories, pricing and claim criteria. In addition, blockchain can also improve the efficiency of the insurance industry. Take life insurance as an example, once an insured event occurs, the smart contract will be automatically triggered to review and pay for the claim according to the policy. The whole claim process will be optimized and significantly improved, without the need for trust-based offline communications, which substantially lowers the underwriting costs and premiums paid by users. In addition, blockchain technology has substantial advantages in a financial settlement. In combination with smart contracts, the accuracy of premium payment and claims settlement can be improved.

- **Innovation in the business model:** Blockchain makes it possible for DAO (decentralized autonomous organization) to act as a virtual decision-making system, i.e., there is no need for the centralized process of decision making. The DAO keeps the premium paid by each insured user, and when a claim needs to be paid, the settlement of the claim will be decided by all the insured users participating in the mutual insurance by voting. Blockchain technology enables the payment, management, and payment of insurance premiums to be voted on by the DAO, providing transparency, security, and efficiency from highly automated execution. One of the DeFi projects, Nexus Mutual, introduces DAO governance in insurance, with a risk-sharing pool of funds, where community members holding NXM token vote on the settlement of claims.

(2) Supply chain and trade finance

Supply chain finance refers to the bank's provision of services to the core enterprise customers while providing loans and prepayments or other services to the enterprise's upstream and downstream suppliers or distributors, which is intra-system financing centered on the core enterprise. Supply chain financing has been especially favored by SMEs in recent years. This is because the relatively low level of SME suppliers' assets and credit often makes it hard to do the funding through loans from banks. Therefore, obtaining loans with the help of supply chain finance is an essential solution for SMEs' financing.

The disadvantages of traditional supply chain finance mainly lie in the fact that it is difficult to verify the authenticity and background of enterprise participants. Problems such as forged contracts and insufficient collaterals often occur in the actual operation of supply chain finance. If the authenticity of invoices and shipping documents, the quality of collateral cannot be guaranteed and the SMEs at both ends of the supply chain lack credit endorsement. In these cases, it is difficult for financial institutions to assess the business background, repayment ability and credit risk of micro-SMEs. Therefore, they will not participate in supply chain financing considering the risk factors, leaving micro-SMEs behind in terms of supply chain financing. In addition to the quality of the collateral and the authenticity of documents, inefficient and opaque information communication within the supply chain finance system is another factor that restricts the development of supply chain finance, which causes enterprises at both ends of the supply chain often not covered by the financial system. The supply chain finance system usually can only serve one layer of upstream and downstream affiliates of the core enterprises because credit is passed through only that one layer.

The most use of blockchain technology in supply chain finance is to digitize documents, such as letters of credit, billing, bills of lading, contracts, and so on, with the non-fungible token (NFT) playing a significant role in the future in putting these documents on-chain. It is almost impossible to tamper with the documents recorded on-chain, increasing the transparency and credibility of the supply chain. The tokenized documents can be split to be used as vouchers to pay to different layers of suppliers for financing. Blockchain builds a credit system that covers the entire supply chain, including financial institutions, banks, distributors, suppliers, and third-party enterprises, instead of being limited to the first-tier suppliers or distributors around the core enterprises. Thus, it can maximize the unity of the four aspects (capital flow, information flow, logistics, and commercial flow), solving the difficulties in financing for SMEs while improving the efficiency of capital use.

(3) Cross-border payments

The traditional cross-border payment relies on the chain of trust built between payment institutions in each country, with intermediaries linked with one another to transfer funds to the next layer. That means the remitter's funds need to pass through an intermediary layer of payment institutions before they can reach the recipient's account. Financial institutions in each country are independent, with each institution having its own separate ledgers. The limited openness and sharing of information lead to a high cost of the chain of trust. At present, the most important cross-border payment method is wire transfer. In addition, there are also specialized cross-border remittance companies, and users can also use international credit cards such as Visa for cross-border remittance.

The drawbacks of traditional cross-border payment models are obvious:

- **High handling fees:** When sending money across borders, each layer of intermediaries will often charge a percentage of the handling fee. There are also exchange rate risks for the remitter to consider.

- **Complex process and long processing time:** The efficiency of handling remittances varies considerably from one intermediary institution to another. The remittance may take a long time considering the time difference and working days.

- **Affected by the regulatory policies of countries around the world:** The process of cross-border payment involves the regulations of foreign payments and transfers in different countries, and the success and efficiency of payments are affected by the regulatory policies of each country.

While with a distributed ledger, distributed storage and other technological features of blockchain, data is transparent and cannot be tampered with. Based on the distributed ledger, recipients and payers can make cross-border transfers without the need for trust and third-party intermediaries, breaking the traditional cross-border transfer chain of trust model. Meanwhile, the use of peer-to-peer payment technology in blockchain networks enables real-time payment and receipt, solving the problems of the long payment cycle, complex process and high fees of traditional payment methods. The payment process is not subject to any time, geographical or regulatory restrictions. Cross-border payments under smart contracts are low in cost, fast and more efficient, promoting the integration and utilization of global capital. Among them, Ripple is an example of the application of blockchain technology in cross-border payments. Payees or payers worldwide can realize real-time payments and clearing through the Ripple blockchain network for low-cost cross-border transfers.

(4) Trust Services

As an old and innovative non-bank financial institution, the trust industry provides investment opportunities for many high-net-worth clients and plays a vital role in maintaining a sound financial ecosystem in society and stimulating the competitiveness of the financial market. However, risk events in the trust industry have been emerging in recent years, with increasing quality gaps between trust companies and defaults becoming more frequent and widespread. The primary deficiency in design at the top of the trust industry is the lack of information transparency in the operation process. The trustees do not know enough about the trust company due to the inadequate information disclosure and difficulty distinguishing the authenticity and reliability of the information. The key to the development of the trust industry lies in trust, where blockchain technology is a master. Embedding blockchain technology into the trust mechanism of the trust industry will greatly improve the shortcomings of the traditional trust industry. Blockchain technology will empower the trust industry in the following two ways:

- **Ensure that the information is transparent and immutable:** As blockchain adopts distributed ledger and storage, the information between the principal, trustee and beneficiary in the trust is transparent, traceable and immutable. Many trust products, especially those for the common good, lose the incentive to invest due to the donors' lack of understanding of the flow of funds. Blockchain technology can effectively help the trustors, beneficiaries and trustees to check the flow of funds in real-time so that the information of funds on the chain is always in an open and transparent state.

- **Lower information sharing cost:** Since blockchain is totally open and transparent for all participants, trustees, beneficiaries, trustors and other participants can review the block data in real-time and do not need to communicate among multiple parties to achieve information sharing, so the cost of information sharing will be greatly reduced, and the authenticity and reliability of information will be guaranteed.

References

Meng Yonghui: "As blockchain matures, the competitive landscape is changing", weiyangx.com, https://www.weiyangx.com/361967.html.

"On the historical parallelism between blockchain and the internet", Jinse, https://m.jinse.com/bitcoin/291171.html.

"Is current blockchain the internet in its infancy?", huxiu.com, https://www.huxiu.com/article/232328.html.

"Compared to the history of the internet, current blockchain has only been in a stage of the internet in 1996", ChainNews, https://www.chainnews.com/articles/657408754750.htm.

Securities and Futures Commission, "Position Paper: Regulation of Virtual Asset Trading Platforms", https://www.sfc.hk/web/files/ER/PDF/20191106%20Position%20Paper%20and%20Appendix%201%20to%20Position%20Paper%20(Chi).pdf.

"Hong Kong to comprehensively regulate virtual assets, exchanges licensed to operate as mandatory requirements", PANews, https://www.panewslab.com/zh/articledetails/D30814439.html.

"SFC releases regulation on digital assets trading - Position paper", ChainNews, https://www.chainnews.com/articles/106230616814.htm.

"The future of blockchain is public chain or consortium chain", Sina Finance, https://finance.sina.com.cn/blockchain/coin/2020-04-17/doc-iircuyvh8346331.shtml.

"The status-quo of consortium chains", Tencent Cloud, https://cloud.tencent.com/developer/news/588336.

"Analysis of blockchain applications in cross-border payment, clearing and settlement", Sina Tech, https://tech.sina.com.cn/roll/2020-04-30/doc-iirczymi9245387.shtml.

"Chief architect reveals what BSN is", PANews, https://www.panewslab.com/zh/articledetails/1591948224930306.html.

Lu Minfeng, "How blockchain technology can empower the trust industry", 01Caijing, https://www.01caijing.com/blog/335203.htm.

"Supply chain meets blockchain", Deloitte, https://www2.deloitte.com/content/dam/Deloitte/cn/Documents/strategy/deloiitte-cn-consulting-supply-chain-meets-blockchain-zh-200825.pdf.

Wang An, "Blockchain technology for insurance application scenarios", Gen Re, https://media.genre.com/documents/iipc1808-1-cn.pdf.

iResearch, "Analysis of the landing policy and development trend of blockchain supply chain finance", Gelonghui, https://m.gelonghui.com/p/299290.

Xiao Sa, "Comparing different countries' regulations on virtual currencies, where is the most regulatory friendly place?", https://www.jwview.com/jingwei/html/m/05-18/400874.shtml.

Putin & Wilson, "The status of the six more regulated regions on the blockchain you need to know", ChainNews, https://www.chainnews.com/articles/696170438370.htm.

PART 2

EMERGING INDUSTRY AND NEW PARTICIPANTS – THE COMPOSITION OF BLOCKCHAIN'S ECOSYSTEM

CHAPTER 6

THE SOURCE OF INNOVATION – THE PUBLIC CHAIN ECOSYSTEM

Blockchains can be categorized into public, consortium, and private chains. Public chains, represented by Bitcoin and Ethereum, hold great economic value due to their decentralized nature. It can be said that public chains and their ecosystem are the biggest sources of innovation to blockchain technology. The public chain ecosystem originates from the consensus mechanism used by blockchains to ensure that all the nodes on the network agree on the on-chain transactions and that participants such as miners are rewarded for their contributions to the blockchain network. In addition, each public chain needs tokens as an incentive layer for node collaboration and economic functions. As the currency in the blockchain world, tokens have the basic functions like a measure of value and a medium of exchange. With the increase of token use cases and types, there will be a greater demand for liquidity, resulting in the emergence of digital currency exchanges (or crypto exchanges). Digital currency exchanges consist of both centralized exchanges and decentralized exchanges, which have their pros and cons, complementing each other to provide trading venues for the users with different requirement and increase liquidity for digital assets. In addition, after acquiring digital currencies, people's primary concern is their custody, for which digital wallets are needed. Depending on whether the user has control of the private key, digital wallets are divided into non-custodial wallets and custodial wallets. However, considering the challenges in managing private keys (e.g., whether the mnemonic words can be kept safely), some new types of wallets, which mainly use technologies including the threshold signature (MPC – Multi-party computing), semi-decentralized management (where the private keys are managed by a centralized party), and smart contract management (e.g., multi-signature wallets), have been introduced in recent years. These technologies have progressed in regards to private key management and have also made security improvements and significantly improved the user experience. Mining, cryptocurrencies, exchanges, and wallets are nowadays essential infrastructures in the public chain ecosystem.

6.1 Public chains – The start of the blockchain industry

Blockchain networks can be mainly classified into public, consortium, and private chains.

6.1.1 Public chains (permissionless chains)

Public chains are open to anyone with no entry barriers. Any group or individual can access the public blockchain network via the internet. These blockchain networks have the highest openness, with open-source code and publicly available immutable data. Anyone can participate in the development and governance of public chains, free from the control of any organization or group. Because of its fully decentralized nature, it often generates network effects, which drive value to the underlying assets, e.g., BTC, ETH.

Public chains are the foundation of blockchain and the core of the ecosystem, and they also have respective public market valuations. Blockchain exchanges, wallets, DeFi, lending, and borrowing, as well as mining, are all expanded around the public chain whose importance cannot be overemphasized.

6.1.2 Consortium chain (permission chains)

Depending on the use cases, consortium chains can be open to the whole world, but they come with additional adoption barriers, which require registration on the blockchain network before being able to use it. Governance is in the hands of the consortium doorman/manager who are often partially centralized organizations, such as companies, foundations, and countries. Depending on their permissions, only pre-designated nodes can keep the books, while common users have only the right to use them. This kind of permissioned blockchains is the ones that typically bring value for some banks and financial institutions. AntChain and Ripple are two examples of consortium chains.

Consortium chains, now also called permissioned blockchains. Due to the fact that public chains are permissionless (anyone can be a participant) which leads to some compliance incompatibilities, the consortium chain has become the preferred choice for enterprises and financial institutions for blockchain adoption. In addition, in terms of consensus mechanism, the consensus architecture of consortium/permissioned chains can be prioritized down since all the participants are known to each other and in small numbers.

Two factors need to be taken into account for the design of public chains: consistency – nodes need to have a mechanism to agree on the state of the blockchain – and liveness – requests/transactions are always be processed in a short time. Both these factors can be satisfied in the design of consortium chains. In China, the consortium chain is also the preferred choice of many enterprises, where the technology provider offers the underlying layer of the consortium chain and makes industry-customized modifications on top, e.g., for traceability, anti-counterfeiting, supply chain finance, and so on.

6.1.3   Private chain

In a nutshell, private chains are blockchains completely closed to the public. The governance and data are kept private, only for the participants on the private chain. This kind of blockchain network is often used by enterprises and is maintained and governed by internal/private nodes. There is not much value for the public but it has practical value for participating enterprises since private blockchains are not part of the public/decentralized blockchain ecosystem. MultiChain, JPMCoin, and Quorum are examples of technologies used by private chains.

Although not considered decentralized finance, private chains are popular among financial institutions. In addition to JP Morgan,

.

Wells Fargo and other banks have also chosen similar private chain solutions to serve their internal customers. Moreover, the blockchain technology enabling CBDC, the central bank's digital currency, which is more similar to a private chain and it doesn't matter whether it uses a chain structure or not. Compared with the consortium chain, a private chain is more suitable for large enterprises to use for their internal cross-regional customer base, while a consortium chain is mainly a business-to-business service, with the typical scenario being that one party needs to trust the other party which improves the trust chain.

Although these three categories of blockchains have similar underlying layers and appear to be just different regarding their main participants, they essentially represent different ways of connecting business networks. Consortium and private chains are better integrated with the traditional institutions and have been commercialized over the last few years. The ecosystem of the public chain is more complex and diverse but, because it is global, the path for commercial mass adoption is also more intricate to build.

6.1.4   Comparison between public chains

Bitcoin is the first public blockchain using the PoW consensus mechanism and the UTXO transaction model, the underlying structure design of which has also been extended or improved by subsequent public blockchains. The Bitcoin network can only record transactions, and the transaction confirmation is based on the longest chain principle, which protects against malicious tampering since the probability of 51% attacks is reduced. There is no such thing as a blockchain state in the Bitcoin network, nor is the concept of finality for transactions, only a state corresponding to the last mined blocked. And Bitcoin's support to dApps and tools is unsatisfied.

Ethereum is the first public chain to use smart contracts, with a PoW consensus mechanism and a state root model, which enables the transactions on Ethereum to have speedy finality. This makes it possible to build an Ethereum Virtual Machine (EVM), which can emulate any computer functions and perform complex contract transactions. This smart contract layer is built with a programming language called Solidity. The Ethereum ecosystem is reasonably diverse, encompassing a rich ecosystem that includes dApps such as wallets, digital IDs, DAOs, games, DeFi, NFTs, browsers, and social media. Nonetheless, the rapid growth of the ecosystem also brings a huge test to Ethereum's current transaction capacity.

Public chains like Polkadot and Cosmos, which focus on cross-chain performance, have also emerged in 2017 and have come online in the last two years. Dozens of public chain networks are now taking Ethereum as a benchmark to improve the underlying structure and enhance network efficiency. Some focus on improving efficiency, some focus on protecting privacy, and others are aiming at enterprise users. They all make their ecosystem construction in their respective fields. The DeFi booming has also exposed the scalability issues of Ethereum, which gives room for the development of some other high-performance public chains, such as BSC, Solana, Polygon, and so on.

Because of Ethereum's insufficient throughput, there is a whole ecosystem surrounding networks that tackle Ethereum's scalability.

As discussed above, many public chains have modified the underlying technology in layer 1, hoping to disrupt and replace Ethereum. In the middle layer (layer 2), there are many projects proposing scaling solutions, which are primarily structured as side chains, moving computation or storage to the side chains in order to reduce the burden of the Ethereum network. According to where the data is stored, the scaling solutions are further divided into two types: off-chain solution (e.g., Plasma, Validium) and on-chain solution (e.g., Rollup). The main problem with off-chain storage is that data is unavailable in real-time. In case of security issues, all off-chain information will need to be transferred to the Ethereum network, putting a greater burden on the network. The Ethereum community has been further adopting the on-chain rollup solution, which only separates the computing process from the main network and makes the data available at any time. Rollup can be divided into Validity proofs (e.g., zk-rollup) and Fraud proofs (e.g., optimistic rollup) according to the validation mechanism, and it can integrate zero-knowledge proofs to enhance data privacy and security. Rollup has been merged into the core of the Ethereum 2.0 roadmap in October 2020 as the core of the scalability solution.

6.2 Tokens – The incentive layer for collaboration

6.2.1 The need for tokens

Tokens represent rights and interests that can be exchanged in the blockchain network. These tokens often carry some economic value on the network. Token holders enjoy some of the rights and benefits of the network (e.g., right of use, governance right, among others). Simultaneously, tokens also create an incentive layer that will motivate the participants to work together on maintaining the blockchain network.

Currently, tokens are mainly used as currency, means of validation, utility inside certain platforms, network adoption incentive, governance, voting, asset ownership, dividend distribution, and financing. The mainstream schools of thought generally recognize the necessity of tokens because token enables and incentivizes on-chain governance and make it easier for blockchain networks to reach a consensus. Few articles discuss the necessity of tokens, but there are still some academics holding an opposite opinion that tokens are not necessary for all blockchain networks. They believe that some blockchain networks should weaken the role of tokens as much as possible, and some tokens' investment and utility value are not consistent. The conflict between the investment value and utility value of tokens may sometimes affect the development of blockchain networks.

Table 6.1: Token classification

	Parameter	Value					
Purpose parameters	Class	Coin / Cryptocurrency		Utility token		Tokenized security	
	Function	Asset-based token		Usage token		Work token	
	Role	Right	Value exchange	Toll	Reward	Currency	Earnings
Governance parameters	Representation	Digital		Physical		Legal	
	Supply	Schedule-based	Pre-mined, scheduled distribution	Pre-mined, one-off distribution		Discretionary	
	Incentive system	Enter platform	Use platform	Stay long-term		Leave platform	
Functional parameters	Spendability	Spendable		Non-spendable			
	Tradability	Tradable		Non-tradable			
	Burnability	Burnable		Non-burnable			
	Expirability	Expirable		Non-expirable			
	Fungibility	Fungible		Non-fungible			
Technical parameters	Layer	Blockchain (native)		Protocol (non-native)		Application (dApp)	
	Chain	New chain, new code	New chain, forked code	Forked chain, forked code		Issued on top of a protocol	

Source: Oliveira, Luis, et al., "To token or not to token: Tools for understanding blockchain tokens."

According to the functionality of the tokens, they can be classified as cryptocurrencies, utility tokens, and tokenized securities. A research paper published by Oliveira, Luis, et al. in 2018 offers several key parameters that influence the different types of tokens and gives a decision tree for the design.

As shown in Table 6.1, the influencing parameters of tokens can be broadly classified into general-purpose, governance, functional, and technical parameters. Each parameter is further subdivided into factors, which can be used to classify and design tokenomics.

6.2.2   Token distribution and incentives

Bitcoin's token model can be classified into cryptocurrency with a scheduled total supply of 21 million coins. It can be mined through the PoW consensus algorithm, with mining rewards being halved every four years in a deflationary model. Bitcoin is a public, permissionless, open-source chain that has transactional value only.

In terms of token model, Ethereum's Ether (ETH) is a cryptocurrency with unlimited token supply, which applies a slightly inflationary model in the design of its tokenomics. Currently using a PoW consensus mechanism, Ethereum will be upgrading to the PoS consensus mechanism and is expected to be complete the transition sometime in 2022. There were pre-mined tokens for Ethereum ICO and for the Ethereum Foundation. Ethereum not only has transactional value but also enables more complex calculations and functions, such as smart contracts.

EOS is a cryptocurrency in regards to its token model, which had its ICO on Ethereum blockchain with an initial supply of 1 billion EOS tokens. It adopts an inflationary economic model with a 5% annual increase, among which 4% is for community guarantee fund, 1% for supernode operators. EOS uses the DPoS consensus mechanism and it inherits the merits of Ethereum in design, which in this case improves the network efficiency but sacrifices some decentralization.

BNB is a platform token issued by Binance (one of the leading crypto exchanges). BNB is also a cryptocurrency, with a total supply of 200 million at the time of ICO. It adopts a deflationary economic model by buying back and burning BNB with 20% of the annual profits. Initially, BNB was a token issued based on the ERC-20 standard of Ethereum, which has now been migrated to its main chain – the Binance Smart Chain – BSC.

DAI is a utility token and it is considered a stablecoin. DAI is issued by makerDao and it has ETH as a collateral asset which is slightly overcollateralized above US$1. Its total issuance is determined by the amount of collateral, with the tokenomics corresponding to the inflation model of the U.S. dollar. DAI is an ERC-20 token, and there are no plans to migrate to other chains.

Security tokens are currently less well known considering that this model is regulated because it is essentially the tokenization of equity. Most security tokens require dividends to be paid to investors and also cannot be traded, destroyed, or burned on the blockchain network at will. We will discuss our approach to classifying and valuing tokens in more detail in the valuation section.

Tokens are often criticized for their massive fluctuations and the financial pitfalls they bring. Some argued that the programmable function of the public chain would not be affected by removing tokens, but in fact, the public chain cannot be separated from its tokens. They are two sides of the same structure. For a token to function as an incentive, it must have a market price and the public chain relies on token incentives to bring collaboration to public chains. Similarly, a company relies on its legal structure to unite its employees and the compensations to motivate them to contribute. The public chain does not have a corresponding legal structure due to its decentralized nature, but there is a set of written rules in the form of code, visible and verifiable by everyone. Taking into consideration that there are many stakeholders in a public chain, the token is essential in order to align incentives, and without it, it would be hard for a public chain to run smoothly, attract stakeholders to collaborate, and provide an effective incentive mechanism.

Table 6.2: Comparison between the blockchain economy and traditional company economy		
	Company	Public Chains
Rules	Law	Code
Objective	Employee	Developers/nodes/users
Management	Managers	Code
Incentive	Compensations	Distribution of tokens
Penalty	System	Token collaterals

6.3 Mining – The upstream of the blockchain ecosystem

6.3.1 The origins of mining

Mining is a process in which individuals are rewarded for their contributions to the blockchain network, more specifically for contributing to the consensus mechanism. The Bitcoin network uses the PoW – Proof of Work – consensus mechanism in order to reach consensus and solve the BFT – Byzantine Fault Tolerant – problem, i.e., putting the majority of nodes on a decentralized network agreeing on the data that is on the blockchain. During the process, network participants need to pack the Bitcoin transactions in one block and solve a complex mathematical problem with their hashrate, ensuring the correctness, consistency, and integrity of the blockchain network.

6.3.2　The evolution of mining rigs

During the early days of Bitcoin, mining could be done with a regular computer. In 2009, the Bitcoin genesis block (the very first blockchain block) was mined by Satoshi Nakamoto. Back then, the Bitcoin mining hashrate was relatively low, with only a few nodes on the Bitcoin network and its value was not recognized by many people. In October 2010, an upgrade to the Bitcoin network allowed for GPU mining which significantly improved the proof of work calculation speed and is more efficient than CPU mining. Bitcoin mining has since entered the GPU era.

Nowadays, with the increasing Bitcoin adoption and higher Bitcoin price, the number of nodes involved in mining has also increased. In June 2011, the first FPGA mining rig was born. FPGA is a chip used by miners to optimize mining based on the Bitcoin algorithm. However, FPGA mining rigs were soon replaced by ASIC mining rigs, which also became the mainstream mining technology that is currently used. As the mining difficulty rises, it is hard for a single mining rig to mine one block within its lifetime. Some miners have pooled together their mining rigs to form mining pools (similar to cooperatives) to share hashrate and mining rewards which increases the probability of being rewarded. The whole development process of Bitcoin mining has been centered around optimizing the Bitcoin algorithm and increasing the hashrate. Current mining machine suppliers (e.g., Bitmain, Canaan) are constantly optimizing and improving the mining machine's performance.

6.3.3　Different cryptographic algorithms

Bitcoin uses the SHA-256 hashing algorithm. SHA-256 is a member of the SHA-2 cryptographic hash function designed by the NSA. LiteCoin replicates the Bitcoin model but replaces the cryptographic algorithm with Scrypt. This memory-dependent hash algorithm takes up a lot of memory space for mining, thus reducing the CPU load. The cryptographic algorithm used by Ethereum is Ethash, which uses directed acyclic graphs (DAGs) for the proof-of-work consensus mechanism, reducing the role of mining rigs by sharing memory. There are many other cryptographic algorithms such as X11, Equihash, NeoScrypt, among others, all of which have their unique uses in the PoW/mining scene.

The biggest problem with the PoW consensus mechanism is the waste of energy. Various consensus mechanisms, such as PoS, DPoS, PoC, PoST, and others, have been created by improving the consensus mechanism. Getting the right to pack transactions into a block on such blockchain networks can also be considered mining but without the need to consume as much energy as PoW.

Mining is still one of the largest industries in the crypto market today due to the existence of Bitcoin and Ethereum. However, as you can see, with the continuous optimization of mining machines, mining has long since shifted from individual work to industrialized operations, namely mining pools and mining farms. Until 2021, the world's largest Bitcoin mining pools were in China, accounting for at least 70% of the world's hashrate.

Miners are incentivized to participate in securing the network, packaging transactions in blocks, and appending these new blocks to the blockchain. Miners can be seen as the guardians of the network as they are rewarded for their stability. Miners are rewarded with tokens, but as miners need to pay for electricity and operating costs, they are also the source of selling pressure on the token market.

| Table 6.3: Global major mining pools' hashrate ||
Pool	Hashrate
Foundry USA	31,272.03 PH/s
AntPool	27,911.22 PH/s
P2Pool	26,991.55 PH/s
Poolin	24,443.00 PH/s
ViaBTC	22,321.29 PH/s
Biance Pool	21,365.64 PH/s
BTC.com	13,150.00 PH/s
SlushPool	10,299.59 PH/s
SBI Crypto	4,894.23 PH/s
Luxor	4,009.94 PH/s

Source: BTC.com as of 2022Q1

Some miners are savvy and will find the opportunity to sell depending on the rise and fall of the token price. While some miners intend to do so but lack trading techniques, thus giving birth to a new category of products, which enables the miners to enjoy token appreciation and avoid market risk. So, serving miners has also become an additional business for some mining pools.

Some miners can invest in mining rigs and buildup farms together while some less sophisticated miners can only buy the rigs and delegate to mine pools. Some mining pools also provide additional services such as helping to select the mining equipment, build the mining farm, set up the machines, and get it up and running for a fee. Some pools also manufacture their mining machines, such as btc.com, Ant Pool, which use their own Bitmain products. Mining pools are the natural extension of the mining machine manufacturer's business.

With the emergence of PoS chains, there came the PoS mining pools. In fact, token holders of PoS chains can also be counted as miners (sometimes also called validators), as long as they participate in the PoS mining process. PoS mining pools provide such a facility by simply allowing token holders to deposit/stake their tokens. PoS consensus mechanism requires the stakeholders to produce the block independently. Additionally, they can also participate in node operation and voting, which cannot be made by individual users. In certain blockchains, stakeholders will also face the risk of slashing if their node is not up and running 100% of the time. That is where professional PoS mining pools, also called staking providers, come into place and provide services that can, in some aspects, resemble cloud providers, in this case, "Staking as a Service".

PoS "Staking as a Service" providers are able to: 1) provide a stable node architecture to ensure consistent block production and uptime; 2) prevent attacks and guarantee the safety of customer funds, as they also ensure safe custody of the funds; 3) actively participate in on-chain governance on behalf of users.

PoW mining is nowadays a corporate game, with large capital investments (buying mining rigs), paying fees (mining pools, operations, electricity), and gaining the token rewards. PoW mining is increasingly occupied by well-funded miners, as the future will be more "arms race-oriented". PoS, on the other hand, is more like a banking service that provides fixed income, not only for institutions but also for retail investors, who can get a fixed income of tokens regardless of how many tokens they hold. It can also be referred to as staking service.

Number	Provider	Staked value	Users	Featured assets	Country
	Blockdaemon decentralized	$918,557,983	2058	+8	
	Midas.Investments custodial	$296,345,482	84062	+29	
	Stake DAO decentralized	$66,908,328	5061	+4	
1	Everstake decentralized	$4,518,285,361	364444	+23	
2	Kraken custodial	$4,483,183,607	1197	+2	
3	InfStones decentralized	$4,172,480,436	33114	+24	
4	Allnodes decentralized	$4,129,695,855	16910	+26	

Table 6.4: Major "Staking as a Service" providers

Source: Stakingrewards.com

6.4   Decentralized exchanges – Lucrative but controversial

6.4.1   The emergence of centralized exchanges

The basic functions of money are to be a store of value and the medium of exchange. With the rapid development of the blockchain industry, the variety of digital currencies has increased. But a currency that is completely secluded from the outside world and unable to perform its basic functions cannot be considered a currency.

In the early days of Bitcoin, there was a demand for trading with digital currencies, mainly through forum posts or private chat rooms, which is a way of OTC (over the counter) trading. However, OTC trading has a high risk of default and lacks an effective price discovery mechanism. Centralized exchanges have become popular for making digital currency trading more secure and stable for the public.

Like the stock exchange, the centralized exchange adopts the traditional order book trading mechanism, where the role in trading mainly includes the broker, traders (the user), the market maker, and the exchange. The specific process can be divided into three stages:

First, traders use their wallets to deposit tokens into the address assigned by the exchange, and they can then place orders through their accounts. Next, brokers will be responsible for matching buyers with sellers and connecting market makers to transmit trading information to other market participants, providing buy and sell prices. Ultimately, the buy and sell prices are aggregated on the exchange, and the transaction is completed under the trading platform.

Most current exchanges allow two-way trading and can execute various forms of trading orders such as limit orders and market orders. Some crypto exchanges also have some of the features of distributed ledgers, such as openness and immutability, which further ensure the security and stability of trading.

In addition, some exchanges have functions similar to financial institutions such as futures tradings, brokerage shops, and fund management. They play a vital role in crypto world.

6.4.2   Mt. Gox – The world's first large Bitcoin exchange

Founded on July 18, 2010, by the American entrepreneur Jed McCaleb, Mt. Gox was the world's first major Bitcoin exchange and it was once the world's top exchange handling approximately 80% of Bitcoin trading volume. Mt. Gox is credited with driving the rise of the Bitcoin market. Especially after the emergence of the Mt. Gox exchange, Bitcoin prices began to rise slow and steadily. With the listing of multiple trading pairs of BTC and different fiat currencies, the Bitcoin market saw its first mini-bull market, reaching a peak price of US$29 on June 9. However, Mt. Gox was hit by a series of chronic technical problems. In June 2011, it suffered a massive hacking attack that compromised over 60,000 usernames and passwords, with US$8.75 million worth of Bitcoin being stolen, causing the platform to shut down for a week. Then, in February 2014, Mt. Gox announced its bankruptcy after suffering an attack that made the exchange lose almost all its cryptocurrency holdings.

6.4.3   Disadvantages of centralized exchanges

Mt. Gox has gone bankrupt, but it played a pivotal role in the development of centralized exchanges. At the same time, the Mt. Gox incident has also led to a growing awareness that centralized exchanges may have a number of security risks.

(1) Asset security

Trading on a centralized exchange requires a certain amount of funds to be deposited in advance and held in escrow on behalf of users by the exchange, which requires the exchange to implement a robust architecture and excellent cybersecurity patterns. If the security of a centralized exchange is breached, the user's assets can be compromised.

(2) Lack of regulation

Cryptocurrency transactions are decentralized and peer-to-peer. However, large, centralized trading platforms attempt to build a centralized system, something that undermines the decentralized nature of the Bitcoin ecosystem, thus giving rise to a vast unregulated profit-seeking space. Retail investors not only have to deposit their assets into the exchange before trading, but also have to pay a fee to the exchange. In addition, the exchanges' stakeholders include users and projects, but all the trading and listing rules are determined by the exchanges, which results in unequal status among users, projects, and the centralized exchanges. In addition, the market is characterized by an oligopoly where some exchanges hold a big market share. These exchanges not only take advantage of their position by raising the threshold for projects to list their tokens but also charge them high listing fees. In addition, if an unethical project wants to manipulate the market, it may join hands with the exchange to raise the fees for the trading of its valueless token, thus greatly damaging the interests of users and increasing the systemic risk of the entire trading market. Therefore, it is unreliable to trust entirely on the self-regulation of trading platforms.

6.4.4   The decentralized exchange boom

The concept of "Decentralized Exchange" (DEX) is starting to catch on due to the lack of "decentralization" principles by centralized exchanges. Simply put, a decentralized exchange does all of this through open-source smart contracts, putting asset custody, market making, and asset clearing on the blockchain, which is more transparent and less susceptible to be tampered with. Users simply need to generate a digital asset wallet with a relatively simple KYC process (or no KYC at all) and keep their assets and private keys secure. Decentralized exchanges bring higher security and meet the needs of users for private transactions.

The official launch of the Ethereum network in 2015 and the launch of the EOS main network in 2018 drove the emergence of a large number of DEXs. Between 2017 and 2018, we saw the peak for the emergence of DEXs, such as Bancor, OasisDEX, StellarDEX, Switcheo Network, Airswap, OmiseGo, and so on. More decentralized exchanges will emerge in the future as the digital currency market grows.

6.4.5   Coinbase – Compliance or profits?

Founded in June 2012, Coinbase is one of the largest digital currency trading platforms in the United States, whose main businesses are the Bitcoin wallet and trading platform. Although Coinbase is ranked low in terms of volume, it scores high in terms of security, transparency, and credibility, and is known as the world's largest compliant/regulated exchange. Its compliance can be seen in three ways:

1. **Strict legal procedures:** Coinbase is very cautious about legal procedures and sets high entry standards for registered users, including KYC (Know your customer) and AML (Anti-money laundering).

2. **Uncompromising listing requirements:** Coinbase uses USDC as the only stablecoin able to be exchanged with fiat currencies. Additionally, only well-known credible cryptocurrencies, such as Bitcoin, Ethereum, Ripple, Litecoin, Bitcoin Cash, Ethereum Classic, etc., can be listed on the exchange, which further ensures the security of the exchange.

3. **Licensed in the U.S.:** One of Coinbase's core competencies is that it is licensed to provide the exchange service to customers by the U.S. government. Coinbase has obtained regulatory licenses for cryptocurrency trading in over 40 states, and a digital asset license in New York State. Users in the U.S. can not only use their credit cards to purchase Bitcoin on Coinbase, but can also easily store Bitcoin in any wallet application and can send Bitcoin to other users via email or even SMS.

As a result, Coinbase can still manage to take a large chunk of the huge market share and build a relatively healthy cash pool.

6.5 Non-custodial wallet – Pure permissionless finance

6.5.1 Basic concepts of blockchain wallet

One of the most important angles to anyone holding cryptocurrencies is the storage of the coins. The application where the cryptocurrencies are stored (in practice, the private keys that control those assets) needs to be of utmost safety and security.

With the rapid development of the blockchain industry, blockchain wallets have also undergone blockchain iterations of 1.0 to 3.0, from the early single-chain wallets to multi-chain multi-asset wallets. From a functional point of view, the current digital wallets can also instantly interact with the on-chain contract, besides the basic storage and transfer function. We can say that a blockchain wallet is the window that allows the users to interact with the blockchain.

There are five important concepts that are part of blockchain wallets:

- **Public key:** The public address is related or the same as the transfer address, which can be disclosed to the public and can be seen as bank account number

- **Private key:** Each address corresponds to a private key, equivalent to the password of the bank account

- **Mnemonic words:** The mnemonic words or mnemonic phrases translate into the private key. They can be used to back up a wallet and they are easy to remember

- **Keystore:** Encrypted private key

- **Password:** To further enhance the security of digital assets, most wallets will take a password that is used for secondary encryption of the private key

6.5.2   Non-custodial and custodial wallets

There are many ways to classify the blockchain wallets existing in the market. However, from the perspective of how they manage the most important component of a wallet, the private key, we can classify the wallets into custodial wallets and non-custodial wallets based on whether the users have control over their private key.

Custodial wallets do not give users access to the private key and will store it in their server, which means users do not have control of the private key. Currently, many centralized crypto exchanges (e.g., Coinbase, Bitfinex, Binance, and others), as well as trading platforms and brokerage services have custodial wallets. For these platforms, custodial wallets simplify the services that they offer and allow users to quickly trade digital assets in a commission-free way on the custody platform without having to remember their private keys. However, those platforms may freeze users' assets for system maintenance or KYC/AML reasons. The security of users' funds is also tied to the security of the platform. For example, if the exchange is hacked, user funds may be stolen.

Non-custodial wallets give users control of their private keys, giving them full control of their assets. Non-custodial wallets do not store any private keys on behalf of the user. However, non-custodial wallets have also some drawbacks. If a user loses the private key and the mnemonic words, he or she will never be able to retrieve the assets. There is also a high risk that the assets will fall under the control of someone else if the mnemonic words or private key is compromised, at which point the user will need to immediately transfer the assets to a new address.

6.5.3 Meaning of non-custodial wallets

Just like the decentralized exchanges mentioned in the previous chapter, the value of non-custodial wallets lies in their decentralization. Decentralization allows non-custodial wallets to evolve into multiple forms, giving users a variety of options.

(1) A wide variety of crypto wallets

The two mainstream wallet classifications currently available are as follows:

- **Full-node wallets and light wallets:** According to the degree of decentralization, crypto wallets can be divided into full-node wallets and light wallets. Full-node wallets need to synchronize all blockchain data, which will take up a lot of memory/storage, but they can be fully decentralized. Light wallets rely on other full-nodes on the Bitcoin network and only synchronize data related to the wallet itself, which basically makes them decentralized. Still, the downside is that transaction validation may be a little slower.

- **Hot wallets and cold wallets:** Wallets can also be classified as hot wallets and cold wallets, depending on whether they are connected to the internet or not. Common hot wallets are desktop wallets, mobile wallets, and web wallets, while cold wallets are generally paper wallets and hardware wallets, which are devices that are not connected to the internet.

(2) The different functions of crypto wallets

Function 1: Digital asset trading. Compared to centralized (custodian) wallets where assets can only be traded on the exchange platform, non-custodial wallets give users the freedom to trade on decentralized exchanges, aggregate liquidity, and OTC trading, improving the way digital assets are traded.

Function 2: Financial products. Many of the existing wallets have already integrated additional financial tools, including mining pools, staking, and other investment options, which can meet users' needs in terms of portfolio management and the value of their assets.

Function 3: Digital asset management. Similar to some banking apps, users can use the wallet to transfer and receive digital assets, as well as view asset and transaction details and other asset management utilities. In addition, wallets can also provide a variety of additional services such as wealth management, funds, insurance, simplified payments, lending/borrowing, and so on, which helps with the unified management of multiple assets.

6.5.4 The evolution of wallets from a key management perspective

As we know by now, private key management is an integral part of a crypto wallet. To a certain extent, private key management is the main component of wallet security. The management of the wallet's private key is the most vulnerable part as to wallet security, and the current wallet products involve several issues: 1) the private key itself is difficult to remember and almost hard to be adopted by ordinary users; 2) It is popular to use mnemonic words for HD wallets (hierarchical deterministic wallets), but still need to be physically stored safely; 3) fully centralized wallets, such as exchange wallets, use the traditional account password model which may be good for user experience, but the trust and security responsibility is entirely on the exchange; 4) ease of use and security is a balancing process between centralization and decentralization.

In addition to the traditional HD wallets using mnemonic words, a variety of new wallets have been born in the last year or two, which have made a lot of progress in regards to private key management without weakening security and significantly improving the user experience. We believe that new types of wallets fall into three categories from a technological point of view:

- **Threshold signature scheme (TSS):** Represented by ZenGo

- **Semi-decentralized management:** Represented by Torus, Fortmatic

- **Smart contract management:** Represented by MYKEY, Argent, Dapper

Each wallet has different technological paths and design concepts. We will take specific products as examples below to introduce their respective features and unique technologies.

(1) Threshold signature

» ZenGo

ZenGo utilizes Threshold Signature (TSS) technology based on Secure Multiparty Computing (MPC). The wallet's private key is split into two parts, one stored on ZenGo's server and the other on the mobile phone, which can be accessed with TouchID/FaceID authorization if the user is using iOS, and with ZoOm® 3D Face Authentication solution if the user is using Android. Control of the wallet (signature of cryptocurrency transactions) is only possible if the transactions are signed by the private key on both the mobile and server.

- **Accessibility:** Users do not need to handle the private key throughout the use of the wallet and do not need to save and record the key themselves. The entire process is controlled through FaceID or TouchID, making it extremely easy to use.

- **Wallet Recovery:** Assuming the user lost his or her device but had the private key stored on the ZenGo server and the decryption key stored via iCloud (for iOS) or Google Drive (for Android), the wallet can be recovered via iCloud or Google Drive. If ZenGo's server is shut down, its Escrow service will then go into recovery mode to help users restore their keys. As long as device loss and iCould/Google Drive server shutdown do not occur simultaneously, wallets and the respective assets can be recovered.

- **Key generation:** Generating private keys with ZenGo also adopts the Distributed Key Management (DKG) method. Each party (two parties involved herein) holds a part of the private key without disclosing it to the other party. The public key generation process here also follows the conventional way.

ZenGo uses the threshold signature technology for key generation and management. Threshold signature technology has certain advantages over the Secret Sharing Scheme (SSS): 1) In the generation of SSS, there will be a single party responsible for the generation and distribution of various pieces of the key, which is not required in threshold signature; 2) The signing process of SSS requires all parties to rebuild the private key. While there is no need to rebuild for threshold signature, the distributed key management can handle the related signing. For example, ZenGo requires users and servers to sign separately, but it is not necessary to rebuild the respective saved pieces first.

(2) Semi-decentralized wallet management

The semi-decentralized wallet uses centralized identity providers such as the account or private key system of Google or Facebook, allowing users to log in and control the decentralized services, which is closer to internet users' habit.

» Fortmatic

Fortmatic is a light web wallet. Different from MetaMask, it is not a browser extension, but a wallet SDK. Users can register an Ethereum account with a mobile phone number, which is much more convenient than traditional mnemonic words. The user can have a Fortmatic account as long as the mobile phone can receive the SMS verification code. Fortmatic is mainly developed for dApps, which dramatically reduces the tedious process of using dApps from docs of Formatic, and the account system can be logged in at any time on the browser with a mobile phone.

Fortmatic's private key management uses a semi-decentralized model with Delegated Key Management (DQM), which was upgraded in November 2019 from a centralized custodial model. The generation and encryption of the user's private key under the delegated private key management are put on the secure enclave of Fortmatic.

The process of delegated key management is as follows: With the adoption of AWS Key Management Service (KMS), Fortmatic enables users to interact directly with Amazon KMS, without any intermediary through Fortmatic. AWS KMS has the Hardware Security Module (HSM) to provide the user with the master key, with the encryption and decryption process to be done entirely in HSM.

- **Generation of the key:** The user completes registration in Amazon Cognito through Fortmatic Relayer, and then generates the private key. The private key is saved in the user's hands after the scoped credential is generated via Amazon Cognito to be encrypted through HSM. The encrypted private key will also be kept by Fortmatic as a recovery backup. Amazon Cognito allows the user to authenticate with services such as Google and Facebook.

- **Use of the key:** The user can interact through the wallet with HSM to decrypt the encrypted key and can use the decrypted key to sign transactions and interact with blockchain applications.

- **Account recovery:** If the user forgets the password, he/she needs to use email for verification and get an access token and get the credentials through Amazon Cognito. The user can then download the encrypted private key from Fortmatic with the access token.

This private key management method makes it difficult for other parties to access the decrypted private key unless there is a bug in Amazon's KMS. It is assumed that users trust Amazon's KMS, that the Amazon infrastructure will be kept secure and it will not be attacked, and that Amazon will not steal users' keys.

(3) Smart Contract Management

In 2019, Vitalik mentioned the concept of the smart wallet, or contract wallet, at the Wanxiang Blockchain Summit in Shanghai. This concept allows the control of tokens in the wallet through smart contracts. As described by Vitalik, it can also support the multi-signature function, distributed storage of keys, and social accounts. As the concept is relatively new, there are currently different definitions of smart wallets in the industry:

1) In a paper by Monika and Gernot, the concept of smart

wallet was defined as one that offers enhanced features such as authorization of arbitrary transactions, the mechanism for recovery of keys after loss, or advanced token standards.

2) MYKEY defines a smart wallet as a wallet that interacts with a smart contract or a set of smart contracts. On top of a local saved private key, a smart contract controls the account, to substitute blockchain's native account system. Through the logic defined by the smart contract, the account has a richer functionality, allowing for splitting and restoring permissions to the account, limiting transfer amounts, etc. The smart wallet achieves a balance between security and usability.

If the criteria are entirely based on whether or not a smart contract account is in place, only those wallet applications that use smart contract accounts can be considered smart wallets. However, from the user experience perspective, wallets with the same security features can also be called smart wallets, such as ZenGo, although it cannot be seen as a Smart Contract Wallet by strict definition.

Technologically, the smart wallet is based on Ethereum (or similar blockchains) prototype account, as Preethi Kasireddy wrote in his introduction to Ethereum's working mechanism: The Ethereum network is comprised of two types of account, the externally owned accounts, and the contract accounts. Externally owned accounts are controlled by private keys (or derived mnemonic words) and have no code associated with them. Contract accounts are governed by smart contracts and have code associated with them.

An externally owned account can send messages to other externally owned or other contract accounts by creating and signing a transaction using its private key. A message between two externally owned accounts is simply a value transfer. But a message from an externally owned account to a contract account activates the contract account's code, allowing it to perform various actions (e.g., transfer tokens, write to internal storage, mint new tokens, perform some calculation, create new contracts, etc.). Contract accounts cannot initiate new transactions on their own. Instead, contract accounts can only trigger transactions in response to other transactions they have received (from an externally owned account or another contract account).

Figure 6.1: Working mechanism of externally owned accounts and contract accounts

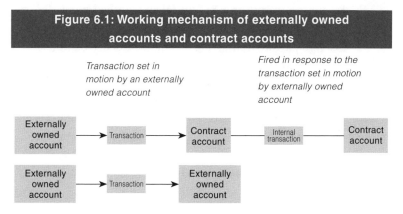

Source: Medium article, "How does Ethereum work, anyway?" https://preethikasireddy.medium.com/how-does-ethereum-work-anyway-22d1df506369

Smart contract operations can be added to the Typically, with externally owned accounts and contract accounts. Typically, smart wallet features include:

1) Social recovery mechanism: Use social connections as the backup to recover lost accounts;

2) Time recovery mechanism: If an account does not make any trade for a period, the funds will be restored to another designated account;

3) Limit transactions: Limit the amount of each transaction;

4) Arbitrary transactions;

5) Batching transactions: Multiple transactions are put and approved in batches. For example, InstaDapp's bridge feature, which allows a single transaction to achieve the transfer of smart contract debt across platforms (e.g., from Maker to Compound);

6) Exemption from the ERC-20 token transaction gas fee (for meta-transactions): use a proxy node to pay the gas or use a token to pay the transaction fee (in the absence of Ether).

There is no unified architecture or standard for the current smart wallet products. Each product follows its own business logic to develop relevant smart contracts with customized functions, and no external smart contracts are called. The wallet developers need to be responsible for the security of the smart contract. Therefore, it is still in an early stage and a prevailing standard for smart wallets has not yet appeared.

For the key management model, the design for smart contracts varies between wallets. For example, some wallets do not give users access to their private keys at all, and still, some consider it necessary for users to keep their private keys (although there is no complex private key management involved). It is difficult to conclude which one is more likely to gain a large number of users in the future.

There are also wallets that claim to be smart contract wallets, but with confusing business logic. For example, they may require creating a smart contract account at the beginning, but the implementation requires the user to pay the gas fee first, which seems to have defeated the original purpose of smart contracts. Smart contracts are supposed to solve problems, not to increase the burden.

6.6 Distinction between coin and token

Coins and tokens are the most crucial part of the public blockchain ecosystem. In the early days, there was no universally and officially recognized name for it, and the categories of digital assets were very different. It is sometimes confusing whether digital assets should be called coins or tokens.

In western countries, cryptocurrencies are generally referred to as crypto assets or digital assets. While in some regulatory contexts, such as the Financial Action Task Force on Money Laundering (FATF) and the Hong Kong Securities and Futures Commission (SFC), they are referred to as virtual asset, as in the *Guidance for a Risk-Based Approach to Virtual Assets and Virtual Asset Service Providers* issued by FATF in 2019, and the *Position paper: Regulation of virtual asset trading platforms* issued by the Hong Kong SFC in 2019.

However, regulatory contexts are kept evolving:

For example, in 2014, the FATF issued the guidance of *Virtual Currencies: Key Definitions and Potential AML/CFT Risks*, where crypto assets were referred to as virtual currencies. In 2018, the FATF introduced a new definition, the virtual asset, which has been used till now.

As for SFC, the earliest official statement on crypto assets is the *Statement on initial coin offerings* issued in 2017, which still referred to crypto assets as digital tokens, but the SFC has made certain distinctions on the nature of crypto assets, classifying some of them as virtual assets, while the remaining as securities, which was further segmented as shares, debentures, or collective investment. In 2018, *Warns of Cryptocurrency Risks* issued by SFC began to refer to it as cryptocurrency and introduced the term utility token. In the same year, the SFC started to regulate the crypto-asset industry with the publication of the *Statement on regulatory framework for virtual asset portfolios managers, fund distributors and trading platform operators*, where formally call it a virtual asset and explained that, a virtual asset is a digital representation of value, which is also known as cryptocurrency, crypto-asset or digital token.

On the other hand, the SEC does not have a specific name for crypto assets, but rather called them ICOs at the beginning and sometimes tokens or digital assets. Due to the regulatory separation between federal and state regulation, they are called virtual currency at the state level, while FinCEN, for example, calls them convertible virtual currencies. The SEC's primary concern is whether such tokens are identified as securities under the U.S. securities laws, and whether the corresponding ICOs are securities offerings, without going into much detail about the functions provided by the token. For example, crypto assets such as Bitcoin and Ethereum, whose characteristics do not match the Howey Test, are not recognized as securities, and therefore do not fall within the SEC's regulatory scope.

Figure 6.2: SEC's position on token regulation

[-]   Tokens sold in ICOs can be called many things.

ICOs, or more specifically tokens, can be called a variety of names, but merely calling a token a "utility" token or structuring it to provide some utility does not prevent the token from being a security.

Source: SEC website

Switzerland's Financial Market Supervisory Authority (FINMA) has had a more detailed classification of crypto assets since 2018. Same as SEC, FINMA started to regulate ICO from their economic function and divided the tokens into three categories:

• **Payment token** is synonymous with cryptocurrency and has no other functionality or connections with other projects. In some cases, tokens may be developed with only the necessary functionality and become accepted as a means of payment for a period of time.

- **Utility tokens** are tokens designed to provide digital access to an application or service.

- **Asset token** represents an asset, such as participation in a physical entity, company, or income stream or the right to receive dividends or interest payments. In terms of their economic function, such tokens can be seen as stocks, bonds, or derivatives.

MAS, the regulator of Singapore, referred to crypto assets as the digital token, or digital payment token.

From a regulatory perspective, when crypto assets are called coins, they are more often referred to in the context of ICOs. Otherwise, they are often called virtual assets, crypto assets, cryptocurrencies, digital tokens, and so on. The terminology varies from one regulatory body to another.

It is a different story when looking from the economic perspective. In the industry's early days, blockchain native tokens such as BTC and ETH were called a coin, while other crypto assets derived from the blockchain are called tokens, such as various dApps and DeFi tokens. The term coin is an emphasis on its financial significance, while token refers to its practical function, such as utility token/securities token/ payment token. The term of the coin is inherited from Bitcoin. All the early crypto assets can be called coins because they are natively based on blockchain. If we use coins to refer to native crypto assets, it would be much clearer to use tokens to refer to blockchain-based tokens.

Also, in the economic sense, most crypto assets fall into the category of asset, not currency. Only a few crypto assets such as BTC, ETH, and stablecoins have the meaning of coin. There is not much difference between assets or tokens in other contexts.

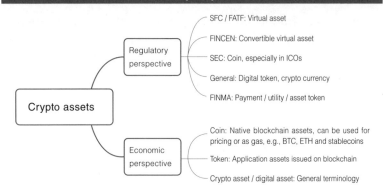

Figure 6.3: Different name of crypto assets from regulatory and economic perspectives

References

Satoshi Nakamoto, "Bitcoin: A peer-to-peer electronic cash system", https://Bitcoin.org/Bitcoin.pdf.

"Ethereum Whitepaper", https://ethereum.org/en/whitepaper/.

Ian Grigg, "EOS – An introduction", https://whitepaperdatabase.com/wp-content/uploads/2018/03/EOS-Introduction-whitepaper.pdf.

"ZkSync overview", https://zksync.io/faq/intro.html.

Toshendra Kumar Sharma, "Permissioned and permissionless blockchains: A comprehensive guide", https://www.blockchain-council.org/blockchain/permissioned-and-permissionless-blockchains-a-comprehensive-guide/.

"The world's largest compliant digital currency exchange: Coinbase", https://www.jianshu.com/p/d55932a0b650.

"The difference between custodial and non-custodial wallets", https://www.jianshu.com/p/bc6c293cbc0d.

"A panoramic view of the blockchain wallet ecosystem", https://www.chainnews.

com/articles/786080731457.htm.

Tristan Greene, "A brief history of Bitcoin mining hardware", https://thenextweb.com/hardfork/2018/02/02/a-brief-history-of-Bitcoin-mining-hardware/.

Androulaki, Elli, et al., "Hyperledger fabric: A distributed operating system for permissioned blockchains." The Thirteenth EuroSys Conference 2018.

Vukoli, Marko, "Rethinking permissioned blockchains." The ACM Workshop ACM, 2017.

Oliveira, Luis, et al., "To token or not to token: Tools for understanding blockchain tokens." 39th International Conference on Information Systems 2018.

Foundation, L. X. L., Legal Counsel at Interstellar and Stellar Development, "Deconstructing decentralized exchanges." *Stanford Journal of Blockchain Law & Policy*, 2019.

CHAPTER 7

REAL PRODUCTS AND
USERS – DECENTRALIZED
APPLICATIONS

A dApp, or decentralized application, refers to an application that uses an architecture where the server maintains interaction with the blockchain, sometimes by running a full node on the blockchain. dApps are one of the most critical components of the blockchain ecosystem. Two main sub-sectors of dApps include decentralized finance (DeFi) and non-fungible tokens (NFT).

DeFi is a transparent financial system open to everyone and implemented entirely by smart contracts. DeFi has made significant breakthroughs and innovations in liquidity, financial freedom, openness, and transparency compared to traditional financial systems, with main fields being decentralized exchanges (DEX), lending, insurance, derivatives, and decentralized asset management. In terms of functionality, most of these fields mirror the traditional offline financial model onto the blockchain while adding innovative logic to optimize the conventional financial service model.

NFT, another dApps sub-sector, gained popularity rapidly in 2021. Favoured by many celebrities and institutions, it is considered the trend succeeding DeFi. An NFT is a unique, non-fungible indivisible token mainly used in games, artworks, social tokens, and other fields. Clear copyright and binding of creators rights and interests are some of the contributors for NFT's popularity. In addition, Metaverse, a space intimately related to NFTs, has gradually entered people's mindspace in recent years. Metaverse, or meta-universe, refers to the virtual world which innovates and upgrades the real world in terms of financing and socialization. In the future, the Metaverse may create an economic volume several times that of the physical world and offer a place for an increasing number of people to explore.

7.1 dApps – Applications that genuinely belong to the blockchain

7.1.1 The emergence of dApp

dApp stands for decentralized application, also known as a distributed application. While conventional apps have only two centralized sides – a server and a client, dApps have an additional side: the smart contracts (blockchain side). A dApp interacts with the smart contracts and the whole blockchain by running full nodes.

Some dApps launch under a model similar to crowdfunding, where the team behind the app writes a white paper to detail the consensus mechanism, token distribution and incentive mechanism. Then, any token holder can directly enjoy the benefits generated by the dApp and can trade the token on relevant exchanges. Therefore, dApp can attract more users into the blockchain world, and the blockchain technology can also be applied to various use cases via dApps.

The rise of dApps can be traced back to the ICO storm in 2017. Later, with the decline of ICO projects, the crypto community entered its cold crypto winter. Yet, dApp projects that could see the actual implementation of blockchain with real use cases, brought new hope to those participants and renewed confidence in the blockchain technology. In 2018, in particular, led initially by a blockchain game called *CryptoKitties*, the total number of dApps on the three mainstream public chains (Ethereum, EOS, and Tron) reached 1,618, with the total transaction volume of the whole dApp market reaching US$7.3 billion.

Although dApp projects cover many spaces, including cryptocurrency exchanges, games, collectibles, marketplaces, quantitative trading, and gambling, in 2019, they were mainly focused on games, gambling, and finance, when EOS and Tron, the two public chains, being once called "gambling chains". After a year of testing, in 2019 the dApp market lacked real users other than for games and gambling applications. The market was lacking large-scale popular dApps. In addition, the poor performance of public chains also limited the use cases of decentralized applications, making it hard for dApps to compete with traditional internet applications.

7.1.2 The DeFi boom

Despite the dampened dApp market in 2019, the rise of DeFi gradually alleviated the apprehensions related to the dApp ecosystem.

DeFi, short for decentralized finance, aims to build a transparent financial system that is open to all without needing a license or third parties. DeFi is highly automated: all lending and clearing processes in economic activities can be executed only through smart contracts, without fear of default and the involvement of third parties. Therefore, compared to the mechanism of traditional internet applications, this mechanism gives users great freedom and convenience. DeFi is also the most efficient marketplace for lending and borrowing and is expected to significantly improve financial inclusion.

At present, DeFi products cover a plethora of use cases such as trading, insurance, stablecoin, and lending. According to DeFi Llama, the total value locked (TVL), the most critical indicator of DeFi ecosystem development, increased over ten times from US$10 billion in July 2020 to approximately US$206 billion in January 2022.

Compound, a well-known DeFi protocol, launched its liquidity mining with its governance token COMP on June 15, 2020, giving rise to another round of DeFi boom that continued in the next half of 2020. Although sometimes the crypto space is often regarded as a zero-sum game, DeFi can create real value by connecting crypto and real assets. That means DeFi can serve the real economy and fulfil the original purpose of dApps – to promote the application and popularization of blockchain. Therefore, whether it is liquidity mining or issuing its own tokens, DeFi has a significant role.

7.2   DeFi – Injecting vitality into blockchain

In the summer of 2020, DeFi market was set off by the liquidity mining and farming ecosystem, engaging the whole Ethereum community. The significance of DeFi is to enable the blockchain to find its native financial applications in the decentralized world. The blockchain is an asset trading network whose liquidity is aggregated by DeFi. With centralized finance as an existing model, DeFi soon brought in a proven mechanism and updated the features of crypto. Here we will discuss the main features and potential of several DeFi's main areas: trading, lending, insurance, and derivatives.

7.2.1   Trading – AMM (automated market maker) solving the listing, cold-start, slippage, and liquidity issues

We believe one of the most important breakthroughs for DeFi is the decentralized exchange use case.

DEX's initial idea was to directly move the CEX order book onto the chain. Despite the features such as asset self-management and KYC/AML free, three problems were overlooked: 1) This mechanism has no advantage over CEX, as the speed of the order book cannot catch up with the centralized order exchange and timely price discovery is not possible; 2) With the current structure of Ethereum, the transaction speed is extremely slow; 3) To create an order, you need to pay the gas fee (not refundable even if there is no transaction). So basically, in the beginning, a DEX could only be seen as a platform trying to mimic CEX but falling short on it.

(1) AMM, liquidity mining and project bootstrap are closely combined

The main advantage of a DEX is the quick and easy access to open market liquidity. Listing on a CEX takes a long and expensive process (at least in the past), making it impossible to get listed for the projects that run with a small, decentralized team or a community-run model. Without additional resources to do a "cold-start", it is not easy to complete the entire process typically required to have a token on a CEX, including financing, development, listing, and market-making.

On the other hand, DEX relates to the model of initial community offering (which has been slowly standardized). Without a solid operating team, a DeFi token is hard to get through CEX, but it can be quickly listed on DEX.

A DEX order book is somehow complex. The market-making team is required to understand not only market making but also the blockchain, smart contract, and wallet interaction. However, AMM solves exactly this "cold-start" problem. With the LP – liquidity provider – token, ordinary people can be rewarded to participate in market making, thus lowering the threshold. By adding the incentive layer (liquidity mining), a series of problems such as the listing process, the "cold-start" and transaction slippage has been (or at least partially) solved.

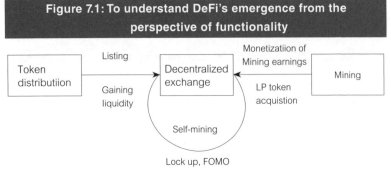

Figure 7.1: To understand DeFi's emergence from the perspective of functionality

Source: HashKey Capital

(2) AMM's price discovery mechanism is still behind that of centralized exchanges

AMM are still evolving, but, having said that, there are issues that need to be tackled. Here we have a comparison of common AMM and centralized order book models.

AMM's biggest problem is the impermanent loss that LPs need to bear. This is because AMM is designed to aggregate liquidity into a pool rather than to actively match orders. In a centralized order book (centralized exchanges), a maker and a taker provide liquidity based on a specific market price and spontaneously work as an oracle. Centralized exchanges are essentially a sorting and matching pool of order books, and the order initiator determines the price.

For AMM, such as CPMM, the popular constant product market maker, the price is determined by the number of tokens in the pool. The constant product of X*Y determines that ΔX can be exchanged back for ΔY. The corresponding token price is only known after the exchange. Therefore, the price estimation provided by AMM before the transaction is converted according to the ratio of ΔX and ΔY.

The real price discovery of AMM can be seen only after trading, unlike centralized order book that spontaneously forms the market price through the maker and the taker. This is where arbitrageurs make profits, resulting in impermanent losses. Some AMMs have begun introducing the oracle mechanism to provide prices, but the frequency of quotes needs to match the transaction frequency which is hard to achieve. Consequently, AMM's prices cannot be adjusted automatically.

7.2.2 Lending – Offering liquidity, leverage, and extra revenue amplifier

Lending is the earliest form of DeFi, kicked off by MakerDao, with Compound, Aave, and bZx being launched later. Compound's liquidity mining ignited the whole community and became a pioneer of the DeFi industry.

The early volume of DeFi lending is also related to the transactions and liquidity mining:

- Mining is available on lending platforms, such as Compound and bZx.

- The lending platform provides a leverage tool with which one asset can be exchanged for another minable asset (usually the platform's token), or liquidity mining is conducted via continuous lending. Typically mining returns are high enough to cover the lending cost. These lending platforms have become new revenue streams for investors.

- Borrowing and lending such as Aave involve even higher leverage.

All of the above starts with the premise that the endpoint of the entire liquidity mining game – the rewards of liquidity mining –

should be relatively stable. Now the industry is constantly expanding the game's space/the use cases of liquidity mining, but without knowing to where it can be developed. Also, centralized exchanges have already begun to take part in liquidity mining, it seems complicated for them to do so.

However, liquidity mining has unlocked the capability of lending protocols: by increasing the types of tokens, adding lending function (credit), and liquidity mining to offer rewards to users, DeFi protocols acquired many new users and made the products more usable.

Some lending protocols try to introduce a centralized approach, i.e., lending using real identity information (similar to KYC information required by banks or telecommunications companies), such as Tellor. This can also be seen as DeFi trying to capture the traditional centralized lending market.

7.2.3   Insurance – Far from maturity despite enormous potential

Decentralized insurance is the most innovative mechanism for DeFi. Compared to other DeFi use cases, it is still early and has a big addressable market. We have discussed the topic of insurance mechanisms in the previous chapter.

The traditional insurance market is dominated by joint-stock companies (50%-70%), with mutual assistance and mutual insurance as secondary players, yet with a proportion as high as 27% of the global market. It is particularly developed in the United States and Europe, exceeding 30% in both, over 40% in Japan, but very low in China.

The advantage of mutual insurance companies over joint-stock insurance companies is as follows: joint-stock insurance companies involve three parties' interests, i.e., managers, policyholders, and shareholders. In a sense, policyholders and shareholders are opposite in terms of interests; let's say, 1 dollar more to policyholder's compensation, means 1 dollar less to shareholder's interest. However, this can be alleviated through checks and balances. If the insurance company has a clear preference towards shareholders, the number of insurances sold will be significantly reduced, affecting the long-term interests.

On the other hand, mutual insurance has only two parties, the manager and the policyholder. The policyholder invests in a pool, and all compensation comes out of this pool without involving other shareholders. This is much simpler. Therefore, the nature of mutual insurance and blockchain is similar in some cases. For example, blockchain projects also involve the team and general token holders.

7.2.4   Derivatives – Synthetic products have many advantages

(1) Synthetic products have more advantages than traditional finance

We call synthetic products to the derivatives created by DeFi. Synthetic products are a special type of product that has been implemented in traditional finance, with a large number of transactions in the open market through CFD (contracts for difference), and many customized services in private markets through investment banks.

The risk of traditional CFD platforms is mainly counterparty risk. One cannot hold the corresponding assets via the CFD platform. The CFD platform offers a hedge in the middle, meaning the user and the platform are counterparties.

Using DeFi, the counterparty risk is reduced. This is determined by the DeFi platform and blockchain mechanisms. Take Synthetix as an example. Since all products are completed based on users pledging the platform's native tokens, excess collateral (750%) is needed to control the risk of synthetic assets. The synthetic assets minters will receive a commission for swapping the assets and can only claim their share of the commission if the collateral ratio is maintained. As more synthetic products and transactions are essential to the platform's success, the platform will be more motivated to excel. In addition, the CFD platform still needs a traditional KYC process to make engagement with the DeFi synthetic assets platform more fluid.

(2) Perpetual contracts have the largest profit margins, but additional design and architecture are still needed

Another trend in DeFi derivatives is that the market begins to target perpetual futures contracts. As previously summarized by ChainNews, six DEX platforms launched decentralized perpetual contract products. Those who choose perpetual contracts have found that in CEX, contract trading develops even faster than spot trading. On March 12, 2020, when the Bitmex server went down, some DeFi projects had issues with smart contract liquidation. DEX for perpetual contracts has not yet been subject to market and technical stress testing. Based on the current Ethereum architecture, the performance may not be good enough.

It is also interesting that DEXs of other high-performance public chains are slowly being developed and getting market share. Products on Cosmos, Polkadot, and Solana are strong competitors which fuel cross-chain trading.

Derivatives are certainly the most profitable part of CEX. CEX will not give up its pursuit of products, market share, and mechanism design, which means DEX's derivatives have met its arch-rival. However, DEX is likely to develop a "para" liquidity mining mechanism that requires additional product development and iterations. Otherwise, there might go like using order book-based

DEX to compete with CEX in the spot market.

Overall, all of the sub-categories of the DeFi market have long-term potential. We are optimistic about automated market makers, synthetic products, decentralized insurance, and other DeFi products. Liquidity mining has heated the industry for a while, but it is by no means without its own issues although it has already been proved to be a valuable business model. DeFi tokens' profitability has been similar to other small altcoins, a characteristic of early blockchain projects. Its alpha earnings are expected to be closely related to the degree of decentralization, valuation, long-term mining earnings, and project fundamentals.

7.2.5   Asset management

Since the DeFi boom, the market has witnessed the development of various DeFi protocols, such as AMM, lending, derivatives, synthetic assets, and so on. Each field has influential and anchor projects. On the other hand, a large category in traditional financial products – asset management – did not follow the steps of the entire DeFi development, given its decentralized form. Despite the slow development, decentralized asset management has initially developed a relatively complete model, and with the increase of asset types, there lies great growth potential for decentralized asset management.

Why does asset management need to be decentralized?

(1) Providing additional returns to regular users

Managing financial assets, both traditional or crypto assets, and especially those with good liquidity and significant fluctuation is time-consuming and laborious. As a result of insufficient investment and risk control capability, it is difficult for individuals to outperform professional asset managers in terms of yield. That is how traditional asset management came into being. Except for mutual funds, traditional asset management entry barriers are high.

Decentralized asset management, on the other hand, offers a more crypto inclusive model with community participation.

After reaching large volumes, asset management starts benefiting from advantages related to advantageous information and resources. Over the years, crypto has created excess returns mainly through information asymmetry. The asset management model also gives retail investors the possibility of benefiting from information asymmetry. Two factors cause the information gap asymmetry in the crypto community: one is the scope of the community. There is a big difference in information transmission between public and private channels. The other is the massive information that is necessary to screen investment opportunities. There is a narrow information gap between institutional and retail investors for major assets such as BTC, and the excess return is relatively low. On the other hand, small assets have a high excess return because sometimes the information is harder to get, thus creating larger information gaps. Therefore, small assets are where bigger asset management rewards can be found.

(2) Decentralized asset management remains a "blue ocean"

Nowadays, we can say that decentralized asset management remains a "blue ocean" considering that not many people have recognized the necessity of asset management:

- There are still many myths about excess returns in the crypto community. Most people are confident that they are capable enough to beat the market, but the hard reality is that they fail to do so most of the time, and it is hard for an individual even to outperform Bitcoin. The market as a whole is still in a zero-sum game where it is difficult for individuals to beat institutions. Regardless of centralization or decentralization, as Bitcoin's market cap gets larger, the returns from holding Bitcoin or other large-cap cryptocurrencies have begun to decrease. Simultaneously, the risk of the altcoins is directly proportional to the earnings.

- There is a lack of understanding and trust regarding decentralized asset management. While traditional asset management relies on reputation and performance, decentralized asset management has been running for a short period. There are practical problems such as lack of transparency, inflexible mechanisms, and the absence of track records, which will be gradually overcome as time goes on.

- The growth of the DeFi and NFT market has driven the rapid development of decentralized asset management and its innovation capacity. Compared to traditional asset management, new DeFi models are emerging.

(3) The rapid increase in the difficulty of investing in crypto-assets provides additional prospects for asset management

In addition to the growing quantity of assets, another important factor that drives the need for asset management is the increasing complexity of asset returns. From Bitcoin to public chain and DeFi/NFT, the complexity is rising, and it may be even higher in the future. Various atypical new assets are now registered on the chain. This, coupled with composability, creates various possibilities in terms of assets/returns.

Different types of protocols create multiple revenue models:

- Gains from price fluctuations

- Lending revenue

- Staking rewards

- LP fees

- Mining revenue (LP fees and token rewards)

- Arbitrage opportunities

- Savings in fees (significant as Ethereum gas fee increases)

- Allocation yield (or opportunity cost) by considering the above factors

With all these revenue models, any approach that can generate new returns will have a market. Here we are not discussing the pros and cons between traditional asset management and decentralized asset management, but in terms of the scope of investment, it is difficult for traditional asset management to participate in the items listed above. Buying altcoins may be the best that traditional asset management can do in the crypto space. On the other hand, decentralized asset management is cutting-edge, and it offers the possibility to participate in all items above.

The more complex the DeFi revenue models are, the greater the space and opportunity for decentralized management. It was in this market that Yearn cut into in 2020. In the beginning, Yearn applied the strategy of comparative yield. For instance, when users deposit DAI, they will seek the highest DAI yield between different pools such as AAVE and Compound.

With the increase of capital volume and the emergence of liquidity mining, Yearn created a product called vault, helping users allocate the returns of different DeFi mining pools allowing additional revenue-generating activities in between (such as mining, token sale, and swap). The entire process is automated, reducing costs for users. Since a major part of the income from liquidity mining is the token distribution rather than transaction fees, how to handle this reward is important. The vault automates this part so that users receive the rewards in the form of the same asset/token they deposited. The vault strategy is decided by the Yearn community through voting. Due to the addition of YFI community tokens, staking yCRV at an early phase can also earn YFI rewards. The emergence of vaults like Yearn also enables matching between multiple protocols. A vault presents a multi-dimensional dynamic distribution of its income with its token distribution. There are high fees for the transfer of tokens between protocols, which is why the one-click vaults are gradually gaining attention from the market.

7.3 NFT – Bridging the physical world and the virtual world

7.3.1 What is an NFT?

In the blockchain space, tokens can be divided into fungible and non-fungible tokens from the exchangeability perspective. Fungible tokens (FT) mostly use the ERC20 as one of their standards. These fungible tokens are interchangeable and can be split or fractionalized infinitely. However, these tokens have some limitations. In real life, unique objects are irreplaceable and cannot be fractionalized. Assets with uniqueness cannot be attached to fungible tokens. Non-fungible tokens are unique, cannot be split, and some of the use cases are in-game items, tickets, artworks, and many others. Most NFTs are issued based on the ERC721 standard, which is followed by the ERC1155 standard. The ERC1155 token standard creates the possibility of each token ID representing not a single asset (which is the case of

ERC721), but a category of assets, allowing multiple tokens to be created in batches and share the same token ID.

(1) NFTs are gaining huge popularity, yet not with a high market cap

The NFT market had existed since 2017 when *Cyberpunks* and the *CryptoKitties* were launched. The top five NFT related tokens in terms of market capitalization are MANA, OMI, AXS, SAND and THETA. As of early February 2022, the total market cap of NFT was close to US$35 billion. The daily transaction volume of NFT related tokens in Q1 2022 exceeds US$5 billion, 3.5 times higher than in Q1 2021. The top NFT collections by volume are the card game *NBA Top Shot*, the *Cyberpunks* NFTs, *Axie Infinity*, *Meebits*, and *Bored Ape Yacht Club*. Simultaneously, the NFT platform OpenSea accounted for more

Table 7.1: Top 10 NFT tokens in terms of market cap		
Ranking	NFT token	Market Capitalization (US$)
1	Decentraland	4,046,662,795
2	Axie Infinity	3,714,178,022
3	The Sandbox	3,426,512,351
4	Theta Network	2,820,020,883
5	ECOMI	2,656,421,926
6	Gala	1,901,879,699
7	Flow	1,889,410,824
8	Enjin Coin	1,367,860,050
9	Chiliz	942,388,985
10	Smooth Love Potion	753,365,278

Source: Top non-fungible tokens (NFT) coins by market capitalization on Coingecko website (February 26, 2022)

than 50% of all the NFT volume. Since early 2021, the average unit price of NFT has continued to rise. The table below shows how the price of NFT tokens has evolved. Despite the growing market cap and continued popularity, NFT accounts only for 1.9% of the entire crypto market. The NFT market is still in its infancy, and it is still considered a niche.

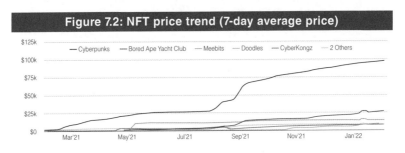

Figure 7.2: NFT price trend (7-day average price)

Source: NFT price trend on the Block website (February 4, 2022)

(2) Majors institutions create NFTs, celebrities joining the craze, and popular projects deliver outstanding returns

Some projects in the NFT space, such as the ones related to *Memes*, *the NBA Top Shot*, *Bored Ape Yacht Club*, *Meebits*, and *Hashmask*, have created enormous economic benefits and performed well, convincing many participants that the NFT space will become the new next big thing. In addition, many influential celebrities are also jumping into NFT, including the artist Beeple with its NFT collage "Everydays: The First 5,000 Days" which sold for US$69.35 million, and Twitter founder Jack Dorsey selling his first tweet as an NFT for US$2.9 million. Some well-known institutions have also joined the NFT game, including Marvel, Disney, the National Basketball Association (NBA), Adidas, LVMH, and other luxury brands. The influence of institutions will effectively drive the further growth of NFT. The following table shows the major events on the NFT market in 2021:

Table 7.2: Major events of NFT in 2021

Date	Event
2021.12.18	Jay Chou's brand Phantaci released "Phantom Bear" series NFT on Ezek platform
2021.12.13	L'Oreal Paris launched NFT lipstick and sold it on OpenSea
2021.11.30	Budweiser beer launches its first NFT series "Budverse Cans: Heritage Edition"
2021.11.29	The Sandbox launched the Alpha Pass
2021.11.01	Cristiano Ronaldo NFT card collection opens auction
2021.10.04	The total revenue of the famous game *Axie Infinity* in the third quarter was US$781.6 million
2021.10.02	Snoop Dogg, a famous American rapper, replaced Twitter avatars with Cyberpunks NFT works
2021.09.23	Edison Chen, the founder of CLOT, shares the heart project NFT works on Instagram
2021.09.03	BAYC auctions at Sotheby's
2021.8.30	Three Arrorws Capital launched NFT fund starry night
2021.8.28	Dom Hofmann created LOOT, the floor price reached 20th in one week
2021.7.15	The NBA Miami Heat auctioned the 2006 championship commemorative NFT
2021.6.25	American rapper Jay-Z auctioned the cover of his debut album NFT at Sotheby's
2021.5.27	Gucci auctioned its first NFT at Christie's
2021.4.20	Rapper Snoop Dogg and Nyan Cat jointly created an NFT
2021.4.07	McDonald's France launched NFT artwork based on food
2021.4.07	Auction house Sotheby's partnered with artist Pak for the first NFT auction on Nifty Gateway
2021.4.05	Gucci and other luxury companies announced to offer NFT soon
2021.3.26	A *New York Times* column NFT sold for 350 ETH
2021.3.21	Twitter CEO Jack Dorsey sold his first tweet for US$2.9 million
2021.3.11	Surrealist artist Beeple sold his NFT artwork "Everydays: The First 5,000 Days" for US$69.35 million

Source: HashKey Capital

7.3.2   Use cases

(1) Crypto games – The earliest commercialization attempt and one of the primary use cases of NFT

We believe that NFTs give players real ownership of game assets, enabling gamers to disintermediate asset transactions or transfers and use them seamlessly across multiple games. Game data can also be safely stored on the chain. At the same time, the game code can be open source, and players that form the community can contribute with their creativity in building the game and setting the rules. In the future, decentralized crypto games will be more advanced, and there will be more game-friendly public chains exclusively for game development.

» History

Since 2013, Bitcoin has been incorporated in some online games, inspiring today's blockchain games. At the end of 2017, *CryptoKitties* emerged, and this event is generally considered as the beginning of the blockchain game industry. *CryptoKitties* even caused the congestion of the Ethereum network back in late 2017. As of February 2022, the total transaction volume was 70,500 ETH, about US$188 million. The number of blockchain games has seen tremendous growth in the following two years, especially on the Ethereum blockchain.

» Main projects

The following table compares some of the major projects and respective features in the blockchain gaming space.

Table 7.3: Main blockchain games

Sector	Name	Overview	Token-related	Features
Card game	Gods Unchained	A great tactical card game with a crypto turn-based system similar to *Hearthstone* and *The Elder Scrolls*	Tactical NFT cards	Cards can be traded on OpenSea. They vary in rarity and value
	Sorare	A fantasy football game based on Ethereum. Players can buy different NFT player cards to form a team and participate in the game	Football card NFT	/
	Cometh	A strategy game with space as the theme	Space card NFT	It has NFTs that generate revenue. It can be combined with DeFi. Players can collect, mine, cultivate and get token income
	Skyweaver	Players may randomly obtain NFT cards and participate in the competition in exchange for gold cards	Spell card and unit card NFT	When players have enough cards, they can use them to build a deck. Players can earn and own in-game digital assets supported by Ethereum

Sector	Name	Overview	Token-related	Features
Card game	NBA Top Shot	It was developed by Dapper Labs (developer of *CryptoKitties*) based on the Flow Chain and has been officially licensed by the NBA. The digital cards recording the "highlights" of NBA stars can be used in the game or traded in the secondary market. Both credit card and cryptocurrency payments are supported	NBA star card NFT	Gained popularity in 2021, reaching a transaction volume larger than *CryptoKitties*
Virtual assets	The Sandbox	It is a decentralized game platform based on Ethereum. Players can create their own virtual world, including NFTs that represent land, in-game items, and so on	Players can use the token SAND to earn assets, tokenize assets, pay for experiences, vote in the community and earn revenue from the game	/
	Decentraland	It is a decentralized VR platform based on Ethereum. Users can freely create environments, buildings, and so on	The token MANA can be used to purchase Land (the negotiable 3D virtual space on the platform). It is the exchange medium of the platform	/

Sector	Name	Overview	Token-related	Features
Virtual assets	Somnium Space VR	It is a cross-platform social VR world. Users can buy land or import objects to shape the virtual universe	The token CUBE is used for microtransactions within the platform, such as paying for items NFTs	Players are free to place purchased NFT assets on their Somnium land and explore them
	Cryptovoxels	A completely open free sandbox game similar to *My World*	Virtual assets NFT	Players have no target task and but they may create content freely
	My Crypto Heros	A game about historical figures, armies and virtual battles	Virtual role, virtual asset NFT	Loom NetWork is adopted in Japan to reduce network delay and supports wallet-free login, making it more convenient
Collection game	Axie Infinity	It is a game of collecting and raising weird cute little creatures	Creature NFT	These pets can not only be collected but also be used for fights inside the game. They are among the earliest NFT pets that can fight
	CryptoKitties	It is the first pet collection game based on blockchain technology. Players can buy and sell crypto kitties with different values and rarities	*CryptoKitties* NFT	/

Source: HashKey Capital

» Featured project – *NBA Top Shot*

(i) Market overview

- ***NBA Top Shot* ranks first in total transaction volume.** The *NBA Top Shot* card collection quickly became popular in 2021. The *NBA Top Shot* was ranked first in crypto collectibles during H1 2021 and has more than 640,000 token holders. Among them, the digital collection card of the famous Los Angeles Lakers star LeBron James' classic dunk shot on the platform sold for US$71,455, making it the highest-priced card sold to date.

In the meantime, other NFT projects such as *Axie Infinity*, *Cyberpunks*, *BAYC*, and *Art Blocks* surpassed *NBA Top Shot's* volume and led the rankings in Q1 2022.

Table 7.4: Top 10 NFT collection projects in terms of transaction volume			
Ranking	Project	Trading volume (US$)	Transactions
1	Axie Infinity	4,009,372,409	14,581,146
2	Cyberpunks	2,069,756,681	20,243
3	Bored Ape Yacht Club	1,373,393,286	24,687
4	Art Blocks	1,198,191,743	143,802
5	NBA Top Shot	932,590,175	17,093,602
6	Mutant Ape Yacht Club	884,621,582	26,354
7	CloneX	441,851,887	13,317
8	Meebits	400,948,298	26,001
9	The Sandbox	365,143,494	48,136
10	Azuki	362,813,884	21,388

Source: NFT price trend on Cryptoslam website (February 26, 2022)

- **Development based on Flow blockchain.** Unlike most NFT projects based on Ethereum and WAX, *NBA Top Shot* is developed on the Flow blockchain, a public chain developed by Dapper Labs, which is also the developer of *CryptoKitties*. Flow achieves better scaling without sharding by removing the nodes from the transaction validation process, and there is a division of labor between nodes that are only involved in the collection, consensus, execution, and validation procedures, resulting in a significant increase in speed and throughput. Flow gets hold of many strong IPs, and the famous NFT exchange, OpenSea incorporated into Flow ecosystem on February 24, 2021.

(ii) Advantages of NFT cards over traditional cards

- **More creativity opportunities and forms of expression:** In addition to the pictures and phrases about stars' profiles on the traditional cards, NFT cards also offer short videos and GIFs that record the "highlights" of NBA stars. NFT cards have forms of expression and content that are more attractive, interesting and of higher value in investment and collection.

- **Easier to store:** Physical cards can be oxidized, discolored, or be damaged during storage as time goes on. The ink on physical cards with stars' autographs may also fade. When NFT star cards are registered on-chain as assets, there is no storage or transportation problem of physical cards. NFT assets can be stored in wallets at virtually no cost.

- **Lower risk of fake cards:** The traditional star card trading market is not regulated. After the official release, the secondary market transactions between individuals are likely to involve counterfeit cards. Players who make a wrong judgment may overpay for counterfeits that cost very little to produce. With smart contracts, the source of NFT cards and every address holding or transferring it can be tracked. Each card is unique and cannot be copied, and the information cannot be tampered with. The chances of fake cards are very low.

(2) Crypto art – The most suitable use case with NFT

» Disadvantages of traditional digital art transactions

In addition to the conditions for registration on-chain, the disadvantages of traditional art transactions are also a significant contributor to the emergence of crypto art. Traditional art has the following two disadvantages:

(i) The low liquidity of the art market

Transactions mainly occur in galleries and auction houses in the traditional art market. The creators display their works in galleries or auction houses through intermediaries. The disadvantages of this transaction model are obvious: low exposure rate, restricted by time, region, and population, low marketability and popularity, and poor liquidity.

(ii) Creators do not have real copyright

After acquiring the works from creators, buyers can make identical copies and sell them on the secondary market. The scarcity of artworks decreases due to the continuous reproduction and dissemination, resulting in the drop of the collection value. Compared to the initial sales revenue, the economic benefit of resale appreciation is objective. Over the years, creators have been fighting for further royalties on resales, or *Droit de Suite* (the right granted to artists or their heirs to receive royalties on future resale of their artworks). This concept was first introduced in France in 1920, where the further royalty rate is usually shallow, with artists in France receiving a 3% share of the resale price. In countries that follow the *Directive 2001/84/EC of the European Parliament and the Council* on the resale right for the author's benefit of an original work of art, artists can get 4% of the proceeds from the resale. In the United States, California legislation recognized the *Droit de Suite* in 1976. In 1991 and 2011, Congress solicited opinions from the public on the system of *Droit de Suite*, but neither passed. In 2012, the *California Droit de Suite Act* was repealed. In addition to inadequate legislation, there are also problems of difficult law enforcement and high legal costs.

» Main NFT projects

The following table compares the main NFT projects in the field of crypto art/NFTs and the respective features.

Table 7.5: Main NFT projects in crypto art				
Field	Name	Overview	Token-related	Features
Collection art	Art marketplaces	SuperRare	Established in 2017, *SuperRare* is one of the leading NFT art marketplaces	Token not issued	Collectors, artists, and critics can interact here. It has strong social attributes. Artists must apply before selling their works on this platform. Smart contracts allow artists to get royalties in resale

Field		Name	Overview	Token-related	Features
Collection art	Art marketplaces	Rarible	A platform for minting and trading crypto artworks launched in early 2020	RARI: mainly as a governance token. Token holders can vote for artworks or participate in platform management	The first NFT trading market that implements community token governance
		Async Art	Artists may mint multiple NFTs for an art piece	Token not issued	NFT is dynamic, and the state can be changed at any time. You may create your own artwork by modifying "layers"
		Makersplace	It is a platform that provides all-round services for artists and creators	Token not issued	Every digital creation is signed and distributed by the creator. Even if it is copied, the copied work will not have the genuine signature of the creator
		Nifty Gateway	Launched in early 2020, it plays an increasingly important role in the NFT art trading market	Token not issued	It is a wholly-owned subsidiary of Gemini, a virtual currency exchange founded by the Winklevoss brothers
		KnownOrigin	A platform for minting and trading NFT artworks	Token not issued	NFT Artists can decide their own pricing model or give NFT to new users

Field		Name	Overview	Token-related	Features
Collection art	Art marketplaces	Cargo	Emerging NFT art trading market	Token not issued	/
		Blockparty	Emerging NFT art trading market	Token not issued	/
	Collections	CryptoWine	Users can participate in Grap mining and obtain NFT collections	GRAP: liquidity mining tokens; bottle collection NFT token	Users will get winemaking points by staking GRAP. Players can get CryptoWine collections for trading or collection
		Cyberpunks	Launched in 2017, it is the first NFT released on Ethereum, with 10,000 different pixel avatars	Pixel avatar NFT token	The first NFT collection set the trend of NFT
		Avastars	It is a virtual avatar with different expressions and images	Virtual avatar NFT	/

Field		Name	Overview	Token-related	Features
Collection art	Collections	Hashmask	Portrait NFT with a total supply of 16,384 pieces. It was released in the form of mystery boxes through auctions. Users participating in the auction can obtain the portrait NFT by the random algorithm after 14 days	Profile picture/Digital portrait NFT	Another popular project after *NBA Top Shop*. Players may name their own works
	Artists	Hackatao	Famous artist on Crypto art platform whose main works are abstract avatars	MORK: community token, mainly used to encourage community members to buy NFT	/
		Matt Kane	Chicago artist, an algorithmic artist who makes good use of code and data	Abstract character NFT	He designed customized software and constructed drawings layer by layer with the adoption of an algorithm
		Francesco Mai	3D digital artist	3D artwork NFT	/

Field			Name	Overview	Token-related	Features
Collection art	Artists		Frenetik Void	An artist good at representing science fiction scenes	Science-fiction-themed painting NFT	/
			Totemical	Crypto artist depicting cyberpunk, magical human forms, nature, and urban landscape	Painting NFT	/
	Mint tools		ethArt	It is a tool for minting NFT artworks. It realizes commission-free token minting by using code customized for DFOhub	ARTE	Users can operate without programming knowledge
	Physical commodities		WiV	/	Red wine NFT	/
			Icecap Diamonds	/	Diamond NFT	/
			Crypto Stamp	/	Stamp NFT	/

Source: HashKey Capital

(3) Social token – One of the most promising increment markets of NFT in the future

We believe that social tokens embody the Web 3.0 peer-to-peer features, which helps reduce creators' dependence on centralized platforms, increase the circulation and liquidity of creative works, and can genuinely realize the binding of creators and respective rights. Compared with physical assets registered on the chain, native assets in internet communities have a higher value capture. So far, people have only touched the shallow potential of social tokens. They may become one of the most promising increment markets of NFT in the future.

» Classification of social tokens

Social tokens are a kind of token supported by personal reputation, brand, or community. It is a relatively new application in the NFT space. Social tokens are based on the premise that community value will continue to rise, roughly divided into personal and community tokens.

(i) Personal tokens

Created by individuals, they can appreciate as the individual grows in value but has limited capture value and is heavily affected by personal branding. Creators can manage the community they create by issuing tokens.

(ii) Community tokens

They are usually used to access communities with specific membership, such as having tokens issued by the creator of the community to access specific telegram discussion groups, information or services, etc. At the same time, these communities will also encourage people to contribute to the community by issuing tokens, which are mostly governance tokens of decentralized autonomous organizations (DAO). Communities usually have more comprehensive achievements and greater growth potential than individuals.

The table below shows the main projects of two types of social tokens and their token use.

	Name	Profile	Additional value to the token
Personal token	RAC	Personal token issued by Grammy artist OurZora	1. Access to early fan groups with membership 2. Have a discount or priority access to events 3. Potential rewards for supporting early creators
	Rally	Tokens issued by individual creators on Rally platform, also platform governance tokens	
	Roll	ERC-20 personal token issued on Roll platform	
Community token	Whale	Community governance token (DAO)	1. Personal tokens' rights 2. DAO community governance right 3. Income from lending or selling assets in the community
	PSG	Tokens issued by the Paris Saint-Germain team in Chiliz Fan	
	Chiliz	The native token of Socios voting platform, in cooperation agreements with 10 top football clubs such as Juventus	
	GG	Counter-terrorism token of GEN. G anti-terrorism E-sports team	

Table 7.6: Main projects of two types of social tokens

Source: Based on articles on the Messari website

» · Value of social tokens

(i) Increase the monetization of creative works

The internet provides a platform for creators to share their works, but the capability of creators in commercialization, work sharing, communication, and value-adding is limited. In other words, their work lacks monetization. However, the emergence of Web 3.0 is expected to solve this problem. Creators can issue social tokens in the community to let supporters share their favorite works, improve liquidity and add value to the works. Moreover, community users may enjoy tokenized rights according to their rankings given by the users on the activity and contribution.

(ii) Binding creators to their rights

Creators may use social tokens to allow fans to access all works of the creator on all social platforms. Fans will no longer be able to rely only on the platform to support creators and their favorite works. Instead, they can support creators with tokenized tools. Creators may enjoy all the profits of the added value of their works and are bound with rights and royalties, which reflects the core of the Web 3.0 peer-to-peer ecosystem.

» Ecosystem environment

Today, social tokens have not only higher value but are also fueling a rapidly growing ecosystem. The table below shows the main components of the social token ecosystem.

Table 7.7: Main components of the social token ecosystem		
Token issuing platform	Token creation accelerator	Adminstration tools
Roll Rally meTokens Zora	Seed Club Kernel Forefront	Collbland Outpost SourceCred

Source: Based on articles on the Messari website

Token issuing platform: Provide a platform for token issuers to mint and issue social tokens.

Token creation accelerator: The primary role is to incubate social tokens, such as helping creators to design token models and create token standards.

Administration tools: Mainly used for community governance. The main functions include group verification, ID authentication, voting, proposal, launching a DAO, airdrop, reward, asset sales, and revenue farming.

(4) Other use cases

In addition to applications in crypto games, crypto art, and social tokens, NFT has many other exciting use cases. The following table compares some of the typical use cases in the NFT ecosystem.

				Table 7.8: Other NFT projects				

Field	Name	Overview	Token-related	Feature
Marketplace/Aggregator	OpenSea	Users can freely trade NFT and view historical data	Token not issued	The largest NFT marketplace. Almost all NFT assets are traded on OpenSea. The community is active and strong
	Mintbase	A platform for free trading of NFT assets	Token not issued	It provides niche NFT assets, such as music, tickets, photography, and so on

Field	Name	Overview	Token-related	Feature
Database	TokenTrove	Users may trade *Gods Unchained*, *Cryptovoxels*, and *Crypto Space Commander* NFT	Token not issued	/
	Nonfungbile	One of the most important NFT data platforms	Token not issued	With complete data, it is the best place to query NFT related data
	NFTBank	NFT portfolio tracking and data analysis platform	Token not issued	/
Decentralized domain name	Ethereum Name Service (ENS)	ENS maps readable names to identifiers recognized by blockchain and non-blockchain resource machines, such as Ethereum addresses	Domain name NFT	ENS domain names can be traded on the secondary market
	Unstoppable Domains	Users may replace a readable address with a crypto address that cannot be tracked	Domain name NFT token	/
DeFi*NFT	MEME	MEME holders can earn pineapple points by staking their tokens. In return, users can exchange for rare NFT collection cards	MEME: provide liquidity mining	Users get NFT collection cards through Proof of Work (PoW)

Field	Name	Overview	Token-related	Feature
DeFi*NFT	Aavegotchi	A cosmic blockchain game built on Ethereum and powered by DeFi-led Aave	GHST: used for community governance and allowing players to participate in DAO. Users can also buy props and equipment with tokens. Each Aavegotchi ghost is an ERC721 NFT token	With DeFi gamification, users can participate in the staking of DeFi tokens for profits and rarity mining
	DEGO.finance	The aggregator of NFT and DeFi. In the DEGO ecosystem, the elements of various DeFi protocols are recombined to form a new system	DEGO: used for community governance. Users can participate in community proposals, voting, and decision-making and get dividends	It provides users with a more diversified portfolio. dApps include liquidity mining, NFT minting, and so on
Project launch platform	Cocos-BCX	It is committed to creating a low threshold and high-speed blockchain infrastructure and on-chain ecosystem for developers. Users have ownership of game assets	COCOS: platform governance token, used for community voting, decision-making, community reward, and so on	/

Field	Name	Overview	Token-related	Feature
Project launch platform	Flow	A public chain developed by Dapper Labs, the developer of *Cryptokitties*, a platform focusing on the operation and development of NFT assets such as games. It incorporated OpenSea into the ecosystem in February 2021	Flow: platform governance token; now listed on Huobi and Kraken	It has its own wallet. Compared with Ethereum, it is by low fees, high speed, and large throughput. The popular project *NBA Top Shot* is developed on Flow
	WAX	A public chain focused on the production and trading of NFT virtual goods. It was initially based on EOS, and later separated from it	WAX: community governance token. Token holders can participate in community voting to determine the proportion of liquidity pool, fees, and so on	Users do not need to create wallets. They rely on opskins, a virtual goods trading market. Rich in traffic and resources in gaming, it is an excellent public chain for NFT
	Enjin	A game development platform based on Ethereum. The company was established in 2009, and it has been running for more than ten years with a complete ecosystem. Enjin wallet can store props, and users can design their own game discussion forum	ENJ: players can mint NFT assets by locking ENJ. ENJ will automatically unlock after NFT assets are burned. Players can also earn tokens in the game	/

Field	Name	Overview	Token-related	Feature
Finance	yinsure.finance	A distributed insurance project of YFI. In addition to self-holding, such insurance policies can also be traded in the NFT market or participate in mining for profits	Tokenized policy: yInsureNFT	/
	NFTfi	Users can obtain ETH or DAI loans by staking NFT assets. Users who provide DAI or ETH loans can get benefits	Loan voucher: NFTfi Promissory Note	The first NFT lending platform
	NIFTEX	Self-service NFT liquidity solution. Users can split an NFT into numerous pieces, and these NFT token fragments can be traded on the open market to improve liquidity	Fragment token: users participate in community governance (DAO) according to fragment token holdings	Community governance rights are more decentralized. The collection threshold has been lowered, and asset liquidity is higher
Content creation	Zima Red Newsletter	NFT related newspapers	Token not issued	/
	DeFi Arts Intelligencer			/
	Play To Earn			/

Field	Name	Overview	Token-related	Feature
Content creation	NonFungerbils Podcast	NFT related Podcasts	Token not issued	/
	Matthew and Rizzle Show			/
	Blockchain Gaming World			/
	NonFungerbils Podcast			/
	Blockchain Gaming World	NFT related videos	Token not issued	/
	DCL Blogger / Short-form Twitter video			/
	NFT Anorak			/

Source: HashKey Capital

7.3.3 Virtual worlds paralleled to the physical world – Metaverse

(1) What is Metaverse?

The word Metaverse was first proposed by Neal Stephenson in his science fiction novel *Snow Crash* in 1992. Meta refers to something transcending, and verse means "universe". Metaverse is a virtual world that parallels and interacts with the physical world. In this virtual world, there are new characters, currencies, assets, ways of socializing, and forms of society. It is independent of and complementary to the physical world. In a broader sense, elements such as AI, AR, VR, MR, cloud, and gaming all belong to Metaverse. Generally speaking, the keywords that define Metaverse include virtual world, digital identity, social interaction, immersion, economy, ecosystem, and online civilization.

The movie *Ready Player One* describes a space similar to Metaverse. In the movie, people can enter the virtual world "Oasis" as long as they wear VR equipment, in which buildings and busy cities are similar to the physical world. It is a world that has an independent social form and economy. In "Oasis", users may also find players and superheroes from different dimensions, socialize and play freely. Another example of Metaverse is the video game *The Sims*, released by Electronic Arts in 2000. It is an open sandbox game where people do not have a clear task. Players simply control the virtual citizen Sims in the game, establish connections with other citizens, build houses, participate in social activities, and so on. One more example is the game *Second Life*, which built an open world. The prices of some items in the game are even pegged with U.S. dollars. The city size and functions are also linked to real life. Corporates frequently use virtual worlds and games for advertisement, promotion, and product placement. Although games seem to be the most suitable direction, the Metaverse can also create different kinds of experiences that mimic the real world, such as digital twin cities and digital twin shopping centers.

(2) Reasons for the Metaverse entering public views

The Metaverse has come into the public eye in recent years for three main reasons:

- **Relevant technologies are now developing to maturity.** VR, MR, AR, AI, virtualization, and graphics rendering have made considerable progress in recent years and can serve as the infrastructure of the Metaverse. Take VR and AI as examples. VR refers to virtual reality technology, a high-tech simulation system that can help players get an immersive experience. VR is of great significance in the Metaverse. Players can feel like they are in the virtual world and have exciting and diverse experiences than in the real world. AI refers to artificial intelligence, which enables machines to show advanced intelligence through medicine, learning, and robotics. It is expected that many jobs will be replaced by artificial intelligence in the future. AI technology has made a significant contribution to Metaverse content creation.

- **Commercialization is more feasible.** Nowadays, new forms of social media such as games, video, live broadcasting, and other streaming media have emerged. Besides, e-commerce, distributed technology, blockchain technology, distributed commerce, and various remote technologies have made the commercialization and distribution of Metaverse platforms possible. There is a falling demand for face-to-face communication in economic activities. Consequently, an "online society" and online communities are being formed.

- **Driven under new economy paradigm.** The Covid-19 epidemic since the end of 2019 has posed restrictions on social distance and interactions. The desire to socialize is sometimes difficult to satisfy in the real world and has to be compensated in the virtual world. The epidemic has promoted the landing of Metaverse and accelerated the process of digitalization.

(3) How NFT empowers Metaverse

Blockchain technology has many advantages, such as distributed, decentralized, traceable, easily verifiable ownership, labor-saving, and cost-saving with smart contracts. In terms of games, the ownership of game assets in traditional games belongs to the game developers, and players only have the right to use them. In crypto games, users can really own the game assets through smart contracts. In addition, it is difficult to hack the distributed ledgers of blockchain games, and the game data can be saved safely. Finally, the code of the blockchain game is open source. Players and respective communities are free to innovate, making the games more exciting and inclusive.

Compared to FT, NFT tokens are unique, and their commodity attributes are greater than the currency attribute. This feature is a natural fit with the Metaverse virtual world, where most items, characters, avatars, and assets in the virtual world are non-fungible, and ownership needs to be verifiable. The batch minting of multiple NFTs represented by the new ERC1155 protocol is also of great use in Metaverse.

The Metaverse virtual world must entail blockchain technology and NFTs. NFT games are among the pioneers, represented by *Cryptovoxels*, *the Sandbox* invested by Whaleshark, who has also purchased virtual real estate on *Decentraland*, whose token MANA has soared 50 times in 2020, and the popular NFT games *Axie Infinity* and

Somnium Space. *Decentraland* and Adidas jointly held a virtual fashion show where all items were auctioned in the form of NFT.

(4) What differences can the Metaverse make to mankind's life?

- **Elevating social life:** The Metaverse offers an experience completely different from the physical world. To some extent, Metaverse has disrupted social life. Imagine that in Metaverse, players can have a 360° view of Beeple's paintings, watch Apple product releases, enjoy fashion shows, and make friends with people from anywhere in the world or with realistic AI characters. They can buy virtual real estate and live in noble neighborhoods in the virtual world. Metaverse is attractive not just for its technological improvements but also for the better social experience and upgraded social interactions it offers. In the future, more of us will meet in the Metaverse.

- **Creating new ways of financing:** The profit-making approaches of players in Metaverse are both related to and innovative from the traditional world, including the auction of game assets such as land, rare items, and precious real estate in the virtual world, the reward for participating in activities and returns from platform token investment. Take the sprite NFT game *Axie Infinity* as an example. Players have many ways to earn in-game revenue. They can buy Axie NFT characters for trading, fighting, or breeding to get SLP (The Smooth Love Portion token) token rewards; buy and develop land and offer services on it for profit; buy functional items specifically deployed on the land and upgrade functions for profit; invest in Axie Infinity Shards (AXS) game governance tokens for returns. The possibilities are endless.

- **UGC gradually rising, competing with OGC/PGC:**

Unlike in the traditional world, in the Metaverse, people do not complete tasks to win the game according to the rules set by the content provider. Instead, they can explore and create content freely. Most of the activities in the Metaverse are people-centered rather than planned around specific game events. This resembles more the video platform YouTube where people may browse without knowing exactly what they want to watch or create and upload their own videos, rather than passively accepting the schedule and content provided by the platform. Content in the Metaverse will be disintermediated, cross-platform, and created by users, for users, which is also in line with the concept of Web 3.0.

Today, the Metaverse is still in its infancy. Only a few games or films showcased prototypes of the Metaverse, providing an image of the future social conditions. It will be long before we see its large-scale implementation.

References

"The Meaning of Decentralization", https://medium.com/@VitalikButerin/the-meaning-of-decentralization-a0c92b76a274.

"dApp Industry Research Report 2018", http://www.199it.com/archives/833512.html.

Coingecko website and data, https://www.coingecko.com/en.

The Block website and data, https://www.theblockcrypto.com/data/nft-non-fungible-tokens/nft-overview.

Messari website, https://messari.io/.

CHAPTER 8

SERVING MAINSTREAM INSTITUTIONS – THE RISE OF THE INSTITUTIONAL CRYPTO FINANCE ECOSYSTEM

In contrast to DeFi, traditional institutional finance is called CeFi (centralized finance). The digital asset boom is bound to bring an inflow of trading and various supporting financial service providers. Moreover, when traditional institutional investors get interested and drawn to the digital currency market, they are also faced with a steep learning curve. This translates into a big market for crypto financial service providers focusing on cryptocurrency, which combines traditional financial model with digital assets features. At present, institutional financial services for crypto assets fall into three categories: custody, insurance, and prime brokerage. Custody mainly includes key management, staking, on-chain governance, and transactions, while insurance services include products launched by traditional insurers and self-insurance services. Prime brokerage services mainly include aggregate transactions, lending business, custodian services, OTC services, and other businesses. In addition to these services, the entry platform for traditional institutional investors is also being improved, such as cryptocurrency ETFs, compliant exchange services, and compliant trust products. As a crypto-asset with the most robust connection to the physical world, stablecoins have been trending and issued by financial institutions or internet companies, including fiat-backed stablecoins, decentralized stablecoins, and algorithmic stablecoins. They are also a type of digital asset that is of great concern to regulators as stablecoins share great similarities with current financial instruments and may disrupt the existing financial system.

8.1 Custody – The uniqueness of virtual asset as opposed to financial asset

Cryptocurrency custody has been a long-standing problem for institutional investors. Custody involves security, technology, compliance, the introduction of institutional investors, among others.

Custody is the foundation on which many products are built, such as stablecoins, STOs, and compliant exchanges, so it is a strategic and highly competitive field. In the sense of traditional financial institutions, custody refers to keeping the clients' financial assets at the entrusted custodian that ensures asset security and offers value-added services such as valuation calculation, performance analysis, asset accounting, and risk control.

There was no such thing as digital asset custody during the early days of crypto. Digital assets are natively self-custodial, and no third party is required to be involved. This is a feature of digital currency, where the private key that can transfer digital currencies is in the hands of users. There was no trusted institution to offer centralized custody or a credible institution to do the licensing.

However, the problems started to occur when institutional investors interested in getting involved dared not to enter the market due to the absence of custodians. Custodian services of institutional funds and assets are a must rather than an option when discussing institutional investors. For example, in the United States, the SEC requires institutions holding more than US\$150,000 to have their assets in a custodian provided. Moreover, institutional investment mandates will also require the use of various custodians. Without them, investors may have no confidence to invest. As far as we know, all mature funds investing in cryptocurrency use custodians.

Features of digital asset custody:

The following four services are unique to cryptocurrency custody:

- Multi-party key management

- Staking

- On-chain governance

- Transactions

8.1.1 Multi-party key management

As the control of the cryptocurrency is in the hands of private key holders, the safe way is to divide the private key into several parts. For example, if it is divided into M parts, then N signatures are needed to operate digital assets (N < M). The custodian and the client each hold different parts of the private keys, which require all parties to operate together. This is not unique to the custodians. Some crypto wallets also provide similar services. However, the multi-party signature is a common practice of custodians, for it can dramatically reduce custodial risks, especially when the counterparty is not so trustworthy. Those with more robust technical capabilities can adopt the secure multi-party computation (MPC) for safer control of private keys. MPC requires different parties to operate within a specific period rather than simultaneously. Besides, there is no need to rebuild the private key. The private key is invisible, so it will not be stolen, thus significantly lowering the security risk. PlatON and Curve are two examples of MPC key management.

8.1.2 Staking

There was no staking when digital assets were born in 2009. Staking gained popularity with the rise of PoS (Proof of Staking) consensus mechanism. As we mentioned before, digital currencies started with the Proof of Work (PoW) mechanism, which was slow and energy-consuming. This is one of the reasons the new generation of public chains is shifting toward PoS consensus.

The rewards of PoS consensus are determined by the inflation level of the coin of that chain. Those who participate in staking (becoming a stakeholder and participating in the block production either directly or through delegation) can get the corresponding proportion of the return. If the PoS token is only stored in the wallet without staking, it will lose the risk-free staking income (in tokens). Therefore, investors holding PoS tokens will certainly participate in staking (rational choice theory) and the staking service becomes inevitable for custodians, with the fittest and most attractive thriving. Investors are unlikely to give up the 2%-20% of annual staking return, as it is enough to cover many expenses. In addition, providing staking service may also have additional technical requirements like setting up nodes, which custodians may choose to outsource.

8.1.3   On-chain governance

On-chain governance resembles the traditional shareholder meetings, where investors participate in voting based on the number of shares they hold. On-chain governance refers to token holders participating in the governance activities, such as upgrades of the blockchain performance, modifications to tokenomics, and other proposals based on the on-chain governance model. Many chains have been shifting to complete on-chain governance, such as Polkadot, while others stick to off-chain governance, such as Ethereum. We have made a detailed analysis of the advantages and disadvantages of on-chain and off-chain governance in "Blockchain Governance and Polkadot's On-chain Governance Practice". (In Chinese, https://www.chainnews.com/articles/399208005832.htm.)

On-chain governance is based on token holder governance but this also means that the more tokens a user holds, the more say they have. Off-chain governance often becomes developer governance which means the original developer team controls the upgrading of the blockchain. So far, there is no agreement on which model is the best. Vitalik, founder of Ethereum, for example, sticks to off-chain governance.

At the same time, assets under custody do not mean transferring the voting rights. The custodian client may continue to vote via the custodian interface. In some cases, custodians are also node operators.

Clients may also delegate the voting rights to them so they can vote on behalf of clients.

8.1.4   Trading via custodians

Trading via custodians is a new emerging service. In this model, the custodian holds clients' assets, but clients may ask the two custodians (buyer side and seller side) to trade directly via the OTC trading platform. This model solves two issues. First, clients' assets do not need to be transferred between the exchange and the custodian, eliminating some risks. Second, trading on the exchange will necessarily cause redundancy of assets, i.e., the number of assets traded is generally less than the amount deposited into the exchange. Therefore, this new service can eliminate the "redundant assets" at different exchanges. All assets can be kept in the wallet of the custodian.

8.1.5   Another custody function – Issuing tokens

Because of some of the unique features of tokens, there are certain types of businesses that must go through a custodian to be compliant. One is the issuance of stablecoins. At present, stablecoins with the largest circulation are fiat-backed. With over 20 billion fiat-backed stablecoins issued by various issuers, there is confidence in the fiat-backed stablecoins. Except for a large deviation of USDT in 2018, other compliant stablecoins are stable in their prices and work like fiat dollars.

An essential condition for the issuance of stablecoin is a qualified custodian. Stablecoins issued by institutions in the United States, whether via BitLicense or MSB, need a qualified custodian. It can be a bank or a qualified trust company. The stablecoin issuer has officially been approved with the license and custodian. Users who wish to buy stablecoins can directly transfer U.S. dollars to the custodian's bank account for the custody of U.S. dollar assets, while the issuer issues the corresponding stablecoins to the users' digital currency account.

8.2   Insurance – An indispensable condition

The frequent occurrence of security accidents in the crypto world has given rise to interest in the crypto-insurance industry. The operation mechanism of traditional insurance companies is 1) Actuaries calculate the probability of various incidents (such as illness, death, disaster, etc.); 2) The product department designs the corresponding products and actuaries price products according to the probability; 3) The applicant purchases products; 4) The policyholder pays the premium during the existence of the policy; 5) In case of claim settlements, the insurance company underwrites, determines the loss, and makes payment; 6) The reserve for the insurance contracts is used for investment.

As far as we know, the decentralized insurance mechanism has no actuary or investment department. Therefore, it is different from the traditional insurance companies operating under the corporate system. It is more like mutual insurance. Of course, mutual insurance has always existed and is the oldest form of insurance in the form of mutual insurance cooperatives. The global mutual insurance market accounts for about 1/3 of all insurance contracts.

In the traditional insurance industry, an insurance product reaches the client (the insured) via product, insurance company, broker, and many other roles. They play different roles as follows:

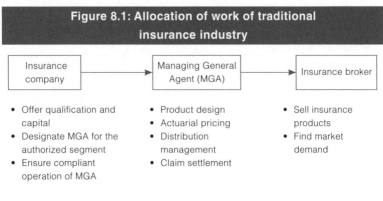

Figure 8.1: Allocation of work of traditional insurance industry

Source: HashKey Capital

8.2.1   Insurance company

An insurance company is a party that provides insurance qualifications for insurance products and undertakes insurance liability. After deducting the commission of other third-party service providers, most of the client's premium goes to the insurance company for active management. It may be used for investment or the payment for the client in case of a claim. Compliant insurance companies generally need to hold insurance qualifications and have a strong balance sheet. To ensure the capacity of paying claims, the regulator usually requires the insurance company to maintain a certain proportion of reserve that cannot be used for investment or operation.

8.2.2   Insurance product designer

An insurance product designer can be the insurance company or an independent third-party supplier. In most countries, third-party suppliers exist in the form of MGA – Managing General Agent. Its role is to design insurance products for insurance companies, involving services including risk identification, product pricing, and subsequent risk management, such as claim settlement review. This can be regarded as a white-label service provider of the insurance company.

MGA was originated in the United States. When the insurance companies on the east coast wanted to enter the western region but lacked local contacts and knowledge, they had to hire a general agent locally. Later, with the maturity of the European and American insurance markets and the high segmented insurance types, professional product designers in various segments emerged one after another, and the MGA model gained popularity in Europe and America.

MGA can help the insurance company design the terms and conditions of the policy, but it is still the insurance company that finally signs on the policy and takes liability. Therefore, MGAs do not need a strong balance sheet or insurance qualification, but they are still regulated insurance intermediaries. Generally, compliant MGAs need either to hold an insurance intermediary license or to be designated and authorized by the insurance company and subject to its supervision.

8.2.3   Insurance broker

Insurance brokers are mainly responsible for distributing and selling insurance products and are an important link between insurance companies and end clients. Insurance brokers are the product of the "separation of product and marketing" trend in the insurance market. In a mature insurance market, an insurance broker can act as an agent for products of multiple insurance companies and provide clients with more choices. At the same time, an insurance company can understand the market demand and get feedback for insurance products through multiple insurance brokers and launch various innovative and even customized insurance products according to the market's needs and sales channels.

8.2.4   Centralized insurance

The basic insurance here refers to the products that can be scaled, underwritten by the insurance company, and sold on a per-policy basis. While the sale of products still relies on traditional licensed insurance brokers, insurance companies work in the following models: 1) Insurance companies develop their own products. In this model, insurance companies conduct due diligence on the clients and product pricing themselves. 2) Insurance companies + MGA. In this model, MGAs design and manage a full set of crypto asset insurance products for insurance companies, which are only responsible for underwriting. 3) Insurance companies are bound to an asset security solution. In this model, insurance companies underwrite the assets only when a specific security solution is adopted.

(1) Insurance products independently launched by traditional insurance giants

Currently, the primary use cases of insurance products are all asset insurance services offered by traditional insurance companies that favor a specific custody solution. Most of them are case by case rather than standardized products.

Lloyd's of London is an essential institution for traditional licensed insurance companies and brokers to enter the crypto community. Many insurance policies in the market are underwritten through Lloyd's syndicates.

Lloyd's is known for its segments and insurance network coverage as a large-insurance marketplace. Syndicates are the pillar of Lloyd's. Each syndicate can be regarded as a small insurer with its own focus. Each can consist of one or more individuals or companies that jointly offer reserves for the policies. Lloyd's adopts a "subscription" model, whereby when Lloyd's receives a policy request, multiple syndicates may subscribe to a policy request, each taking only its share of risk and paying only its own percentage of the claim. If taking all syndicates of Lloyd's as a whole, the risk-bearing capacity is relatively high. Lloyd's is regarded as a large insurance company with its net assets worth US$45 billion.

In addition to syndicates, Lloyd's also has its own insurance brokerage network. Brokers need approval from Lloyd's to do business in Lloyd's marketplace. World top insurance brokers mostly run their business on Lloyd's in the form of subsidiaries. In addition, Lloyd's has its MGA members to meet the demand of member companies in cross-border trade. This way, members can carry out global business without building a global office network. Lloyd's Syndicate Arch Insurance and broker Marsh jointly launched Blue Vault, a cold wallet insurance product. In April 2019, Lloyd's provided insurance services with an insurance policy amounting to US$255 million for Coinbase's hot wallet security. Previously, Lloyd's also provided insurance services for custody companies such as Kingdom Trust.

(2) Traditional insurance companies + security technology provider

Unlike the above insurance companies providing insurance for the client of custody service providers, security technology providers are also involved in the research and development of insurance products, similar to external consultants or vendors of insurance companies. But they are also different from MGAs. Technology suppliers do not need to conduct risk due diligence for the clients or provide product pricing and claim settlement for insurance companies. They only offer asset security that can be recognized by the insurance company or the authorized MGA, leaving pricing and claim settlement to the insurance company or the authorized MGA. Cooperation with insurance companies is a good channel for customer acquisition and endorsement for security technology providers.

(3) Traditional insurance companies + MGA

In the crypto-insurance space, MGAs need to connect with upstream insurance companies to provide product management, channel management, and service management for lower costs and higher efficiency. They also need to connect with downstream brokers to offer customized product, marketing, and claim settlement solutions and support them in sales activities.

Currently, there are very few professional MGAs focusing on crypto. However, their emergence may accelerate the pace of traditional insurance companies to enter the crypto assets field.

Established in 2017, Evertas is a crypto-insurance service provider headquartered in Chicago. Currently, it is the most well-known Crypto MGA. Evertas itself does not provide any technical services related to asset security and only focuses on insurance products. It conducts risk audits and due diligence for insurance clients and prices insurance products based on risk on behalf of the insurance company. In case of a claim, it also needs to review the rationality of the claim on behalf of the insurance company and complete the compensation process. Its unique advantage lies in its understanding of crypto-asset security and private key management.

With a business license issued by Bermuda Monetary Authority, Evertas is a licensed insurance broker.

8.2.5　Captive insurance

Captive insurance refers to the model in which the insured company, such as an exchange, establishes a separate insurance subsidiary to provide services for the business of the insured company.

The biggest difference between captive insurance and self-insurance is that the insurance subsidiary is also licensed and regulated, and its capital reserve must meet the mandatory requirements of regulators. Therefore, captive insurance offers more professional and trusted protection for institutions.

The disadvantage of captive insurance lies in difficulty of scaling up, for it can only provide small-scale insurance for its own business and not beyond. Besides, the underwriting limit of captive insurance is based on the company's balance sheet, and usually, the balance sheet of exchanges or custody companies is not enough to cover their AUC.

A captive insurance subsidiary is a perfect channel of risk transfer from the parent company. The subsidiary can directly participate in the re-insurance market as a licensed insurance company. Moreover, the compliance threshold for establishing a subsidiary is much lower than for an independent insurance company.

8.2.6   Self-insurance

Usually, self-insurance does not involve a traditional insurance company. It is essentially a promise made by the asset management side, including custodians and exchanges, to the clients. For example, after the wallet was hacked in May 2019, Binance exchange lost more than 7,000 bitcoins worth about US$41 million. Finally, Binance compensated clients for their losses with its asset security fund, which is 10% of the platform's commission and was established to protect clients in extreme cases. This is essentially self-insurance. Usually, it is based on the platform's own credit and can be used to supplement basic insurance and captive insurance, but it is not a compliant institutional solution.

8.3 Prime broker – Infrastructure serving institutional investors

8.3.1 Main business of traditional prime brokers

The clients of prime brokers in the traditional financial industry are institutional investors, mainly hedge funds and high net worth clients. These brokers specifically provide services including trading, clearing, custody, leveraged finance, technical services, and other types of support. The emergence of prime brokers is attributed to the heavy workload of hedge fund trading data, positions, and earnings calculation. Prime brokers provide one-stop management, freeing fund managers from the heavy workload and providing additional capital efficiency value-added services. Arguably, the development of prime brokers is inseparable from the prosperity of hedge funds, and their main businesses are classified as follows.

Table 8.1: Traditional prime brokers business model		
Core prime services		Synthetic prime services
Margin financing	SBL	
• PBs provided financing to their clients, allowing them to obtain the leverage required to support their trading strategies. • This could be achieved through the provision of a margin loan within a credit limit calculated through a defined margin methodology and collateralized by assets posted by a client to a PB.	• PBs provided their clients with access to lenders, such as institutional investors with deep portfolios of securities which could be used by hedge funds to cover their short positions and facilitate short selling strategies. • Securities were lent to a collateralized basis. Transactions were managed by PBs and governed by a securities lending agreement.	• PBs allowed clients to synthetically obtain exposure to a certain share without buying or borrowing the physical share, especially in restricted markets. This was often done through a total return swap transaction. • Synthetic transactions may be margined on a transaction-by-transaction or portfolio basis.

Source: Reports on SFC website

(1) Main businesses – Capital-based

The main businesses of prime brokers are those that contribute the most to the company's revenue, such as traditional services, including margin financing and securities lending, and new services of synthetic prime brokerage. Synthetic prime brokerage mainly refers to the use of derivatives such as swap agreements to help clients establish corresponding underlying asset positions, thus saving the cost of direct purchase and resolving the difficulty of direct positions in specific types of markets.

The purpose of such services is to help clients save capital. A prime broker lends assets against its own balance sheet or other sources to earn income, increasing the client's leverage level.

(2) Other businesses – Fee-based

Other businesses include trading execution, settlement, custody, account management, cash and position management, the introduction of funds, and business consultancy. Other businesses are not the main source of income but the basic services of prime brokers, which rely on the solid backstage administration system and prime brokers' professional institutional client service team.

In addition, based on the strong client relationship network, some prime brokers are leading match-book or intermediate businesses, i.e., matching the trading orders of clients in opposite directions. Prime brokers can do it internally without going to the external market for inquiry with a fee charged. Therefore, on the one hand, prime brokers are required to have a high standard in their services. On the other hand, it is difficult for clients to migrate when the network is established, so the market share of prime brokerage is in the hands of several large investment banks.

Figure 8.2: Source of business revenue and global market share of prime brokers

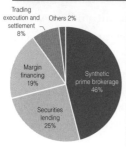

Rank	Prime Broker	Exclusive	Non-exclusive	Total	AUM (million dollars)	Market Share
1	Goldman Sachs	139	482	621	293,004	15.49%
2	J.P. Morgan	134	403	37	288,472	15.25%
3	Morgan Stanley	89	408	497	240,673	12.72%
4	Credit Suisse	41	275	316	186,213	9.84%
5	BoAML	24	221	245	135,964	7.19%
6	Citigroup	25	183	208	127,923	6.76%
7	Deutsche Bank	18	213	231	123,280	6.52%
8	Barclays Capital	3	155	158	84,470	4.46%
9	UBS	25	231	256	74,977	3.96%
10	BNP Paribas	26	84	110	47,830	2.53%
	Others	607	705	1,312	289,174	15.28%
	Total	1,131	3,360	4,491	1,892,021	

Source: Reports on SFC website and Hedge Fund Association website

8.3.2   Main businesses of cryptocurrency prime brokers

The so-called cryptocurrency prime brokers are slightly different from the traditional prime brokers. At the current stage, a more proper definition might be brokers. To adapt to the characteristics of cryptocurrency transactions, cryptocurrency prime brokers provide services including aggregate trading services, funds and digital currency lending, custody services, and OTC services.

(1) Aggregate trading

One of the more significant differences between crypto aggregation and traditional aggregate trading is that the separation of liquidity and the scenario in which aggregation occurs is completely reversed.

In the **traditional standard financial trading scenario:** few exchanges, many brokers, liquidity aggregated on exchanges.

In the **crypto scenario:** few brokers, many exchanges, brokers aggregate and distribute liquidity.

There are many liquidity aggregations in foreign exchange markets similar to crypto because the structure of foreign exchange markets is also fragmented. There are banks, dealers, prime trading firms (PTF) and retail traders. The crypto market is also fragmented, but differently. There are many exchanges but few liquidity aggregators, many types of tokens, and trading pairs, resulting in too many segmentations of liquidity and an urgent need for liquidity aggregation services.

(2) Lending services

Both brokers and prime brokers generally provide lending, but it is optional for brokers in the crypto space, which is related to the project nature. For example, FalconX, which is known for its trading, provides a low credit line, but some brokers shifting from custody or lending provide higher credit lines, such as BitGo and BlockFi.

Capital efficiency is an important demand of clients, especially institutional investors who can use leverage. According to an SFC survey, in traditional finance, 90% of the clients of prime brokers choose margin financing, and nearly 90% prefer securities lending. Lending ranks first among all demands.

Figure 8.3: Usage of different prime brokerage services

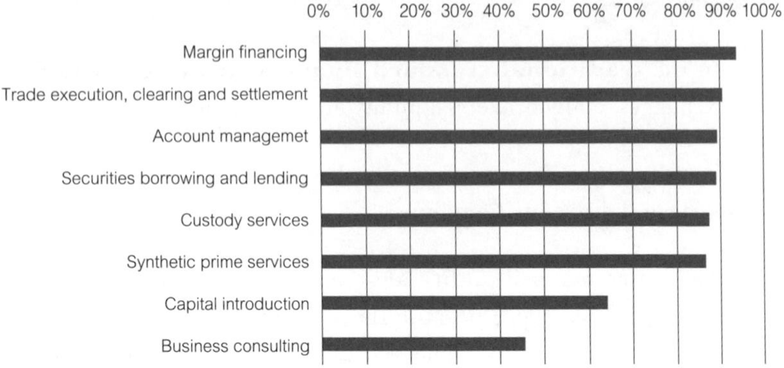

Source: Reports on SFC website

These figures, of course, are related to the customer structure. More than 80% of the prime brokers are hedge funds. However, hedge funds usually cannot be counted as large capital, so they need various lending services to obtain positions.

(3) Custody services

Custody services usually are not the main source of income, considering that they do not generate too much income. Crypto custody was in high demand initially since it was not easy to get a license, so the custody was expensive. However, as the number of players increases, the profit margin of custody-related services has declined. Some custodians are under business transformation, such as BitGo and Anchorage. A significant advantage of custody services is that custodians hold a large number of customer assets. Besides, the risk of crypto means a high customer stickiness in custody. Therefore, the custodian may offer some value-added services for profits.

(4) OTC services

OTC services represent a large volume. Bloomberg once estimated that the OTC service volume is two times the exchange trading volume. There are mainly two types of OTC services.

One is the principal desk, where the desk bears the risk of buying coins. Clients place an order and quote, and then traders complete the order at the market based on the respective quote. The desk takes the mismatch risk between quoting price and the final execution price.

The other is the agency desk, where clients give a price scope and order size, and the desk looks for a seller. Clients bear the price risk between placing the order and finishing the deal.

OTC exchange is not necessarily provided by prime brokers, but also by large exchanges. Large OTC traders include Genesis Trading, Coinbase Prime, and Kraken OTC desk, the former Circle Trade sold to Kraken.

(5) Other services

» Synthetic prime brokerage

Synthetic prime brokerage is common in traditional finance but not much in crypto. B2C2 is, for example, one of the leading liquidity providers that are offering this service. Traditional institutions that want the risk exposure of digital currencies but do not want to hold them directly will need this service. Basically, all the tokens can be traded with the help of OTC traders.

» Portfolio margin services

Prime brokers involved in derivatives trading can provide portfolio margin services. The portfolio margin corresponds to the general margin, which is calculated according to each position opened by the trader. Portfolio margin is the sum of all investment portfolios, especially derivatives. Since there are always occurring opposite trading directions, the margins required can be offset, so the margin demand is greatly reduced. It is a method of margin calculation based on the whole portfolio, not on a single position. In short, it is also a capital efficiency method. The key to portfolio margin is the calculation. Traditional calculation methods have gone through non-offsetable margin systems, strategic portfolio margin systems, intra-group offset margin systems, and portfolio margin systems based on a global risk view. Horizontally, various exchanges have different portfolio margin mechanisms, such as span of CME, Stan of OCC, Prisma of Eurex, and Genium Risk of Nasdaq.

» Multi-account management

Multi-account management is closely related to the characteristics of the digital currency market. Since the beginning of the digital currency market, exchanges have always assumed the role of traditional exchange + brokerage, offering various services including listing, trading, clearing and settlement, account management, custody, and derivatives. All parties are involved in the construction of the exchange. Users can trade directly on the exchange without the need to pay an intermediary. However, the existence of many exchanges gives rise to the demand for brokers. The problems faced by users are: 1) Multiple exchange accounts may be needed; 2) Each account needs to have some balance; 3) In the case of an institution, additional OTC trading and low-cost leveraged fund are needed. Now, the prime broker may trade on multiple exchanges on behalf of users. Clients do not have to worry about the differences among exchanges. They can rely on the capital of the prime broker to open positions and trade derivatives so that the capital can be greatly saved.

8.3.3 Huge potential

There is no doubt that prime brokers mainly serve institutional investors. They can save them from the heavy workload of account management and position management. However, the cryptocurrency prime brokerage relies on the booming of crypto funds and the growth of the derivatives market.

Now, there are still too few crypto hedge funds with a low amount of assets under management (AUM). According to PWC, the AUM of crypto hedge funds totaled US$3.8 billion by the end of 2020, accounting for less than 1% of the entire cryptocurrency market. This is far from the minimum to do prime brokerage. Based on the current market cap, it can be assumed the ratio will not exceed 5% or US$85 billion, even including high-net-worth and wealthy accounts.

The derivatives business has been one of the biggest cryptocurrency trends in the last four years, with futures and options flourishing one after another. Since 2017, the derivatives market has developed rapidly, with the futures trading volume very close to that of spot trading. 2020 was a year when prime brokers began to emerge. Many players publicly announced their entry in press releases such as Coinbase, Genesis Trading, Nexo, Bequant, and BitGo. It shows that this segment has begun to receive attention. The participating prime brokers have much better qualifications than exchanges in previous years. Many have a background in traditional investment banking, and some are from custody and lending. They have a solid customer base, a deep understanding of the industry, and have obtained VC funding. Now in light of the early stages of the industry, the problem is too few institutional clients and underdeveloped derivatives. It is believed that in another two to three years, these prime brokers may form regional monopolies and oligopolies, following the pattern of traditional prime brokers.

8.4 Learning from traditional finance

The digital ecosystem itself is a huge financial system, with trading, payment, and lending products popping up from the day Bitcoin was born. The inflated and volatile trading prices quickly attracted a lot of trading before knowing what was the purpose that digital assets actually serve and their use cases. As long as there is a type of asset, there is a trading market for it. According to the development of typical finance path, there will be service providers, analysis and decision-making systems, and broker-dealers. This is how the digital asset market is approaching traditional finance.

Another factor that has driven the digital asset market toward traditional finance is traditional institutional investors' attention. They already have a well-established service system, with various business forms born from banks, custodians, brokers, and traders. Entering the digital assets market, they found a significant gap in the investment process when compared to stocks, bonds, and foreign exchanges. They had to first adapt to the status quo of digital assets, which created a high threshold and learning cost.

8.4.1 Onboarding tools gradually improving

A high threshold usually means business opportunities. Some service providers for traditional institutions see this opportunity and apply some traditional finance models in the new field. One of the factors that institutional investors value much is compliance. For them, a question as simple as "how to invest in Bitcoin" can be tricky.

Currently, there are several optional solutions in the market:

- Bitcoin ETF

- Compliant exchanges

- Trust funds / private equity funds

An ETF is the most compliant and yet most challenging to apply for. But an ETF is the most accessible channel for institutional investors to enter the Bitcoin market. Listed on traditional exchanges, an ETF can be traded directly like stocks. Settlement, trading, and custody all look familiar like stocks. This has always been a direction asset management companies are working on. Once successfully adopted, it can generate enormous business volume and incomparable advertising effect.

However, commercialization of an ETF may not be straightforward. It needs the regulator's approval. Therefore, how the regulator sees crypto assets remains a problem.

Since 2018, at least five companies have submitted their ETF application for SEC approval, including Vanrek, Bitwise, Phoenix, Winklevoss. But they were rejected by the SEC on the following two grounds:

- The applications do not conform to Exchange Act Section 6(b)(5).

- The applications fail to prove that the Bitcoin market is free from price manipulation.

There are mostly no counterarguments regarding the rejections. For example, SEC Commissioner Hester Peirce, argues that such rejection has raised a heightened standard on the market.

However, these applications are not in vain. In October 2021, SEC approved the first derivative-based Bitcoin ETF – ProShares Bitcoin Strategy ETF, opening the gate to a wider investor base. It is a huge step forward for digital assets and a bridge linking the traditional finance world and crypto. After that two other same kind ETFs were approved to be traded on Nasdaq and the market is expecting the spot Bitcoin ETF to be available this year.

8.4.2   Compliant exchanges – Legit but incomplete

In the U.S. there are two types of compliant exchanges. The exchanges that are more compliant at the moment are the few companies licensed by BitLicense in New York State, represented by Coinbase, and those licensed by MSB in other states. But still, they are not comparable to traditional exchanges.

Founded in 2012, Coinbase is the world's largest compliant digital asset exchange, having operations in many countries worldwide and with more than 56 million registered users. It was listed on Nasdaq through a direct listing on April 14, 2021. There are several contributors to the rapid growth of Coinbase: 1) Complete compliance, holding various digital currency licenses; 2) Strong shareholder structure, including Tiger Global, Union Square Ventures, IDG and SVC, and having banks and payment companies as partners such as Visa and MasterCard; 3) Diversified business, in addition to the exchange, having eight business lines including wallet, trading, stablecoin, VC, broker, and retailer payment processing. Coinbase's rapid development is also attributed to the U.S.-based startup culture and solid development philosophy. Unlike other technology businesses, exchanges must be sound and compliant as they offer financial services. Listed on Nasdaq since April 2021, Coinbase's valuation was approximately US$42 billion as of February 2022.

The other type of compliant exchanges is the futures exchanges, including CME and Bakkt's Bitcoin futures with physical delivery that is tradable on ICE Futures U.S. This type of exchange is entirely compliant, for CME is a futures trading platform that traditional investors can access. In early 2020 when legendary investor Paul Tudor Jones actively invested in Bitcoin, he was engaged in CME futures rather than holding a spot via the new virtual asset exchange above, demonstrating that spot Bitcoin is not the best choice for traditional traders.

8.4.3   Compliant trust products – Formal and sizeable

The Grayscale fund is a well-known digital currency investment product in the industry. Grayscale Asset Management, established in 2013, is a renowned business under the Digital Currency Group, a lead blockchain investor.

The Bitcoin Trust, Grayscale's first product, also the most popular flagship product of Grayscale, was launched in 2013 and got the exemption from registration of private placement by SEC (targeted private placement without the need to be registered as security). In 2015, with approval from the U.S. Financial Industry Regulatory Authority (FINRA), it was allowed to make public offers on OTCQX[1] (code: GBTC). Since then, eligible investors may trade the trust shares publicly on this market. This Bitcoin trust was officially registered with SEC in January 2020, becoming the first SEC reporting company engaged in cryptocurrency investment.

8.4.4   Information service providers – Is it possible to build another Bloomberg?

Bloomberg, Reuters, and Wind are all long-existed business models in the financial information community and there are similar service providers in the blockchain market. In the beginning, they struggled with their business as most participants were not used to referring to data for trading or paying for data and information. Many high-quality products did not survive, which was unfortunate.

---

1   General information of GBTC product: https://www.otcmarkets.com/stock/GBTC/
overview.

Data service providers fall into the following categories:

1) On-chain transaction data: the data that lives on the blockchain ledger, which includes addresses, transfers, blocks, hashes, smart contracts, and other on-chain data.

2) Transaction data services: corresponding to the real transaction data from current exchanges.

Blockchains are public databases, so why do we need on-chain data service providers? Data on the blockchain is not directly available. The simplest way is to build a blockchain node to save all on-chain data for analysis. But the cost and threshold to run full nodes are too high for ordinary users. Raw blockchain data is hard to read for regular users without the appropriate tools. That is where on-chain data service providers step in. They use analysis tools on their own nodes or rent third-party nodes. Bloomberg and Wind have a mature service model in traditional finance, so it is common to borrow these tools from them directly.

Considering that blockchain's data is public and free to access, the only barrier is the user interface.

Why institutional investors cannot use blockchain data on a large scale? Here are the reasons:

- There are too many homogeneous services. Data service is a direction easily thought of, where many traditional data service providers rush into the market with similar products.

- There are not many valuable services to institutional investors. They need comprehensive tools directly linked to profit generation rather than a pure data service. Even with well-formatted data, institutions still struggle with further structurization and strategic development, which is time- and effort-intensive.

- Exchanges themselves also provide data. Trading data can be acquired directly from the API of exchanges and is essentially free to retrieve. Data of exchanges is essentially helpful for quantitative trading teams, especially market-making teams.

8.4.5 Data quality issues

Some institutions have started to integrate the data services of exchanges. Users can quickly establish historical exchange data by looking for third-party data sources. However, the liquidity of digital assets is scattered. Except for leading exchanges, most exchanges have insufficient liquidity, so they have to bring in market makers. Some exchanges have started to set the rates for market makers to negative values to encourage them to accumulate volume on the platform, thus building brand and attracting users for exchanges. But compliant exchanges such as those in the United States will not do so, as more volume also means more taxable income.

Fake volume is a serious problem with non-compliant exchanges. Through analysis, some institutions, including Bitwise, Coin Metrics, BTI, and Alameda, have found some ways to identify the ones providing fake volume.

Experience in traditional finance tells us that there will not be many data providers, especially for integrated products. DeFi's development has given birth to new service providers such as Dune Analytics and Nansen that focus on DeFi data. This is also a volume dividend brought by the expansion of underlying products. But eventually, it will concentrate on the top players. We have seen many data providers failing to survive, although some of them deliver good outcomes, which is pretty unfortunate. However, they are all predecessors to the emergence of future giants.

8.5 Stablecoins – Real use cases but arousing regulatory concern

Stablecoins are classified as an institutional financial service. On the one hand, stablecoins have been gradually issued by financial institutions or technology companies and on the other hand, stablecoins are increasingly attracting attention from central banks and global regulators, including Fed, ECB, BIS, and G7 members. They will probably be subject to strict regulation in the future. Unlike general native assets on-chain, stablecoins are similar to existing financial instruments and may be disruptive to the current financial system. This trend will be even more evident if Facebook's Libra (now called Diem), in the meantime acquired by Silvergate is issued. The stablecoin market will be entirely dominated by institutions.

8.5.1 Types of stablecoins

Generally speaking, there are three types of stablecoins:

- **Fiat-backed stablecoin**, referring to stablecoin backed by fiat currencies such as the U.S. dollar. Tether is the earliest fiat-backed stablecoin but criticized for its compliance issues. Subsequent fiat-backed stablecoins, such as USDC, GUSD, and PAX, have complete regulatory structures. They adopt MSB and/or trust structure to meet the legal framework of U.S. state regulation.

- **Decentralized stablecoin**, represented by MakerDao, an Ethereum-based lending protocol, with stablecoin DAI being its byproduct. DAI has also ushered in a new era of stablecoins with a fully decentralized issuance model, pegged to real assets. It is a delicately designed mechanism. DAI's emergence indirectly drives the growth of the DeFi market at both protocol and tool levels.

- **Algorithmic central bank-like stablecoin**. Emerged in 2018, it is one of the three major stablecoin types. Leading players are stablecoins with multiple use cases and reserves like Terra. These algorithmic stablecoins are not mainstream yet, but they are gradually gaining importance in the market.

The table below shows the stablecoin classification by ECB, but different institutions may have their own classifications.

Table 8.2: Stablecoin classification			
	Underlying assets	Collateral	Redemption
Tokenized fund	Funds	Funds or low-risk assets	Market value or face value
Off-chain staking stablecoin	Assets held by institutions	Assets held by institutions	Market value
On-chain staking stablecoin	Digital assets held by distributed ledger	Digital assets held by distributed ledger	Market value
Algorithmic stablecoin	Digital assets might be distributed for free	No collateral	Non-redeemable

Source: Stablecoin reports of ECB

8.5.2   Regulation and risks of stablecoins

Stablecoins grow fast and it saw a significant expansion in 2020, with less than 6 billion market-wide at the beginning of the year, and over 25 billion by December, a near three-time increase in one year. In the meantime, this amount surpassed 150 billion in 2022.

The significant increase in stablecoin demand is an evidence of its store of value capability. The Federal Reserve keeps printing money, leading to surging liquidity. The reason for stablecoin's expansion in 2020 is still unclear but we estimate that a large portion of the money printed ended up in the stablecoin market.

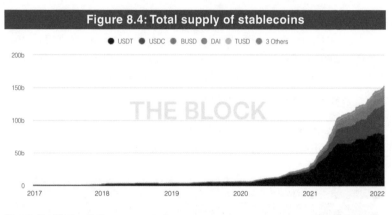

Source: The Block website

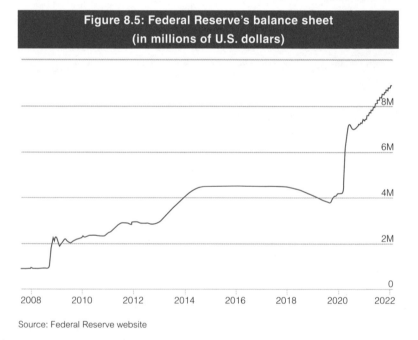

Source: Federal Reserve website

Money entering the stablecoin market can be used to buy other crypto assets. Although this is just an extrapolation, if we compare the diagram of Bitcoin and Ethereum exchange volume with that of the stablecoin, we will see the connection between the two.

The development of stablecoins seems to attract more attention from the regulator than Bitcoin is. After years of observation, it has been recognized that Bitcoin's impact on the financial system is actually inferior to that of stablecoins. According to the research report on stablecoins by BIS and entrusted by the G7, Bitcoin has not become an effective means of payment or store of value. Though the latter is open to discussion, the former is agreed by most of the people in the industry that there is a long way for Bitcoin to become a means of payment.

However, stablecoins are in line with both features, especially as a means of payment, which is mostly a regulated activity.

Stablecoins begin to attract attention from global regulators for the following reasons:

1) Digitalized U.S. dollars appear for the first time beyond the current regulatory framework. It is unclear whether it will pose financial risks.

2) There are various types of stablecoins under different themes. Some are decentralized, without a clear regulatory body.

3) The development of stablecoins is so fast that their commercial value runs ahead of regulations.

4) Large commercial companies such as Meta (Facebook) and JP Morgan have also entered this field, shocking global regulators, particularly Libra (now called Diem). Assuming that global regulation is to be adopted, there is indeed no effective regulatory approach yet.

Currently, stablecoins have the following recognized risks:

- **Impact on monetary policies.** As an alternative store of value, stablecoins may endanger monetary policies and policy execution. For example, the interest-free feature of stablecoins would bring up an essentially zero interest rate policy.

- **Impact on financial stability.** The interaction between the internal vulnerability of stablecoins and other financial systems may cause impacts such as migration of liquidity to and from stablecoins.

- **Impact on infrastructure and market.** The current stablecoin system is similar to the payment system, yet without proper regulation.

- **Impact on the banking system and macro-prudential regulation.** Banks may also need to play a role in the stablecoin market. Pillar 1 (capital adequacy requirements) and pillar 2 (supervisory review) of the Basel Agreement will also need to be included in measuring the risks of stablecoin.

8.5.3 Development of stablecoins

Currently, stablecoin development is at two levels. One is driven by the blockchain industry, which is industrial innovation/demand-oriented, that drove the stablecoin explosion in 2020. The other is the strong interest of traditional businesses in stablecoins and blockchain. Stablecoins can be used as both a means of payment and an accounting unit. The former is represented by Diem (formally known as Facebook's Libra), now a Silvergate product, while the other one is issued by banks for settlement, represented by JPM Coin.

The biggest event of 2019 in the industry was Facebook's (now rebranded Meta) plan to issue stablecoin Libra. Back then, we reckoned that Libra (rebranded Diem) could go in two directions.

First, it could become a financial infrastructure play, as stated in the white paper. Second, if the first was too hard to achieve, it might become a general-purpose public chain similar to current ones but with more users and use cases. The most recent Libra/Diem iterations seem to go in the second direction. Libra Association released white paper 2.0 on April 16, 2020, which included some major changes based on version 1.0 and visions. Libra showed the regulator its greatest goodwill to comply with regulations in the paper. The changes were regulatory/compliance and economics oriented, and even economics were under the regulatory/compliance structure. Technical changes (abandoning the non-licensed public chain structure) are also to serve compliance. It is fair to say that Libra is essentially not a technology product but an economic architecture that is constantly making trade-offs to accommodate multilateral regulation.

As things stand now, ≈USD is likely to be the first to satisfy the market's compliance requirements and practical demand.

» JPM Coin

JP Morgan started testing Quorum (a consortium chain)-based stablecoin in February 2019. JPM Coin is a digital currency that uses blockchain technology for instant payment. A digital currency is needed to exchange value (such as currency) between different parties via blockchain. JPM Coin is not money per se. Instead, it is a digital coin representing the U.S. dollars held in the accounts designated by JP Morgan Chase. In short, a JPM Coin is always worth one U.S. dollar. When a client remits money to another via blockchain, JPM Coin will be transferred and immediately exchanged for the equivalent value in U.S. dollar, thus shortening the typical time needed for settlement.

The following chart shows how it works. In step 1, a JP Morgan client commits deposits to a designated account and receives an equivalent number of JPM Coins. In step 2, these JPM Coins are used for transactions over a blockchain network with other JP Morgan clients (e.g., money movement, payments in securities transactions). Finally, in step 3, holders of JPM Coins redeem them for U.S. dollars at JP Morgan.

Figure 8.6: How JPM Coin works

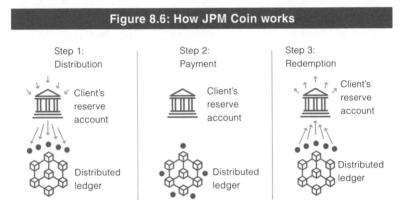

Source: JP Morgan website

JPM Coin is now a prototype to be tested with a small number of JP Morgan Chase's institutional clients with plans to expand the pilot program further. JPM Coin is designed for the money movements between businesses. It is still in the testing stage, so they currently have no plans to make it available to individuals. In other words, lower costs and higher efficiency will benefit the end-users of institutional clients and it is only used for accounting as a stablecoin.

References

Report on Prime Brokers by SFC, https://www.sfc.hk/-/media/TC/files/ER/Reports/sfocircular19031_chi_report.pdf.

Report on Prime Brokers, Hedge Fund Association, https://www.hedgefundassoc.org/wp-content/uploads/2019/08/Article-Prime-Brokerage-survey-Absolute-Returns-HFM-07-15-2019.pdf.

Report on Stablecoin, ECB, https://www.ecb.europa.eu/pub/financial-stability/macroprudential-bulletin/html/ecb.mpbu202005_1~3e9ac10eb1.en.html#toc8.

SEC Rejects Latest Bitcoin ETF Bid, CoinDesk, https://www.coindesk.com/sec-rejects-latest-bitcoin-etf-bid.

The Block, https://www.theblockcrypto.com/data/decentralized-finance/stablecoins.

Federal Reserve website and data of Balance Sheet, https://www.federalreserve.gov/monetarypolicy/bst_recenttrends.htm.

Introduction of JPM Coin, JP Morgan, https://www.jpmorgan.com/solutions/cib/news/digital-coin-payments.

CHAPTER 9

ACTIVE PARTICIPATION AND ENTHUSIASM OF TRADITIONAL INSTITUTIONS

There is a stereotype that most traditional institutions are conservative about new technologies. However, the reality is that many regulators, including central banks, started blockchain research a long time ago. As for central bank digital currencies – CBDCs, the Bank of England announced it started researching on it in 2015, and relevant papers have been published since 2018, indicating that central banks are very sensitive to digital currencies. The Monetary Authority of Singapore (MAS) also launched its Project Ubin in 2016, mainly studying distributed ledger technology (DLT) in the modern financial system. It analyzes the role of the distributed ledger in digital fiat currency, real-time clearing system, Delivery versus Payment (DvP), and payment systems, and has reached some valuable conclusions.

In 2019, Facebook released the Diem (formerly known as Libra) white paper, which was the beginning of large private enterprises trying to develop a global payment network using blockchain. Later, the project was renamed because of strong opposition from regulators. However, these traditional institutions still show us the prospect of blockchain, which also reflects the inclusiveness of this technology. The adoption of blockchain technology by institutions marks a step towards its practical application. On the other hand, the digital RMB of the People's Bank of China (PBoC), or DC/EP for short, does not use blockchain as the underlying technology but draws on the design idea of blockchain, and is also the first member of the PBoC's digital currency family, which will have far-reaching impacts.

Large traditional institutions and central banks of various countries have been actively involved in research on and application of blockchain over the past few years and have achieved meaningful results. Facebook with its Project Libra (in the meantime renamed Diem and moved to Silvergate) proposes a financial infrastructure that empowers billions of people. Central banks, including the European Central Bank (ECB), the Bank of Japan (BOJ), and the MAS have carried out research projects such as Stella and Ubin to explore the application of blockchain technology in areas such as improving the efficiency of payment systems, enhancing security and inclusive finance. The digital RMB (e-CNY) issued by the PBoC has been tested in several areas in China, namely Shenzhen, Suzhou, Xiong'an New Area, Chengdu, Shanghai, Hainan, Changsha, Xi'an, Qingdao and Dalian.

9.1   Diem (Libra)

On June 18, 2019, the Facebook-led Libra Association released a white paper on the project, claiming to enable a simple global currency and financial infrastructure that empowers billions of people (Libra Association, 2019).

9.1.1   Mechanism of Libra 1.0

Libra was designed to be a synthetic currency backed by a reserve of assets including the U.S. dollar, the Euro, the British Pound, and the Japanese Yen. The Libra Association claimed that Libra would bring together the attributes of stability, low inflation, wide global acceptance, and fungibility. The price of Libra currency was designed to be pegged to the weighted average exchange rate of these reserved assets, which can also enable low volatility, although it is not pegged to any single currency.

Libra is fully backed by a reserve of fiat currencies, which will be held by a geographically distributed network of custodians with investment-grade credit rating and be invested in a basket of bank deposits and short-term government securities. Interest on the reserve assets will be used to cover the costs of the system, ensure low transaction fees, and pay interest for early investors (the Libra Association), and so on. Users of Libra do not receive a return from the reserve.

The Libra Association will authorize a certain number of resellers to enable them to trade directly with the Libra Reserve. The price of Libra will be then pegged to the weighted average exchange rate of the currencies in the Reserve through the two-way exchange between Libra and fiat currencies.

The Libra Blockchain is a permissioned blockchain. Libra white paper states that it planned to recruit 100 validator nodes at the initial stage and support 1,000 transactions per second to meet the daily financial needs. The 100 validator nodes would come from the Libra Association, an independent, not-for-profit membership organization that was previously planned to be headquartered in Geneva, Switzerland. The association is governed by the Libra Association Council, which comprised of one representative per validator node. Together, they make decisions on the governance of the network and reserve. All decisions are brought to the council, and major policy or technical decisions require the consent of two-thirds of the votes, the same supermajority of the network required in the BFT consensus protocol.

The Libra Association did not disclose the rebalancing and management mechanism of the fiat currency reserve pool (Libra Reserve), and the two-way exchange mechanism between Libra and fiat currencies. Therefore, Libra is exposed to market, liquidity, and cross-border capital fluctuation risks.

First, if Libra's fiat currency reserve pool implements a more aggressive investment strategy in pursuit of investment returns, it may not have enough liquid assets to fulfill the squeezed large amount redemptions, and the Libra Association may have to sell its fiat currency reserve assets urgently. This may put pressure on asset prices and worsen Libra's liquidity and even solvency. Since there is no central bank acting as the lender of last resort, a run on Libra could trigger systemic financial risks. Therefore, Libra's fiat currency reserves will be subject to prudential regulation in bond type, credit rating, maturity, liquidity, centralization, and so on.

Second, despite that Libra's fiat currency reserves are held by a geographically distributed network of custodians with investment-grade credit rating, it does not mean there is no risk, and the custodians selected by Libra should meet certain regulatory requirements. If one or more central banks are serving as the custodian(s) of Libra's fiat currency reserves, then Libra would be said to be an equivalent of the "synthetic CBDC (central bank digital currency)" as proposed by Tobias Adrian in 2019.

Third, Libra boasts also the cross-border payment function, which can be used as a multi-currency cross-border payment instrument by financial institutions. Due to corresponding risks, it will have complex impacts on cross-border capital flows and will be subject to prudential regulation.

Fourth, if Libra-based deposit and lending activities are accompanied by money creation, Libra will be regulated accordingly due to its impact on the implementation of monetary policy.

Libra, as a currency involving multiple countries and fiat currencies, should meet the compliance requirements of relevant countries. For example, it should be subject to the existing regulatory frameworks for issuing stablecoins in the U.S. and the Eurozone. Additionally, for USDC, it should at least meet the following compliance requirements: first, obtaining the Money Services Business (MSB) license granted by the Financial Crimes Enforcement Network (FinCEN) within the U.S. Department of the Treasury; second, obtaining the currency transfer license for operations in a state; third, U.S. dollar reserves should be held in banks protected by the FDIC; fourth, the realness and adequacy of U.S. dollar reserves should be regularly audited and disclosed by a third party; and fifth, comply with KYC, AML and CFT requirements. In particular, in terms of AML and CFT, the Financial Action Task Force – FATF, an international intergovernmental organization – published the *Guidance for a Risk-Based Approach to Virtual Assets and Virtual Asset Service Providers* on June 21, 2019.

9.1.2   Libra 2.0

On April 16, 2020, Facebook released the second version of the Libra white paper with four main changes: 1) offering single-currency stablecoins in addition to multi-currency coins; 2) improving the security of the Libra payment system through a robust compliance framework; 3) transitioning to a permissionless system while maintaining its key economic properties, and 4) building strong protections into the design of the Libra Reserve.

We can find that all the major changes were compliance and tokenomics oriented. All the technical changes (e.g., abandoning the permissionless public chain architecture) are to serve the compliance requirements. This has transformed Libra from a technical product to an economic architecture, constantly making trade-offs to accommodate multilateral regulation.

Libra 2.0 has adopted a variety of means in order to establish a compliance framework: 1) established a comprehensive compliance framework to meet local legal requirements; 2) relevant members of the Libra ecosystem should be subject to VASP certification; 3) members of the Libra Association and authorized resellers are subject to regular due diligence by the Libra Association; 4) different types of users are subject to transaction limits and account balance limits; 5) all constraints will be written into the protocol in a technical manner; 6) the Libra network activity will be monitored.

9.1.3 Diem

On December 1, 2020, Libra was renamed Diem, and the digital wallet Calibra was also renamed Novi. Both new names are related to Latin words, "Diem" means "day" and "Novi" means "new". The name changes were intended to reinforce the project's independence while obtaining regulatory approval.

For Diem, it is very opportune to start from a single-currency stablecoin in terms of commercial launch. For stablecoins in USD, EUR, JPY, GBP and SGD, many institutions have done related experiments before the Libra Association, and the regulators have initially established a regulatory framework.

For monetary authorities, as a legally compliant single-currency stablecoin is mainly a payment instrument without money creation, it will not affect their monetary sovereignty, and financial risks are controllable. Moreover, due to the openness of the blockchain, the single-currency stablecoin will help to expand the use of their domestic currencies abroad. It will also strengthen the position of strong currencies and weaken the position of weak currencies. For example, some countries that are unstable economically and politically are already experiencing a trend towards "dollarization", which will be further advanced by legally compliant dollar stablecoins.

9.1.4 Silvergate takes over Diem

In January 2022, Facebook (Meta) announced the sale of its Diem network to Silvergate Bank, which seems a temporary setback for Facebook's global payment network plans. After more than two years of wrestling with regulators, Diem is narrowing its expansion into areas ranging from open networks to licensed networks to a single currency stablecoin, a sign that global regulators are worried about the tech giants' attempts. For example, in November 2021, the U.S. President's Working Group on Financial Markets reported that cooperation between stable currency issuers and wallet providers or commercial companies could lead to excessive concentration of economic power, a combination that could adversely affect competition.

Facebook and Silvergate have been working together since 2021, and Silvergate will be the exclusive distributor of Diem's stablecoin, Dime USD. Silvergate has been committed to promoting the combination of traditional finance and crypto, its Silvergate Bank becoming one of the few crypto-friendly banks. Silvergate Exchange Network is also the most well-known blockchain product, which can provide 24/7 non-stop inter-user fund transfers. Diem's transaction target is only US$180 million, which is not a big deal in the crypto market right now (the threshold for the top 100 coins is US$700 million now). However, selling the Diem project only includes intellectual property and other technology assets related to running a blockchain-based payment network, excluding Novi (formerly Calibra), a digital wallet, shows that Facebook still has a strong vision for digital payments. After all, Facebook, which has been renamed to Meta, also needs a payment platform to support the construction of a grand metaverse.

9.2   In-depth research of central banks worldwide

From the targeted users and accessebility perspective, CBDCs can be divided into wholesale CBDCs and retail CBDCs. As for wholesale CBDCs, they can be used only between central banks and financial institutions and are not open to the public. They have fewer participants, and the participants are all regulated financial institutions, allowing for better risk control. This type of CBDC can improve the efficiency of large-value payment and settlement systems and reduce the cost and complexity of existing payment systems. Retail CBDCs are also referred to as general-purpose CBDCs. This type of CBDCs is intended for public use, so there are many participants and variables that greatly impact the economy. On the other hand, retail CBDCs can improve financial inclusion and expand inclusive finance.

According to a survey conducted by the Bank for International Settlements (BIS), out of 66 central banks worldwide (corresponding to 75% of the world's population and 90% of the economic output), 15% of the central banks have been working on wholesale CBDCs, 32% have been studying retail CBDCs, and nearly half of them have been working on both types. The following part will introduce the Project Stella of the ECB and BOJ and the Project Ubin of the MAS.

9.2.1 Project Stella

Stella is a research project jointly carried out by the ECB and the BOJ, which focuses on the applicability of DLT in payment systems, securities settlement systems, real-time cross-border transfers, and balancing confidentiality and auditability capabilities. Four phases of research have been completed under Project Stella. The table below shows the research objectives, DLT platforms, and research results of each project phase.

Project Stella focuses on the research of financial market infrastructures such as payment systems, securities settlement systems, and synchronous cross-border transfers and also carries out extensive research into the confidentiality and auditability of transaction information, indicating the major future applications of DLT by the ECB and the BOJ. However, the project is not intended to replicate or challenge the existing systems, and official research reports have repeatedly stressed that the practical application of DLT is subject to legal and policy regulations.

	Research objectives	DLT platforms	Research results
Phase 1	To assess whether the specific functions of existing payment systems, such as Liquidity Saving Mechanisms (LSMs), can be performed safely and effectively in a DLT environment.	Hyperledger Fabric (V0.6.1)	DLT-based solutions can meet the performance requirements of Real-Time Gross Settlement (RTGS) systems and potentially enhance the resilience and reliability of payment systems. However, the performance of DLT is influenced by the network size and the distance between nodes.
Phase 2	To study whether the settlement between two related reimbursement obligations, such as Delivery versus Payment (DvP), can be conceptually designed and implemented in a DLT environment.	Corda, Elements and Hyperledger Fabric	DLT can be conceptually designed and implemented in a DLT environment, providing a new design method for settling cross-ledger DvP without connection between the ledgers. However, due to the specific design, the implementation of cross-ledger DvP in a DLT environment is complex to a certain extent and may cause other challenges that need to be solved.
Phase 3	To provide new solutions for cross-border transfers and improve the security of the transfers.	Use Five Bells Ledger as the centralized ledger and Hyperledger Fabric as the distributed ledger	There are five main methods of transferring funds between participants: trustlines, the on-ledger escrow with HTLC – Hashed Timelock Contracts, third party escrow, simple payment channels, and conditional payment channels with HTLC. For security, there are mandatory mechanisms for on-ledger escrow with HTLC, third-party escrow and conditional payment channels with HTLC.

Table 9.1: The four phases of Project Stella

	Research objectives	DLT platforms	Research results
			For liquidity efficiency, the five payment methods are ranked as: 1. trustlines 2. on-ledger escrow with HTLC 3. third party escrow 4. simple payment channels, and 5. conditional payment channels with HTLC From a technical point of view, the security of cross-border transfers can be improved by using synchronous payments and locking the funds.
Phase 4	To balance the confidentiality and auditability of transaction information, introduce and classify privacy-enhancing technologies (PETs) applied to DLT, and assess whether transaction information can be effectively audited by authorized audit institutions.	Corda, Hyperledger Fabric, off-ledger payment channels, Quorum and Pedersen commitment, zero-knowledge proof, one-time address, mixed currencies, and ring signature technology	These technologies and platforms differ in terms of whether unauthorized third parties can view and analyze information about senders, receivers and transaction amounts, and auditability. In many cases, effective auditing relies on centralized and trusted data sources in the network. However, over-reliance on these data sources may lead to a single point of failure during the audit process, and specific implementation schemes will also affect auditability.

Source: Compiled by HashKey Capital according to the ECB and BOJ websites

In addition to payment scenarios, digital currencies are also used in financial transaction scenarios that cannot be separated from digital assets and financial transaction post-processing. We cannot fully understand digital currencies and digital assets without studying financial transaction post-processing. Therefore, many research experiments have been conducted on financial transaction post-processing in the project. The ECB and the BOJ have not officially announced the plan to issue a central bank digital currency so far, but the extensive research results of the project are very important in technical accumulation if the two banks issue a CBDC in the future.

9.2.2   Project Ubin

Project Ubin of the MAS has completed five phases of research in the areas of tokenized SGD, payment systems, DvP, synchronous cross-border transfers, and application value, laying a foundation for further practical application in business scenarios. The objectives in each phase of the project have been completed with different members. The table below shows the five phases of the project.

Table 9.2: The five phases of Project Ubin			
	Participating units	DLT platforms	Research methods and results
Phase 1	MAS, Merrill Lynch, DBS, HSBC, and JPMorgan	Ethereum private blockchain, with MAS and banks as nodes	The use of the RTGS system and DLT to complete inter-bank transfers helps to deal with the credit risk between the two sides of the transfer, and there is no liquidity risk.

	Participating units	DLT platforms	Research methods and results
Phase 2	MAS, Association of Banks in Singapore (ABS), Accenture, 11 financial institutions, and 4 technology partners	Corda, Hyperledger Fabric, and Quorum, with all nodes deployed on Microsoft's Azure cloud platform	Using DLT to simulate the interbank RTGS system can reduce the inherent risks of centralized systems such as the single point of failure and improve security and tamper-evident performance while protecting privacy.
Phase 3	MAS, Singapore Exchange (SGX), Anquan Capital, Deloitte, and Nasdaq, etc.	Quorum, Hyperledger Fabric, Ethereum, Anquan Blockchain and Chain Inc Blockchain	DLT is used for the settlement of tokenized assets, such as DvP for Singapore Government Securities (SGS) and China Depositary Receipts (CDRs) issued by the PBoC on different ledgers. DvP smart contracts can ensure that investors exercise their rights and fulfill their obligations, with multi signatures, smart contract locks, time limits, and arbitrators in the design. In addition, the use of DLT can shorten the settlement cycle, and the application of HTLCs (Hash TimeLock Contracts) makes assets unavailable for other transactions during the locking period.

	Participating units	DLT platforms	Research methods and results
Phase 4	Between Project Ubin of MAS and Project Jasper of BOC (Bank of Canada)	Canada's distributed ledger is based on the Corda platform, and Singapore's distributed ledger is based on the Quorum platform.	Synchronous cross-border transfers are made using DLT and the HTLC. As a result, atomic transactions across borders (Canada and Singapore), currencies (CAD and SGD), and platforms (Corda and Quorum) were successfully made. There is no need for a third party trusted by both sides of the transaction in this process.
Phase 5	MAS, JPMorgan, Accenture and partners in the financial industry	Quorum	JPMorgan uses the enterprise blockchain platform Quorum and its digital currency JPM Coin to develop payment networks. Different currencies can be used on the payment network in phase 5 of the Ubin project. Accenture conducts secondary research on use cases and identifies 124 use cases that can benefit from the Ubin payment network.

Source: Compiled by HashKey Capital according to the MAS website

During the research process, MAS has attached great importance to cooperation with other central banks, financial institutions, and technology companies and has drawn on the research results of the traditional financial sector or existing DLT projects. In the final phase, Project Ubin focuses on proving the application value of blockchain and studying its application in use cases across different industries, including capital markets, trade and supply chain finance, insurance, and non-financial services.

9.3 Digital RMB – The world's leading CBDC DC/EP – Global leading CBDC initiative led by PBoC

In April 2020, the People's Bank of China (PBoC) began to test the digital RMB in Suzhou, Xiong'an New Area, Chengdu, and Shenzhen. It has also launched pilots in other regions, including Shanghai, Changsha, Hainan, Qingdao, Dalian, and Xi'an.

To own and use the digital RMB, the public is required to use a digital RMB wallet, the core of which is a pair of keys, namely a public key (corresponding to the wallet address) and a private key. Commercial banks play an important role in the public opening of digital RMB wallets and the Know Your Customer (KYC) review of the wallets.

9.3.1 Mechanisms of digital RMB

On November 27, 2020, Zhou Xiaochuan, PBoC's former governor, further elaborated on the idea of the digital RMB. He mentioned that the digital RMB means a two-tier R&D and pilot project plan rather than a payment product and that the final payment product would be named e-CNY, which, to some extent, draws on Hong Kong SAR's note-issuing system that is also known as the Linked Exchange Rate System (LERS).

PBoC has selected commercial banks with strong capital and technology (currently the six major state-owned banks in China) as the designated operating institutions to take the lead in providing e-CNY exchange services. These designated operating institutions are similar to note-issuing banks in the LERS or CBDC banks on the indirect CBDC.

The e-CNY is issued based on the deposit reserves of designated operating institutions with PBoC. These deposit reserves are similar to the foreign exchange reserves under the LERS. In addition, the designated operating institutions can obtain the certificate of provision or the letter of comfort issued by the PBoC. Such a certificate or letter is similar to the certificate of indebtedness issued by HKMA – the Hong Kong Monetary Authority. According to the revised draft of the *Law of the People's Republic of China on the People's Bank of China*, e-CNY, a digital form of RMB, will have the same value characteristics and legal tender nature as the physical form of RMB.

RMB notes and coins represent users' claims on the PBoC, while e-CNY does not necessarily constitute users' claims on the central bank. Therefore, the relationship between the PBoC and commercial banks can be regarded as that of wholesale and retail in terms of RMB notes and coins, while PBoC and designated operating institutions go beyond the relationship of wholesale and retail in terms of e-CNY. This arrangement provides flexibility for e-CNY exchange services and e-CNY promotion and applications led by the designated operating institutions. Still, these institutions need to follow the PBoC's unified management of the e-CNY quota.

The e-CNY wallets are managed by PBoC, and e-CNY retail payment is handled by the designated operating institutions in the lead. The wholesale payment links concerning e-CNY are handled by PBoC. Therefore, e-CNY is similar to an indirect CBDC in terms of payment, clearing, and settlement. In this way, PBoC does not need to provide real-time gross settlement for retail users and scenarios, effectively easing the pressure faced by PBoC in e-CNY clearing and settlement.

Although e-CNY does not necessarily constitute users' claim on PBoC, the interconnection of e-CNY exchanged by different designated operating institutions is crucial to the orderly circulation of currencies. PBoC guarantees this mainly through three aspects:

First, the interconnection of value characteristics. PBoC conducts regulation on designated operating institutions and sets requirements for the issuance reserve and the capital adequacy ratio in order to ensure that the value of e-CNY is stable and equivalent to other forms of RMB.

Second, the interconnection of circulation links. PBoC improves the payment and settlement infrastructure, making it easy for e-CNY to circulate across different designated operating institutions and wallets and for users to switch e-CNY services between different institutions and wallets.

Third, the interconnection of risk disposal. PBoC provides contingency plans and alternative emergency plans for the designated operating institutions in extreme situations such as a run on them or withdrawal problems. According to Zhou Xiaochuan, "the responsibilities of the central bank vary according to the specific design scheme".

9.3.2 Digital RMB for cross-border payment

Foreign residents and institutions can use digital RMB cross-border payment by simply opening a digital RMB wallet and establishing direct contact with the People's Bank of China without domestic and foreign banks as intermediaries. Because of the natural openness of the digital RMB system, the requirements for opening a digital RMB wallet are much lower than those for opening an RMB deposit account, which helps overseas residents and institutions own and use digital RMB. These residents and institutions should follow KYC procedures and requirements different from domestic residents and institutions when opening digital RMB wallets. From the PBoC perspective, however, there is no difference between domestic and overseas digital RMB wallets.

Peer-to-peer transactions can be made between any two digital

RMB wallets, and there is no distinction between domestic, cross-border, and offshore digital RMB transactions. It is just like any two people in the world can communicate with each other by email without having to know which country the email server is in. Generally speaking, the digital RMB cross-border payment, is completely different from using UnionPay, Alipay, and WeChat Pay overseas in terms of the business logic. It can theoretically be used without relying on SWIFT's processing of cross-border payment information, which helps to maintain China's monetary sovereignty.

Digital RMB cross-border payment can turn on our imagination of overseas use of RMB. Overseas residents traveling in China can open digital RMB wallets and enjoy China's mobile payment services without the need of opening mainland bank accounts. In addition, overseas businesses can apply for a digital RMB wallet without having an account with a commercial bank in China as long as they are willing to accept RMB, and Chinese residents can use digital RMB for cross-border payment.

Two issues need attention. First, in terms of cross-border payment and clearing infrastructure, digital RMB is not intended to replace the current model of agent banks and clearing banks or the cross-border interbank payment system (CIPS) but to complement them. Second, if overseas residents and institutions want to exchange their foreign currency for digital RMB, it means new requirements for RMB convertibility.

As for digital RMB cross-border payment, two issues also need to be studied. First, the opening of digital RMB wallets for overseas residents and institutions should be facilitated while improving KYC procedures and requirements. Second, suppose the digital RMB is in high demand from overseas residents and institutions. In that case, it is necessary to cooperate with the central banks of those countries to respect their monetary sovereignty. Digital RMB should go global in an open and friendly manner.

The digital RMB will boost the internationalization of RMB. Currently, there is already a significant proportion of RMB settlement in China's foreign trade. And digital RMB cross-border payment will enhance the function of RMB as a settlement currency for international trade. But it should be noted that the internationalization of RMB is not only a technical problem but also an institutional one. On one hand, we should give full play to the role of the digital RMB in promoting the internationalization of RMB. On the other hand, the institutional development supporting the internationalization of RMB should keep up with demand.

In addition to the above traditional institutions participating in the "experiments" of blockchain and cryptocurrency in various ways, many commercial organizations have been eager to engage in this field, especially some high-tech enterprises in the United States. Here we share two cases, PayPal and Tesla.

How Paypal joined the cryptocurrency field

Paypal began its involvement in crypto assets in 2019, with great interest and various ways.

- *In 2019, PayPal joined Facebook's stablecoin project Diem (formerly known as Libra), briefly acted as a member of the association, and later withdrew due to regulatory and compliance concerns.*

- *In October 2020, PayPal announced its support for cryptocurrency trading and acceptance of cryptocurrency payments. As a result, some investment banks estimated that at least 17% of PayPal users had purchased cryptocurrencies through PayPal.*

- *On February 4, 2021, Daniel Schulman, CEO of PayPal, said that a department of blockchain and cryptocurrency was being built with heavy investment.*

- *On March 8, 2021, PayPal announced the acquisition of Curv, a provider of cryptocurrency asset custody using Secure Multi-Party Computation (MPC) technology.*

- *On April 20, 2021, Venmo, a subsidiary of Paypal, began to provide its customers with cryptocurrency trading services, and the users can directly purchase Bitcoin, Ethereum, Litecoin, and Bitcoin Cash.*

- *On April 29, 2021, PayPal Ventures participated in the Series D round of financing for US$300 million, led by a stablecoin issuer, Paxos, with the valuation reaching US$2.4 billion.*

- *On April 30, 2021, Coinbase, an American cryptocurrency exchange, allowed users to use PayPal to purchase cryptocurrencies with a daily limit of US$25,000.*

- *On May 3, 2021, Paypal was studying the possibility of using its own stablecoin.*

PayPal, an established payment company in the U.S., may have felt the pressure from its peers, such as the fellow fintech company Square. The mobile payment software Cash APP of the company added buying and selling Bitcoin as early as 2018, with a transaction volume of nearly US$2 billion per quarter. In addition, Square announced in October 2020 that it had purchased 4,709 Bitcoins worth about US$50 million at the time. In February 2021, it purchased additional Bitcoins at the cost of US$170 million. The number of Bitcoins it holds has reached 8,027, with an at then value of about US$440 million as of December 2021. Square was founded by Twitter's co-founder Jack Dorsey, who has a more advanced understanding of crypto assets and blockchain and is also a long-term supporter of crypto assets.

It is a natural choice for payment companies to support cryptocurrencies.

Source: Compiled by HashKey Capital

Tesla and cryptocurrencies

The story of Tesla and Bitcoin is also related to its founder Elon Musk. In early February 2021, Tesla announced that it had bought US$1.5 billion worth of Bitcoin. On March 24, Elon said that Tesla began accepting Bitcoin as payment for its cars. At the end of April, Tesla stated in its first quarter financial report that it had sold 10% of its Bitcoin for US$272 million and that Bitcoin contributed about US$101 million in net profit for the quarter while the company earned US$438 million during the quarter. As of the end of the first quarter of 2021, Tesla owned US$2.5 billion worth of Bitcoin. However, some reversals arose. In May, Tesla suspended the Bitcoin payment because of the environmental impact of Bitcoin mining. In June, the company said it could restart Bitcoin transactions as long as mining transitions to clean energy.

Among listed companies, Tesla is not as "crazy" as MicroStrategy in Bitcoin purchases. However, due to the presence of Elon Musk and Tesla's position in the electric vehicle industry, it has a great influence. What will influence other technology companies is that a leading technology company has truly participated in the Bitcoin game by including it long-term on their balance sheet, instead of just buying and selling Bitcoins.

Source: Compiled by HashKey Capital

References

ECB report on Project Stella phase 4, https://www.ecb.europa.eu/paym/intro/publications/pdf/ecb.miptopical200212_01.en.pdf.

BOJ report on Project Stella phase 4,

https://www.boj.or.jp/en/announcements/release_2020/rel200212a.htm/.

Facebook Diem stabilization currency white paper, https://www.diem.com/en-us/white-paper/.

MAS introduction on Project Ubin, https://www.mas.gov.sg/schemes-and-initiatives/Project-Ubin.

PBoC introduction on digital RMB, http://www.gov.cn/xinwen/2020-04/17/content_5503711.htm.

PayPal introduction on Bitcoin, https://www.paypal.com/us/smarthelp/article/cryptocurrency-on-paypal-faq-faq4398.

CNBC report on Tesla and Elon Musk, https://www.cnbc.com/2021/06/14/bitcoin-btc-soars-after-musk-says-tesla-could-accept-the-crypto-again.html.

PART 3

FRAMEWORK, STRATEGIES AND IMPLEMENTATIONS

CHAPTER 10

BLOCKCHAIN ASSET VALUATION METHODOLOGIES

This chapter serves as a guide on how we see and classify digital assets. To begin with, we divide crypto assets into three categories: securities, payments, and utility cryptocurrencies. The valuation for security tokens resembles that of the traditional stocks, while the valuation for the utility tokens is like a coupon. The classification is for the convenience to apply different valuation models. In addition, the crypto sector is starting to introduce derivatives, which play a pivotal role in the price discovery of crypto assets and will be the most crucial part of crypto payments in the future. Regarding the specific valuation models, we focus on the models themselves and the application boundaries of the cost-based pricing, equation of exchange, NVT (Network Value to Transactions) ratio, and Metcalfe's Law.

In general, the crypto market is still in its early stage, and each valuation model has its own flaws and limitations. These models will further evolve as the crypto asset market matures. Unlike the already established stock market with hundreds of years of history, crypto assets have only been introduced for over a decade. Therefore, there is still very little compelling empirical data. The mainstream valuation models have not yet been developed, so we cannot simply apply those models in the stock market but need to analyze and study the crypto assets and blockchain with their own characteristics.

10.1 Classification of cryptocurrencies

Since blockchain projects involve a wide range of fields and cryptocurrencies are issued in different ways, there has been no unified definition of the attributes of cryptocurrencies worldwide, and there are even dissimilar views within the same country. However, in terms of the current way of classification, cryptocurrencies are mainly classified as security, payment, and utility cryptocurrencies.

10.1.1 Security cryptocurrencies

Security cryptocurrencies are regulated in the same manner as traditional securities. In this case, the issuance and trading of cryptocurrency are subject to the country's securities law in which they are issued. As for the method of determining whether cryptocurrencies are securities, there is no uniform standard among governments.

Take the United States as an example. The U.S. Securities and Exchange Commission (SEC) uses the Howey Test to determine whether a financial instrument is a security. The Howey Test consists of four criteria: 1) If there is an investment of money; 2) In a common enterprise; 3) With the expectation of profit from the investment; and 4) To be derived from the efforts of the sponsor or a third party. The higher the score on the Howey Test, the closer the financial instrument's attributes are to security. In April 2019, the SEC issued a framework for analyzing investment contracts in digital assets based on the Howey Test to provide official guidance on whether a cryptocurrency is a security. The SEC believes that most cryptocurrencies currently on the market meet the criteria of "an investment of money" and "investment in a common enterprise". For the other two measures, the SEC notes that a cryptocurrency is considered a security if its development is dependent on the efforts of a company or centralized entity and if there is an expectation that the buyer will receive a reasonable profit from the investment. It is important to note that a cryptocurrency is not a security if it is sufficiently decentralized and has a clear application scenario. The price change is related to the application rather than the investor's profit expectation. The SEC has confirmed that Bitcoin and Ethereum are not securities.

10.1.2 Payment cryptocurrencies

Payment cryptocurrencies are also known as trading

cryptocurrencies, which can be used as a trading tool to purchase goods and services. Some typical payment-based cryptocurrencies include BTC and ETH, among others. Payment cryptocurrencies are more decentralized and widely accepted, and their issuance and transaction do not need to be regulated. Still, regulators need to have relevant regulations in place in the fields such as anti-money laundering and anti-terrorist financing.

10.1.3 Utility cryptocurrencies

Although the regulators in different countries did not set a criteria to identify utility tokens, we draw on the SEC's approach to identify security cryptocurrencies, if a cryptocurrency scores low on the Howey Test, the cryptocurrency shows less security properties and thus will be classified as a utility token.

Utility tokens are issued by projects for their services or products and are mainly used within the project ecosystem with a relatively small range of applications. Generally speaking, projects issue utility tokens for the purpose of raising funds, which is somehow similar to the pre-sale of a service or product. At the same time, project owners will design their utility tokens to have a limited appreciation so that users can be encouraged to use rather than speculate. For example, if a game or gaming project on a smart contract platform such as Ethereum or EOS blockchain issues a cryptocurrency that can only be used within the project, and the purpose of the buying is to spend it in the game or gaming, then this cryptocurrency can be considered a utility token.

In addition to the three categories of security, payment and utility tokens, cryptocurrencies are sometimes viewed as commodities. In December 2013, the People's Bank of China and five other ministries and commissions issued the *Notice on Preventing the Risks of Bitcoin*, in which Bitcoin was considered a virtual commodity with significant risks. In addition, the U.S. Commodity Futures Trading Commission

(CFTC) considers cryptocurrencies to have the characteristics of commodities under the *Commodity Exchange Act*. In October 2017, the CFTC released its *Primer on Virtual Currencies*, defining cryptocurrencies as commodities.

10.2 Cryptocurrency valuation models

With the rapid development of cryptocurrencies, studies on the valuation of cryptocurrency projects are increasing with main valuation models of cost-based pricing, equation of exchange, NVT ratio and Metcalfe's Law.

10.2.1 Cost-based pricing

The cost-based pricing model is the most intuitive way to estimate the value of crypto assets, whose core concept is to consider the production costs of crypto assets as a lower bound indicator of the value of crypto assets. Only when the production costs are lower or equal to the market price of the crypto asset, the producer will continue to produce; while when the production costs are higher than the market price of the crypto asset, a rational producer will stop production to prevent continuous losses. Take Bitcoin as an example, miners are the producers in the Bitcoin ecosystem, whose production costs include electricity, mining machine costs, maintenance costs, and labor costs, among which electricity accounts for a large percentage. Therefore, miners will only continue to participate in the production when the market price of Bitcoin is higher than the cost of production.

Cost-based pricing can only value crypto assets that use the PoW consensus algorithm. For crypto asset projects using other consensus algorithms, such as PoS, DPoS, and PBFT, which do not require the use of electricity for mining, the cost-based pricing is not applicable.

The cost for the projects using other consensus algorithms is mainly reflected in the fact that participation in the consensus algorithm requires locking of stakes, which is a temporary waiver of the right to sell their stakes according to the market conditions and can result in liquidity costs. The liquidity cost is difficult to quantify and is positively related to the amount and timing of locked-in stakes and more so to the strategy for holding them.

However, the cost-based pricing approach assumes that miners are only incentivized by profit expectations is oversimplified. It is not a completely frictionless process for miners to enter the market; miners need to buy mining machines, build mining farms, sign agreements with power plants, etc. After investing a lot of time and money upfront, a short-term loss will not cause a miner to shut down and leave the market immediately. If miners continue to lose money, they are pressured to exit, but the triggering point for miners to exit might be different. Competition among miners cannot be given equal treatment. There will be a significant difference between miners in terms of electricity costs, mining machinery costs, and performance, so their production costs will not be the same.

The claim that Bitcoin's price is supported by its production cost has also been questioned. The supply of Bitcoin at a given time is determined in advance by the algorithm and has nothing to do with the amount of computing power put into mining. If the price rises, more computing power will be put into mining, but the supply of Bitcoin will not increase. At this point, more computing power competes for a given number of new Bitcoins, leading to a higher cost of production. Similarly, if Bitcoin's price falls, less computing power will be devoted to mining, but the supply of Bitcoin does not decrease as a result, which means the price of Bitcoin will not be supported. At this point, there will be less computing power competing for a given number of new Bitcoins, which will result in a reduction of production costs.

In general, there are significant limitations to the cost-based pricing model. However, it can still provide a helpful reference indicator for miners who have a lot of mining data at their disposal for a lower valuation limit.

10.2.2 Equation of exchange

The equation of exchange is expressed in the formula $M \cdot V = P \cdot Q$, where M represents the quantity of currency, V represents the frequency the currency is used, P represents the price, and Q represents the transaction volume of goods and services. Burniske uses the equation of exchange to value crypto assets, where he considers the network value (M) of a crypto asset to be proportional to the size of the economy it supports ($P \cdot Q$) and inversely proportional to the frequencies it is used (V), i.e., $M = P \cdot Q / V$.

From the above equation, when valuing the expected future network value (M) of a token, it is necessary first to get the price (P), the transaction volume (Q) and the frequency of usage (V) in the expected time. After obtaining the network value, if you want to estimate the unit value, you can divide the network value by the number of tokens in circulation. Meanwhile, considering the token's future value and expected risk, the discounted cash flow method needs to be applied with an appropriate discount rate.

The equation of exchange is usually used to value a utility token. Taking the native token A of a crypto assets exchange as an example, the first step is to calculate the annual economic size ($P \cdot Q$) supported by A in the next five years. The second is to calculate the usage frequency of each A token (V). While the third is to calculate the network value of A per year (M) by the formula $M = P \cdot Q / V$. Then comes the fourth step, which is to estimate token A's circulation per year. The fifth is to get the unit value of token A in the next five years with the annual network value divided by the circulation. Sixth, calculate the current value of token A by the discounted cash flow method with an appropriate discount rate.

In the process of using the equation of exchange, there will be a lot of assumptions in terms of market size, market share, etc., since it is unavailable to access or work out the data, which may make it much harder to calculate the economic size $(P \cdot Q)$. At the same time, it is hard to calculate the usage frequency of the token (V) precisely. Therefore, an estimated value will be taken. However, V will be affected by multiple factors such as users' usage frequency, expectations on the future price of the token, and project incentives, which go beyond the scope of economics and thus cannot be predicted in advance. Especially since the crypto market itself is at an early stage with minimal empirical data, the estimated value of V is likely to be inaccurate.

The equation of exchange is commonly used to value utility tokens. Still, the number of utility tokens in the crypto market that have application scenarios and are adopted at scale is relatively small. Many crypto asset holders are motivated by speculation rather than use. Currently, the reasonably appropriate target for valuation is the exchange platform's native token.

10.2.3 Network value to transactions ratio model

The Network Value to Transactions (NVT) ratio represents the ratio between network value and transaction volume, whose core concept measures the ratio between network value and network value in use. The NVT model considers transfer transactions as the primary value in cryptocurrencies, so the NVT model takes transaction volume as a fundamental metric.

The calculation of NVT is relatively simple. The numerator is the network value of the crypto asset, similar to the market capitalization of a listed company; the denominator indicates the transaction volume, which is mainly a measure of the on-chain transaction volume of the crypto asset in fiat currency. Since the daily on-chain transaction volume of many crypto assets varies greatly, in order to smooth out the fluctuation of NVT, the average transaction volume over a period of time is taken to calculate NVT.

NVT is a relative valuation model. When comparing the NVT of different crypto projects, if the NVT of a particular crypto project is significantly high, then you can determine that there is a possibility that the project is overvalued.

It is worth noting that the NVT model also has many flaws. First of all, it is difficult to determine a benchmark value to judge whether a crypto project is overvalued or not. Secondly, the calculation results can vary significantly from one time period to another. For example, calculating 30-day NVT and 90-day NVT separately will get two different results, which will affect the conclusion and validity for judgment. Meanwhile, NVT calculates only the on-chain transaction volume. However, some transactions do not occur on-chain, which can cause the actual transaction volume to be underestimated, such as the transactions in the Bitcoin Lightning Network. Finally, the NVT model also does not consider the fact that the current main application scenario of crypto assets is trading on exchanges rather than on-chain payments, and the transactions on centralized exchanges do not have corresponding transaction records on-chain.

10.2.4 Metcalfe's Law

Metcalfe's Law is about the network value and the development of network technologies. The core idea is that a network's value is proportional to the square of the number of users within that network. In other words, the more users a network has, the greater the value of the entire network. Since cryptocurrency has a network effect, the more users and application scenarios of crypto assets, the higher their value will be. Therefore, it is argued that Metcalfe's Law can be used to assess the network value of crypto assets in the medium to long term.

Metcalfe's Law was initially expressed in the formula of $NV = C\,n^2$, where NV represents the network value, n represents the number of users, and C represents the coefficient. When evaluating crypto projects, n can be taken as the number of active addresses per day. Researchers have proposed improved formulas for applying Metcalfe's Law to cryptocurrencies, including $NV = C\,n^{1.5}$ and $NV = C\,n\cdot log(n)$.

Metcalfe's Law can only be used as guidance on the long-term trend. In the short term, the validity of Metcalfe's Law has been questioned, with several expressions being relatively simple and only fit well with the price curve of cryptocurrencies in specific periods. The idea of Metcalfe's Law is that all nodes are interconnected with each other. However, for crypto assets, each user will only interact with a limited number of other users in the ecosystem in terms of information and value. Some users will even take the initiative to minimize their contact with other users for security reasons.

10.2.5 Factors affecting the valuation of cryptocurrencies

The valuation models for cryptocurrency listed above give a framework for the valuation of cryptocurrency in a relatively static or short-term approach. In terms of specific applications, the price of cryptocurrencies is greatly influenced by sentiment. Moreover, some fundamental factors that determine cryptocurrencies change very quickly, forming a mutual influence process between price and fundamental aspects.

(1) Indicators

In the case of Bitcoin, market sentiment on a given day can be generally measured by some basic factors such as daily trading volume, number of transfers on the network, and number of active addresses. In addition, if you consider the circulation of cryptocurrencies between available wallets and exchanges, you can have a more directional judgment of the price, i.e., if it flows into an exchange, it generally creates selling pressure, and if it flows out of an exchange, the selling pressure decreases.

SEBA has done some analysis on some BTC networks and proposed a comprehensive model[1]:

$$P_t C_t = U_t^n H(d_t)^i \left(\frac{C_t}{C}\right)^s \left(\frac{C_t}{T_t}\right)^g \tag{1}$$

Where $P(t)$ is the unit value, $C(t)$ is the number of cryptocurrencies in circulation, $P(t)C(t)$ is the market capitalization of the network in circulation, $U(t)$ is the number of users, $H(d,t)$ is the hash ratio, $C(t)/C$ is the proportion of circulating supply, and $T(t)$ is the proportion of transaction.

After rearrangement, equation (1) becomes:

$$\underbrace{p_t + c_t}_{p_t^l} = b_0 \underbrace{\left(1 - \frac{c_t}{c}\right)}_{m_t} + b_1 u_t + b_2 h_t + b_4 (t_t - c_t)$$

After applying the regression equation of the principle of Maximum Likelihood to the above formula with the data from the past 3,613 days, we can get:

---

[1] The specific model of SEBA can be found on https://www.seba.swiss/research/A-new-fair-value-model-for-Bitcoin.

Table 10.1: Bitcoin regression analysis results						
Number of Observations	3,613		s=1.84	i=0.1		
R^2	0.9989		n=1.26	g=0.06		
Adjusted R^2	0.9986					
Variables	Parameters	Standard error	t stat	P-value	95% conf. interval	
m(t)	-31.05	1.09	-28.52	0.00	-33.19	-28.92
u(t)	1.26	0.04	34.46	0.00	1.19	1.33
h(t)	0.10	0.01	8.15	0.00	0.07	0.12
t(t)-c(t)	0.06	0.03	-2.43	0.02	-0.11	-0.01

Source: SEBA research

The explanatory power of R^2 reaches 99%, which is very impressive, and probably no other model with such a high degree of explanation can be found. The point of citing this model here is not to show how well it matches Bitcoin. As there are so many parameters in the Bitcoin network that each can be a dependent variable or an independent variable, if each of them is included in the linear equation, the explanatory power will be extremely high, which can also cause the problem of "multicollinearity".

The introduction of the model is not to price precisely for BTC, but to understand the determining factor to BTC. It is better to have more independent variables in the linear model. The benefit of this model is that only the three most significant numbers are used: i.e., the number of users, the hash rate, and the number of transactions (because the circulation ratio does not change drastically from day to day).

This model is a dynamic pricing model. That is to say, the observable BTC network value is obtained directly on the basics of the number of users, the hash rate and the number of transactions, rather than a static pricing paradigm. To simplify this model with three parameters applied to ETH, we will see that the result is not as good.

Table 10.2: Ethereum regression analysis results			
3-year		5-year	
Related coefficient	0.966	Related coefficient	0.730
R^2	0.934	R^2	0.532
Adjusted R^2	0.934	Adjusted R^2	0.532

Souce: HashKey Capital

Although the R^2 range is acceptable, the standard error is too large, indicating that the variation is predictable but not precise enough and the fluctuation range is too large.

In addition, the hash is a parameter specific to PoW chains, and a similar value will not be available after most chains have started to adopt a PoS-like mechanism. Hence, the model is a unique model for a store of value PoW chain like Bitcoin. Although Ethereum is also a PoW chain, the DeFi ecosystem of Ethereum has grown exponentially over the past two years, and ETH is no longer a network that can be framed with the store of value, so there are more factors left to be examined for the model.

(2) Sentiment model

In the absence of certain fundamentals for digital currencies, some have also turned to sentiment models. The well-known alternative index in the market, for example, uses five variables to describe changes in market sentiment: volatility (25%), momentum (25%), social media (15%), surveys (15%), market share (10%) and

Google Trends (10%).

We run a regression of the BTC market capitalization against this alternative model and get the following results.

Table 10.3: Bitcoin and sentiment indicator regression analysis results	
A 3-year regression	
Related coefficient	0.641
R^2	0.411
Adjusted R^2	0.411
Standard error	15.912
Number of observations	1,056

Source: HashKey Capital

The explanatory power is not as good as the previous SEBA model, but it is convincing enough to show that at least 40% of Bitcoin's price fluctuations can be represented by sentiment. In the SEBA model, the number of users and transactions is a reflection of market sentiment.

(3) An analysis of DeFi tokens earning

Here, we will do a very preliminary analysis to find what factors are responsible for the fluctuations in the price-earnings of DeFi tokens. We apply the methodology used by Zayn Khamisa in his article, "An analysis of the factors driving performance in the cryptocurrency market"[2].

---

2   Reference: https://www.researchgate.net/publication/333967521_An_analysis_ of_the_factors_driving_performance_in_the_cryptocurrency_market_Do_these_ factors_vary_significantly_between_cryptocurrencies.

We do not use any individual DeFi token as the dependent variable to prevent large fluctuations of the token from having too much impact. Instead, we choose the DeFi index on the exchange FTX as the dependent variable, which contains 11 tokens in the sector of DeFi.

The independent variables we selected fall in several categories: 1) DeFi mining yield; 2) BTC price; 3) ETH price; 4) Alt, a relatively large altcoin index; 5) Mid, a medium altcoin index; and 6) Small, a small altcoin index.

The independent and dependent variables, all of which are selected as daily returns (i.e., a daily rate of change), have been smoothed so that an OLS regression can be used, following the approach in Zayn Khamisa's article. The simulation results are as follows:

Table 10.4: Statistical results of regression analysis of DeFi returns and variables						
Regression statistics			Coefficient	Standard error	t stat	P-value
		y-intercept	0.00348	0.00521	0.66670	0.50546
		Yield	(1.06660)	1.73008	(0.61650)	0.53802
Related coefficient	0.808	BTC	0.38072	0.07218	5.27448	0.00000
R^2	0.652	ETH	(0.30677)	0.07749	(3.95903)	0.00009
Adjusted R^2	0.645	Alt	0.11421	0.09391	1.21618	0.22484
Standard error	0.033	Mid	0.21367	0.08300	2.57434	0.01051
Number of observations	316	Small	0.49295	0.07088	6.95483	2.10995E-11

Source: HashKey Capital

We found significant effects of the four variables (p-value < 0.05), so it is simplified as follows:

$$R_{DeFi} = 0.38R_{BTC} - 0.31\,R_{ETH} + 0.21\,R_{Mid} + 0.49\,R_{Small} + Alpha + \varepsilon$$

Our understanding of this earning model is as follows:

1) DeFi tokens are positively correlated with BTC earnings but negatively correlated with ETH earnings, which is counter-intuitive. If we had to find an explanation, the rising price of ETH could cause the gas fee to rise, which would affect the DeFi experience. But the synchronization of BTC and DeFi is indeed unexpected and has a more significant impact than the index of medium-sized altcoins, which seems to be explained only from the perspective of capital expansion, but cannot explain the negative correlation between DeFi and ETH.

2) The earnings of DeFi tokens are highly similar to those of medium and small altcoins.

3) The dependent variable setting of this model also has some shortcomings. Because of the lack of data, we use the random series instead of the mining yield, which could be more accurate if there is actual data. At present, we do not see any strong relationship, which may also be related to the diversity of varieties and yields. Theoretically, the mining yield will be a two-dimensional space with date and names as axises.

4) The model has an explanatory power of 0.645, meaning that close to 2/3 of the variation can be explained. The remaining 1/3 of the variation that cannot be explained is attributed to the Alpha of DeFi token yields. There should be roughly four sources of earnings. The first is the qualitative evaluation, where the community gives higher ratings to the more decentralized projects, such as founders and teams, without initial token allocation or pre-mining. The second

is the valuation, where new topics are always hotly anticipated by the market, and valuations naturally become higher. The third is expected to be the long-term stable mining yield. Logically the higher the mining yield, the greater the purchasing power, the more valuable the token is, similar to a fixed income product. The fourth is the fundamentals of the project, including the technical infrastructure, team, code quality, community activity, long-term operating time, etc.

5) It is also possible to include more independent variables, such as other external factors. However, due to the niche nature of DeFi tokens, the selection of different factors such as VIX, petrol, gold, etc., as chosen by Zayn Khamisa in his article, is of little significance. If the other independent variables are more explicit, the factors can be further stripped from the Alpha.

(4) Relative valuation of DeFi

DeFi has become a relatively established industry, and some institutions have also proposed using the relative valuation method to determine the valuation of DeFi, since DeFi's fees are transparent and can be measured in a similar way to P/E (actually P/S), as the following statistics given by Eloise.

Table 10.5: DeFi fundamental data			
Project	Market cap (US$)	Annualized protocol revenue (US$)	P/E ratio of DEX
SpookySwap	$282.1m	$68.7m	4.1x
dYdX	$5.2b	$662.2m	7.8x
PancakeSwap	$1.7b	$153.2m	11.4x
GMX	$337.7m	$29.3m	11.5x
Trader Joe	$550.0m	$40.9m	13.4x

Project	Market cap (US$)	Annualized protocol revenue (US$)	P/E ratio of DEX
QuickSwap	$158.4m	$8.8m	18.0x
SushiSwap	$795.0m	$36.6m	21.7x
Cap	$10.6m	$445.1k	23.7x
Pangolin	$141.7m	$4.9m	29.1x
Perpetual Protocol	$643.5m	$21.4m	30.1x

Source: Tokenterminal, Feb, 2022

We can see from the chart above that DeFi's P/E ratio can range from 4.1 to 30.1, which is a vast range. With the launch of more DeFi projects in the future, the categories of valuation models can be defined and further estimated by sub-sectors such as DEX, Lending, synthetic assets, etc. It is a good framework, but like securities, the valuation model is only a framework, not a result.

To sum up, the crypto market is still in its early stage, and each valuation model has its own flaws and limitations. As a result, these models will further evolve as the crypto asset market matures.

Unlike the established stock market with hundreds of years of history, crypto assets have only been introduced for over a decade. There is still very little compelling empirical data. The mainstream valuation models have not yet been developed, so we cannot simply apply them in the stock market but need to analyze and study the crypto assets and blockchain with their characteristics. By understanding the elements of crypto assets, we know that consensus is an essential basis, the scope and degree of which will affect the supply and demand, and further affect the value of the crypto asset.

Meanwhile, the main characteristics of each crypto asset project and the factors that may affect the market capitalization are not the same. The vision of the project, development progress, team members, the number of tokens in circulation, the number of active addresses and other factors may all have an impact on the market capitalization of a crypto asset project. Different projects may need different valuation models, and there will not be a universal valuation model.

Regardless of the final form of valuation methods and models, it essentially still requires crypto assets to have their value. However, many crypto assets on the market currently lack a viable business logic and cannot truly capture the value of the network, resulting in the value of crypto assets not being able to be effectively supported. The price changes mainly come from the influence of market liquidity but lack support from fundamental aspects.

References

"SEBA: A new fair-value model for Bitcoin", https://www.seba.swiss/research/A-new-fair-value-model-for-Bitcoin.

"P/E ratio for cryptocurrencies", https://medium.com/coinmonks/p-e-ratio-for-cryptocurrencies-63dad08d26fc.

DeFi projects data, https://www.tokenterminal.com/terminal/markets/exchange.

The fear & greed index for Bitcoin, https://alternative.me/crypto/fear-and-greed-index/.

"An analysis of the factors driving performance in the cryptocurrency market", https://www.researchgate.net/publication/333967521_An_analysis_of_the_factors_driving_performance_in_the_cryptocurrency_market_Do_these_factors_vary_significantly_between_cryptocurrencies.

CHAPTER 11

THE FRAMEWORK FOR BLOCKCHAIN ASSET INVESTMENT MANAGEMENT

This chapter will introduce a framework for blockchain asset investment management. Blockchain asset management is no different from traditional asset management in the adopted principles. Blockchain venture capital (VC) benchmarks traditional VC, and digital currency hedging can benchmark traditional funds. However, we have found that blockchain asset management is more reliable than traditional asset management because it expands the investable target scope by integrating the token. On the other hand, the complexity, operability, and management requirements are also higher. Most Blockchain investment funds are in the form of shares plus tokens, requiring great familiarity with both types of targets

Moreover, due to the vague boundaries of the primary and secondary token markets, the high returns on mainstream digital assets such as Bitcoin also put pressure on fund management. In addition, a compliant, formal, and transparent blockchain investment institution should not only explore its way within an immature regulatory framework but also seek an optimal solution among extremely immature service providers. All of these make blockchain asset management challenging and complex. From the perspective of an investment fund, the investment in blockchain assets is very similar to that in the traditional financial sector. It can also be divided into four phases: fundraising, investment, management, and exit.

11.1   Fundraising – Investment opportunities and asset allocation

In the fundraising process, the most important thing is to show investors the existing industry opportunities. In other words, it is imperative to answer the investors' question of "why should I invest in blockchain funds".

11.1.1 Macro background: Great opportunities on the blockchain track

In order to raise blockchain funds, the priority is to let investors realize the value and opportunities in the blockchain field or make them aware of the current situation that everything is ready in the blockchain field.

Right time: The existing regulatory environment has been built. Various countries began to introduce policies related to blockchain and crypto assets a few years ago. And in recent years, the relevant policies have become more explicit in major global financial markets such as the United States, Hong Kong, China and Singapore, which means that investors can participate in the market through more compliant channels. Besides, clear regulatory frameworks for subdivided fields, including stablecoins, security tokens, custody, asset management and trading, have been set up. As a result, the whole industry has been progressing towards compliance. In fact, the regulation requires global efforts. As countries' regulatory frameworks have similarities, other countries will follow suit once a country's policies become clearer. Many international organizations, such as the International Organization of Securities Commissions – IOSCO, the G20, and the Financial Action Task Force – FATF, have started working on global regulatory policies and conducted regular exchanges between countries. As a result, in the future, the whole industry will move closer towards compliance, undoubtedly providing a boost for limited partners (LPs) of funds.

In May 2019, IOSCO, a global cooperative of securities regulatory commissions of major countries globally, published a consultation document entitled "Issues, risks and regulatory considerations relating to crypto-asset trading platforms". The document sought public opinions on a series of issues, risks and other major considerations relating to crypto asset trading platforms – CTPs

– that had been identified by IOSCO. IOSCO is mainly responsible for regulating financial conducts from the perspective of securities assets and securities investment transactions, and the consultation and suggestions on crypto assets in this paper include what type of token offerings needs to be registered as securities and what kind of trading platforms need to hold a license issued by the global organization.

On May 22, 2019, FATF also issued regulatory guidance on virtual assets service providers (VASPs) to its member states, requiring digital currency exchanges and wallet providers to implement KYC/AML processes similar to those in the traditional financial sector and even implement the Travel Rule like banks, which means that digital currency exchanges must inform each other of customer information when transferring money to each other. Unlike IOSCO, the regulatory framework of FATF is to regulate the flow of funds with anti-money laundering regulations. Anti-money laundering regulation is broader and more profound than securities-related regulation in terms of the regulatory scope.

Although the two international intergovernmental organizations have no law enforcement power, they represent an agreed code of conduct for governments to cooperate well and restrain themselves. If a member state fails to act in accordance with the agreed code, other countries may refuse to conduct financial transactions with that country. Therefore, such regulatory guidelines as those of IOSCO and FATF are likely to serve as international regulatory standards.

At present, Hong Kong, China and Singapore have a clear direction of regulation in Asia.

The Securities and Futures Commission (SFC) of Hong Kong initially issued the *Statement on Regulatory Framework for Virtual Asset Portfolios Managers, Fund Distributors and Trading Platform Operators* in November 2018, with other documents attached, including the

Regulatory Standards for Licensed Corporations Managing Virtual Asset Portfolios, the *Conceptual framework for the Potential Regulation of Virtual Asset Trading Platform Operators* and the *Circular to Intermediaries on the Distribution of Virtual Asset Funds*. It put forward the basic regulatory framework for virtual asset investment, trading and other related businesses. The organization issued the *Statement on Security Token Offering* in March 2019, further explaining the regulation of security tokens. Later, it adopted FATF's recommendations and may regulate all platforms involved in digital assets, including OTC, wallets, transfer payment, custody, and related financial services (such as digital asset issuance).

OSL, a digital asset service provider in Hong Kong, obtained the virtual asset exchange license issued by the SFC in December 2020, and its parent company BC Group (00863.HK) received the placement investment from institutional investors in early January 2021. Early in February 2020, the group obtained the placement investment from Fidelity International, one of the world's largest asset management companies. The change in regulation not only encourages practitioners but also successfully attracts the attention of institutional investors.

Singapore has conducted regulation of digital currencies for several years. As for securities regulation, the MAS issued *A Guide to Digital Token Offerings* on November 14, 2017, offering regulatory guidance for capital market asset issuance and services. The guide was updated in November 2018 to subdivide the various business scenarios that demand regulation. In addition, as for anti-money laundering regulation, the *Payment Services Act* involving regulatory methods of digital currencies was first submitted to the Parliament for initial reading and research on November 19, 2018. More than a month later, the MAS announced on its official website that the bill, the *Payment Systems (Oversight) Act (PSOA)* issued in 2006 and the *Money-changing and Remittance Businesses Act (MCRBA)* issued in 1979 were combined into the *Payment Services Act* on January 14, 2019. As for the digital currency market, the *Payment Services Act* will fully regulate digital currency exchanges and digital wallets in Singapore in terms of risk control and compliance. Its regulation also focuses on AML compliance, which is very similar to the VASP regulatory framework proposed by FATF.

Infrastructure ready: The blockchain infrastructure has been increasingly improved in recent years, and the performance of the underlying public chain remains stable. The number of decentralized applications typified by DeFi has increased sharply, and some large-scale applications such as decentralized lending have already emerged. Meanwhile, Web 3.0 infrastructure and interoperability protocols (e.g., Polkadot Ecosystem) have also begun to emerge and is ready to sprint towards the next-generation internet. It can be argued that blockchain has completed the transformation from 0 to 1 and is preparing to start the explosion from 1 to 100.

Ethereum, currently the biggest smart contracts blockchain, was used to develop decentralized games initially, but it broadened the scope, and many other dApps started to develop on Ethereum in 2017 and 2018 have turned into a surging wave of DeFi in 2020. As a result, real-word applications of public blockchain became possible and the goals of 2017 and 2018 have begun to be realized, although this is mostly on Ethereum.

In addition to crypto native players, participants in the public blockchain, such as Diem (formerly known as Libra) launched by Facebook, have also been involved in infrastructure, not to mention stronger players such as central banks with their CBDCs.

Massive inflow: Currently, many mainstream institutions and many practitioners from traditional financial and internet sectors have entered the blockchain field. The industry participants have been gradually professionalized, and the risks related to "people" have been significantly reduced. Moreover, the management and investment of funds have also become more experienced, which no longer like operating small workshops in the era of chaos.

Since August 2020, many listed companies, including MicroStrategy, Square, PayPal, Meitu, Tesla, and Nexon have announced that they have purchased Bitcoin as an asset. Statistics show that more than 35 listed companies worldwide have held Bitcoins as of December 2021. Furthermore, more companies are involved in crypto assets.

Figure 11.1: Timing of Bitcoin purchases by listed companies

Source: https://www.fxstreet.com/cryptocurrencies/news/institutional-investors-are-here-to-stay-and-they-want-all-your-Bitcoin-202012011121

For example, payment institutions typified by PayPal and Square support the direct purchase of Bitcoin on their own platforms, making the investment threshold very low for individual users in the United States.

There are also trust structures such as the Delaware statutory fund. They hold their own Bitcoin and represent digital currencies with fund shares. This model is similar to Grayscale's Bitcoin trust, and it provides a compliant entry point for high-net-worth users and larger capital holders.

Other traditional financial institutions, especially licensed digital currency banks in Switzerland such as SEBA and Sygnum, can provide on-ramp services for customers in full compliance. Therefore, it is necessary for them to hold a large number of cryptocurrencies in order to ensure liquidity.

The participation ways of the institutions are also varied.

- Paul Tudor Jones, a traditional investor, purchased Bitcoin futures directly through the CME.

- MicroStrategy disclosed that it had purchased Bitcoin through Coinbase Prime, with more than 122k Bitcoin on the balance sheet.

- MassMutual purchased US$100 million worth of Bitcoin for general investment accounts through NYDIG, a fund management company in New York.

- Square's Cash App purchased US$180 million worth of Bitcoin in the third quarter of 2019. By the third quarter of 2020, the single-quarter purchase of Bitcoin had increased to US$1.63 billion, an increase of 8.3 times. Cash App is estimated to have 30 to 40 million monthly active users (MAUs), while the number was 15 million in the second quarter of 2019, indicating that the purchase volume grows faster than the number of users. In addition, Square disclosed several OTC service providers of Venue in the U.S. in its purchase of Bitcoin using the balance sheet: itBit, Genesis and Cumberland.

- PayPal has been granted the BitLicense with exclusive

conditions issued by the New York State Department of Financial Services – NYDFS – which is consistent with the licenses of many compliant cryptocurrency exchanges such as Coinbase. PayPal works with the Paxos Trust Company to provide cryptocurrency trading and conversion services. Now customers can buy cryptocurrencies on PayPal, but they cannot pay and transfer with cryptocurrencies. In 2021, PayPal allowed its customers to pay merchants with digital currencies through Venmo, and PayPal will be responsible for intermediate clearing.

•   ARK Investment, a well-known investment fund managed by excellent investor Cathie Wood, has believed that the prospect for Bitcoin is good since 2017. Its flagship fund ARKW obtains the position of cryptocurrencies by holding GBTC.

11.1.2   Micro opportunities: Asset allocation

In addition to the advantages of the track itself, blockchain assets also have their uniqueness.

Strong asset liquidity: Compared with traditional VC, many blockchain projects have more flexible exit methods. For example, liquidity can be achieved by issuing tokens.

Contrasted with traditional investments, the token model breaks down boundaries between primary and secondary investments, with better liquidity and liquidity premium.

Moreover, the return cycle of the token model is shorter than that of equity investment projects. We can see that equity projects that generally take at least five years can exit in two to three years under the token model. In this way, the VC investment cycle can be significantly shortened, and the capital reuse rate can be increased.

High potential return on investment: With strong asset liquidity, the return on blockchain investment is also higher than that of traditional VC. First, it is a high-growth field. Second, it has many side benefits in addition to investment income. For example, circulated tokens that holders do not want to sell immediately can be used in staking or mining to earn corresponding income. Even tokens that are not in circulation can be pledged in some decentralized agreements to obtain liquidity in advance.

Less correlation with other assets: In recent years, as Bitcoin has been converted to a store of value, it has become increasingly correlated with traditional assets such as gold and crude oil. However, most other blockchain assets remain less correlated with traditional assets such as stocks, bonds, crude oil, and gold. And it can participate in asset allocation, serving as a valuable hedge against other assets.

Table 11.1: Correlation coefficient between virtual assets and traditional assets								
Asset Class	Bitcoin	Gold	S&P	Nasdaq	MSCI EM	US 10Y	Crude Oil	DXY
Bitcoin		17%	2%	3%	-5%	14%	-1%	-4%
Gold	17%		-10%	-6%	24%	61%	-13%	-47%
S&P	2%	-10%		88%	66%	-34%	49%	-21%
Nasdaq	3%	-6%	88%		61%	-18%	34%	-20%
MSCI EM	-5%	24%	66%	61%		-9%	31%	-64%
US 10Y	14%	61%	-34%	-18%	-9%		-40%	-14%
Crude Oil	-1%	-13%	49%	34%	31%	-40%		-17%
DXY	-4%	-47%	-21%	-20%	-64%	-14%	-17%	
Avg	4%	4%	20%	20%	15%	-6%	6%	-27%

Source: Advisor Perspectives website

11.1.3　Why invest in us?

Recognizing the opportunities in the blockchain field is just the first step, which can be regarded as a flexible choice for the industry. Fundraising in all industries naturally cannot avoid the corresponding rigid requirement. It is essential to answer investors, "why should they choose us when there are so many blockchain funds in the market."

(1) Architecture and governance

For investors in the traditional financial sector, the preferred fund must have a compliant architecture and be operated according to the ethics in the traditional financial sector. For example, investment policy statements should be developed and strictly implemented, regular audits should be conducted, and investors should provide written reports. Furthermore, processes including investment decision-making, payment and returns should be faithfully recorded and kept for necessary disclosure.

In addition to process matters, selecting the currency for fundraising is also critical. For example, funds raised in the fiat currency will undoubtedly be more friendly to traditional investors who do not know much about crypto assets.

(2) Team

The professionalism and ethics of the team are also important factors for investors to consider. A professional team needs to have a track record in the industry and research-driven investment strategies. Ethical standards are a prerequisite for the team to remain neutral in the face of potential investment opportunities.

(3) Performance

For a team with a track record, performance is the best proof of its ability to manage funds. If you happen to have beaten the market or invested in unicorns, it will be a plus point for investors. On the other hand, the bull-bear cycle in the blockchain field is shorter than that in other industries. Therefore, when referring to the historical performance, it is necessary to compare with other asset categories and the whole macroeconomy and refer to the periodicity of the blockchain industry, comparing with the benchmark in the industry.

Due to the particularity of the blockchain industry, there were a large number of so-called "funds" that once made easy money in a short time, but they vanished quickly. We can see that many of the so-called capital companies have disappeared since 2017 or 2018 and that few investment institutions can last for one cycle, let alone more cycles. So, the fact that those established crypto funds can endure is because they have withstood multiple tests, they build more valuable brands, proving their investment ability and determination to participate in the industry for a long time.

Investors will make detailed requirements for the whole team. There is almost no difference between the process of accepting investors' investigation and that of performing due diligence of the project. It is no longer the era of chaos when achievements could be made by only relying on relationships, luck and chance. Today, we need to work as a group to achieve stunning results, and we need the group army to get excellent results.

11.1.4　Who else is investing?

When arranging blockchain funds, investors often consider the approach of other investors. In other words, they may ask, "who is investing in blockchain funds at present?"

As for crypto assets, most participants are high-net-worth individuals, family offices, and small and medium-sized financial institutions. They are already aware of the high profitability of crypto assets, and it is relatively flexible for them to redirect their investments. Large financial institutions are now increasingly interested in crypto assets. Most of them are starting to participate in the secondary market by trading, while the investment in the primary market may be some way off.

In terms of blockchain technology, there are a wide variety of investors, including traditional industrial capital and government funds. As blockchain is an investment area for traditional VC/PE, many LPs, such as Skybridge, have participated in funds investing in blockchain technology.

Table 11.2: Statistics on Bitcoin purchases by listed companies				
Company	Code	Bitcoin amount	Value (US$)	%Proportion of total
MicroStrategy	MSTR:NADQ	92,079	$3,032,240,814	0.44%
Tesla, Inc.	TSLA:NADQ	42,902	$1,412,799,829	0.20%
Galaxy Digital Holdings	BRPHF:OTCMKTS	16,400	$540,066,132	0.08%
Voyager Digital Ltd.	VYGR:CSE	12,260	$403,732,364	0.06%
Square Inc.	SQ:NYSE	8,027	$264,336,027	0.04%
Marathon Digital Holdings Inc.	MARA:NADQ	5,518	$181,712,495	0.03%
Coinbase Global, Inc.	COIN:NADQ	4,482	$147,596,122	0.02%
Bitcoin Group SE	BTGGF:TCMKTS	3,947	$129,978,111	0.02%

Company	Code	Bitcoin amount	Value (US$)	%Proportion of total
Hut 8 Mining Corp.	HUT:TSX	3,233	$106,465,476	0.02%
Riot Blockchain, Inc.	RIOT:NADQ	2,000	$65,861,723	0.01%
NEXON Co. Ltd.	NEXOF:OTCMKTS	1,717	$56,542,290	0.01%
Bitfarms Limited	BFARF:OTCMKTS	1,114	$36,684,980	0.01%
Argo Blockchain PLC	ARBKF:OTCMKTS	1,108	$36,487,395	0.01%
Hive Blockchain	HVBTF:OTCMKTS	1,033	$34,017,580	0.01%
BIGG Digital Assets Inc.	BBKCF:OTCMKTS	788	$25,949,519	0.00%
Meitu	HKD:HKG	765	$25,192,109	0.00%

Source: Data on the Bitcoin treasury website

In addition, listed companies merit attention. In particular, those listed companies in the United States are directly involved in purchasing and selling Bitcoin, including leading MicroStrategy and Square.

11.2　Investment – All-round and multi-angle participation

The investment in blockchain and crypto assets is similar to the traditional VC investment to some extent, which is mainly reflected in the investment decision-making process and methodology. Blockchain investment funds sometimes adopt the top-down decision-making method. For example, it may start from industry mapping, sort out the opportunities in the whole industry, and then look for the leading companies of each subdivided track. Or conversely, a bottom-up approach may be adopted. A preliminary screening will be conducted after contacting the project, and in-depth research on relevant fields will be conducted to rule on the prospect after communication with the team. Of course, due diligence on the company should be still conducted after the track, and the company confirms the valuation. Then they will enter the formal decision-making and investment process.

It should be noted that the due diligence in the field of crypto assets is different from that in traditional VC business. Because many financing projects of crypto assets require communitization, special attention should be paid to the community activity of such projects when conducting due diligence. For some early projects that have not formed a user community, building and operating a community is very important. Open source and community development often mean that core technical advantages are not very important, so the consideration of technical threshold may sometimes be weakened in the investment. Due to the special attributes of blockchain, the degree of open source and community size of projects is also the key to ecological prosperity in the future.

The main difference between a blockchain investment fund and a traditional VC investment is reflected in the way of investing. In this respect, blockchain funds offer more choices.

11.2.1 Primary market

Equity investment: Equity investing is a traditional VC investment method. With the growth of the invested company, the equity value becomes higher and higher, and VC benefits from a high exit price. This method also exists in the blockchain and crypto assets space. Many companies with centralized business, such as institutional-level compliance financial service providers, raise capital mainly in the form of equity. Although some projects may plan to issue crypto assets to empower their own ecosystem in the future, they may choose to finance in the form of equity before the token/crypto asset issuance. After issuing cryptocurrencies/tokens in the future, they will map the equity held by investors. This method is called "equity for coin", which is also equity investment in essence.

Private token investment: Generally, token investment in the primary market will be conducted with the Simple Agreement for Future Token (SAFT) or the Token Purchase Agreement (TPA). TPA, similar to the Shares Purchase Agreement of equity investment, will stipulate the lock-up period and unlocking method of the token founders and the rights and obligations of both the investor and the founders before the token is fully unlocked. On the other hand, SAFT is simple, which hardly involves the rights and interests of the investor other than the agreed price and amount of the investment. Therefore, token investors generally try to avoid SAFT and invest mainly through TPA or equity for coin.

Public token investment: In addition to the investment opportunities in the primary market, there are many investment opportunities in the secondary market in the token world, such as the initial coin offering (ICO) and the initial exchange offering (IEO). However, both individuals and funds must undergo the KYC verification process if they want to participate in such financing events. Only users who pass KYC verification can participate in the investment within the compliance framework. Of course, tokens that have been circulated in the secondary market can also be directly purchased low and sold high.

In fact, equity investment and token financing have always been running in parallel. Some non-token projects have always adopted equity financing before the establishment of the Ethereum ICO model. The most famous example is Coinbase which got its first equity financing in 2012 and conducted a direct listing on Nasdaq on April 2021.

There are several considerations in deciding whether to make equity or token investment in a project.

1) Whether to be listed. Generally speaking, in the capital market and traditional IPO model, equity model should be considered, for example, Coinbase and BlockFi. Because direct issuance of tokens is generally in the form of exemption, such as Blockstack and Props, which are exempted in the form of Reg D. They have been regarded as equity but represented by tokens. However, few projects can achieve U.S. compliance, while the token and the scale are not clear outside the country. Therefore, the equity model or the IPO model is more often chosen to list or be merged and acquired by traditional institutions without touching tokens or issuing tokens in the form of exemption. It is said that Coinbase will issue tokens in compliance with its IPO.

2) Whether the business model needs tokens. Although the token has good value and liquidity, it needs to be combined with a specific business. For example, using tokens in a public chain and DeFi is appropriate, while centralized services require traditional business models rather than tokens. If tokens are required, it is necessary to establish a business model, token economics, a reward model and design the relevant token distribution models (time, allocation, and so on).

Business model: Whether it is a centralized or decentralized service. Centralized services can proceed without considering tokens, while decentralized services can issue tokens.

Reward/Motivation model: What is the role of tokens and how to motivate users to use them without encouraging speculation unduly, and deal with cold start.

Token distribution model: Project tokens for decentralized services are usually distributed according to the following roles: the founding team, foundation, inventory, community participants, investors, retail investors, and rewards to liquidity participants. Tokens will also involve the unlocking/vesting period, which lasts for decades or years from the project's launch. The token distribution model requires great attention. The token is a model where stakeholders can be well balanced, but balancing merits attention. Generally speaking, the more decentralized token without pre-excavation is the most popular and owns higher value. However, the start-up project requires teams and funds, and it is impossible to start solely with the community unless it has star founders as AC does. In addition to distribution, the unlocking model is also worth considering. The unlocked token can easily increase sell pressure, and stakeholders' interests will be inconsistent.

Therefore, although the token model looks more attractive, it is not necessarily the best choice to choose the model hastily because there is no mature standard for the design pattern. Of course, the "equity for coin" method is a relatively reliable choice. It mainly depends on which kind of products and companies are more valuable.

11.2.2 Secondary market

(1) Direct investment

Mainstream crypto assets such as BTC and ETH can also be purchased directly through compliant channels in the secondary market.

This basically reflects the logic of allocation. As BTC and ETH determine the minimum basic rate of return of the industry, the direct allocation of BTC and ETH can ensure that the fund's income follows the overall digital asset market.

In general, VC will not directly participate in the trading of BTC and ETH, which is more the approach of hedge funds. In terms of traditional VC investments, it is relatively easy to beat the stock market. However, it is difficult for cryptocurrencies to outperform Bitcoin. In terms of long-term returns, most funds have a hard time to outperform BTC. Therefore, adding BTC and ETH is an anchor for market returns.

In addition, some other mainstream digital currencies can be allocated, such as Polkadot and Filecoin, which have unique positioning in the blockchain world. However, the purchase of digital currencies by VCs is more about asset allocation than swing trading.

(2) Indirect investment

In addition to the direct investment methods mentioned above, there are many indirect investment methods in the fields of blockchain and crypto asset.

Buying a mining machine: For PoW cryptocurrencies such as Bitcoin, holding a mining machine (and connecting it to the network) is actually holding the call option of the tokens. As the fixed cost of mining remains unchanged, consisting mainly of electricity and operation and maintenance costs, if the currency price rises, the upside return of the mining machine owner can be very high. If the currency price falls to the cost line, the mining machine owner can choose to turn off the machine to avoid losses.

The operation and maintenance of a mining machine cost a lot, and there are many uncertainties. If there is no strong technology, operation and maintenance capabilities, or local resources, joining a mining pool is better than operating one independently. Moreover, trading skills are required as the costs need to be covered by digital currencies.

Staking: Staking is a very common way to obtain income in the crypto asset field and exists in various scenarios. As for the mining of PoS currencies, the token holders can stake their tokens in a PoS mining pool. Income will be distributed according to the holding proportions after the staking pool generates rewards. As for DeFi, liquidity is usually required in trading, lending and other scenarios. Therefore, token holders can stake their tokens to automated market makers in exchange for rewards to ensure liquidity.

Staking is great to obtain additional returns in the form of tokens, which is a very good and stable income for investment institutions that want to hold the currency for a long period of time. In addition, staking allows for governance participation. For institutions that wish to be active governance players (similar to active management of listed companies in stocks), it may be a good option to strengthen their voice by staking, which can be seen as different application scenarios for the token. As for other projects, that have their institutional investors' tokens locked-up, but will still allow them to participate in staking, this would become a necessary choice for institutions.

Buy blockchain stocks: For investors in traditional finance that may not know how to invest in crypto assets and select assets, it is probably best to invest in blockchain-related assets in the field of traditional finance. For example, the trust products such as GBTC and ETH issued by Grayscale, the world's largest crypto asset management company, can be purchased through U.S. brokerage accounts. These assets are supported by the value of crypto assets such as BTC and

ETH. Investing in such assets can obtain the exposure of crypto assets without the need to have the technical knowledge to manage crypto wallets, keys, and so on. In addition to Grayscale's trust products, some listed companies are engaged in blockchain and crypto assets, such as Canaan in the traditional stock market, and investing in the shares of such companies can also get into the crypto asset field indirectly.

Other alternatives are listed companies mentioned previously. For example, MicroStrategy, whose business spans business intelligence, mobile software and cloud services, has purchased more than 114,000 Bitcoins (as of December 2021). Judging from the performance of the stock price, people prefer to regard the enterprise as a Bitcoin investment company because the market value of the Bitcoin it owned is close to its market capitalization (current currency price to current market capitalization). And some people think that it is something close to Bitcoin ETF, although it is not a complete 1:1 match. Buying stocks of such companies can sometimes resemble buying Bitcoin.

Some enterprises have gradually participated in blockchain assets, such as Square and PayPal. Square began to provide Bitcoin purchases on its Cash App in 2018, which is similar to a simple mobile exchange. Although the Bitcoin service only contributes a small amount of revenue, it is labeled as "cutting-edge technology". Moreover, we can see that the number of Bitcoin purchases has been increasing significantly due to the ease of use in the cooling-off period and the wide customer base.

When purchasing blockchain stocks, it is necessary to calculate the "content" of blockchain of those stocks and how much risk exposure the institution is willing to accept. That is because the company represented by the stock is not 100% engaged in blockchain or 100% in digital currency in their business. The investment may deviate from mandate or IPS.

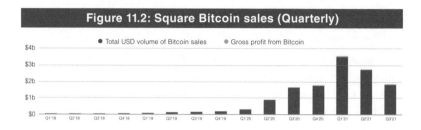

Figure 11.2: Square Bitcoin sales (Quarterly)

Source: The Block website, https://www.theblockcrypto.com/post/95882/square-bitcoin-2020-cash-app-results

11.3 Management – An important phase to increase value

Blockchain funds, like traditional VCs, also require post-investment management. Both the fund and the invested company often earn profits together in terms of post-investment management. If the company runs well, the fund will get high returns. So, the fund is often quite willing to help the invested company. Post-investment management is mainly reflected in operation follow-up and resource assistance.

- **Business management:** including strategic planning, management systems, organizational structures, process systems, business value chain management (R&D, marketing and so on), human resources, and financial management. Organizing course exchange and training in finance, entrepreneurship, and commercial operation training. Providing development and planning suggestions for funded enterprises, helping the company organize its daily operation processes, conducting business connection and resource support with relevant companies.

- **Capital support:** assisting enterprises with gaps in their business ecosystem to find M&A targets, providing financing schemes and financial support for those with financing needs, focusing on support and guidance when assisting invested enterprises that lack experience in finance or capital, and formulating reasonable exit schemes to ensure fund returns without affecting the development of the enterprises.

- **Resource connection:** venture capitalists have at their disposal many resources that can be provided to the invested enterprises. For the invested enterprises that want to have a deeper understanding of some industries' strategic investment value or targets, we can assist in providing industry analysis and investigation of relevant targets. Besides, we can provide business introductions of the invested enterprises to each other, share our research reports, and technically provide integrated solutions in a consultative manner. If the group's ecological subsidiaries, strategic partners, and participating companies have blockchain needs in supply chain finance, insurance, agriculture, and other industries, we will arrange for them to connect their businesses so that they can build more suitable business lending solutions. We are also able to connect the invested enterprises with the industrial resources they need through events like conferences. For example, we can help the founders enhance community users' trust through institutional brand endorsement in terms of community-based projects, or we can provide it with media and PR resources, which is particularly important in cross-border investments. In our investment process, we often see some enterprises investing in well-known projects overseas and exploring the Asian market. Then we can help them connect with local communities and media in Asia or invite the founders to participate in several sessions when we hold our own events to increase their exposure. For centrally operated projects, it may be necessary to try to introduce customers or industrial resources. Of course, there will never be enough assistance media and exposure.

- **Risk assessment:** regularly following up governance of the board of shareholders, board of directors and board of supervisors in the invested enterprise, paying attention to the latest business performance and actual operations, and staying vigilant against major risks of the invested enterprise.

- **Daily operation:** keeping communication with the invested enterprises, paying attention to the daily operation and maintenance of the enterprises, evaluating the needs of the enterprises as soon as possible, and offering corresponding assistance. In line with the attitude of being responsible to the investors, the fund management teams need to regularly follow up on the operation of the invested companies. Once operational difficulties are found, they need to be remediated in time to help the invested companies overcome the difficulties and lower the probability of fund loss.

11.4 Exit – Token investment has its own special way

Blockchain funds and traditional VC are also quite different in the exit process. The exit methods of funds for blockchain and crypto assets are more flexible.

In traditional VC investment, the common exit methods mainly include old stock transfer, M&A, listing, repurchase, and so on. The cycle from investment to exit is generally very long, and the fund usually starts to exit investment after entering its own exit period.

Pure equity investment in blockchain and crypto assets is almost the same as traditional VC investment. However, token investment or investment in "equity for coin" can exit directly by issuing tokens, and the first token offering (i.e., partial exit) is not far behind the investment. The founders even have a time plan to be listed on a crypto exchange when investing. Therefore, for many crypto asset funds, the investment period may be far from over, but there are already fund returns because there is price discovery due to the fact that the tokens are listed on exchanges. These funds can also be used for further investment during the investment period to earn greater returns.

It should be noted that although the investment can be recovered by using the method of "equity for coin", and the actual usufruct is transferred from the shares to the tokens, the fund still holds the shares of the invested company. Therefore, complete exit has not been finished from the perspective of fund exit liquidation. Finally, it is necessary to transfer the held shares. Part of tokens and equities can also be transferred to a third party, or the shares can be transferred back to the founding team at an agreed price to realize the complete equity exit.

11.5 Compliant fund structures

A compliant fund structure has several important elements: a qualified asset management team, fund asset custody, fund administration, legal counsel, and fund auditing.

Asset management team: Recently, the regulatory policies for blockchain funds in some major countries and regions worldwide have become clearer. The management team needs to have specific qualifications for different blockchain underlying assets. For example, the SFC has set up a Type 9 license for asset management. And the license will limit the scope of asset management, investing in primary market equities, or investing in secondary market securities. Similarly, there are restrictions on the proportion of investments in crypto assets. For most Type 9 license holders, the investment in crypto assets cannot exceed 10% of the total asset investment. If the 10% limit is to be exceeded, it is necessary to apply to the SFC to adjust the business scope limited by the license. In addition to the qualifications, the asset management team also needs to strictly follow the compliance requirements in the process of asset management. For example, it should actively reallocate funds when the market value fluctuates sharply so that the scale of crypto assets meets the requirements of the license. In addition to the rigid qualification requirements, the asset management team also needs to be fully functional. For example, it should have the post-investment management function, the risk control, and internal control functions or processes in addition to the investment function, to ensure the neutrality of investment and post-investment management.

Fund asset custody: For compliant funds, customers' assets need to be held with an independent custodian. For funds raised in fiat currency, the custodian is usually a bank. For funds raised directly in crypto assets, finding an independent and compliant third-party crypto asset custodian is necessary.

Fund administration: Including the creation of documents and contracts related to the fund creation, fundraising account management, and fund clearing, fund share registration, fund accounting, fund valuation calculation, fund information disclosure, and so on. It covers the complete fund operation phases and can improve fund managers' credibility and operation efficiency. As for blockchain fund administration, there are still some challenges now because these funds have a variety of investment methods, such as participating in staking or mining to earn income. Special accounting treatment methods are also needed in the phases of capital accounting and net value estimation. At present, as compliant blockchain and crypto asset funds are still at an early stage, and accordingly, there are no professional administration providers in subdivisions in the markets, compliant crypto funds still use the service providers in the traditional fund sector.

Fund audit: Like ordinary funds, blockchain funds also need regular external audits in order to display transparency to investors and enhance credibility. At present, EY, PwC, and other large accounting firms have also moved into the field of crypto funds.

Legal counsels: Investment funds also requires legal counsels, who are responsible for reviewing the legal documents of project investments and pointing out potential legal risks and the business compliance and risk of the fund.

Other compliance service providers: Compliant share sales channels are required for public funds or share subscription asset management products. At present, the existing blockchain funds in the market are mainly private funds, and share subscription products account only for a small part. However, strict compliance qualifications are required once share sales are involved, especially sales to the public.

11.6   Diversity of asset management

There are many forms of crypto asset management, including hedge funds, venture capital funds, trusts, deposit products, and so on.

Hedge funds: Crypto hedge funds are usually raised from a small number of high-net-worth individuals and invested in the secondary market of crypto assets according to certain quantitative strategies, such as high-frequency trading and the CTA strategy. As the barriers to entry in this field are relatively low, a small hedge fund can be established as long as there are good strategies and a certain amount of capital. Therefore, there are great differences among participants in this field, including both top hedge funds such as Citadel and small strategy funds managed by individual traders. And it is difficult to unify regulatory standards, which need to be based on the agreements between investors and management teams as well as the teams' moral standards.

Venture capital funds: Venture capital funds in the primary market need certain industry resources in order to obtain high-quality and stable project sources. From the regulation perspective, there are still no challenging compliance requirements, and regulation is more based on the trust between private equity investors and the management teams as well as transparent operation processes. HashKey Capital and Fenbushi Capital are categorized as crypto asset venture capital funds.

Trusts: The regulation on trusts are rather strict. Currently, the most famous trust products in the crypto asset field are passive trust products like GBTC and ETHE launched by Grayscale in the United States. The principle of the products is to build a trust architecture where qualified investors can subscribe for shares of the trust products with fiat currency, and trust managers will purchase crypto assets such as BTC and ETH with all the subscription money received. Then, after a certain lock-in/lock-up period, these trust shares can be publicly listed and traded in the OTC market. As of November 30, 2020, the assets managed in the form of Grayscale's crypto asset trusts have reached US$12.2 billion.

Deposit products: There are many time deposits and wealth management products similar to bank deposits in the area of crypto assets. Users can subscribe for the shares of such products with crypto assets and receive their capital and interest after the products mature. The underlying assets of such products are often high-quality institutional loans or low-risk quantitative trading products. These products are usually launched by B-side/end platforms like exchanges and centralized wallet platforms, such as HashKey Hub, Binance, Matrixport, and Cobo. The return of capital and interest mainly relies on the endorsement of credit of the platform without mandatory regulatory requirements. In recent years, the regulatory policies worldwide have gradually become clearer, and some countries have put such deposit products under regulation, which makes the platforms gradually move to more complaint frameworks.

References

FXStreet website, https://www.fxstreet.com/cryptocurrencies/news.

Advisor Perspectives website, https://www.advisorperspectives.com/commentaries/2020/03/27/diversification-is-key-and-the-only-free-lunch-in-these-markets.

Bitcointreasury website, https://www.buybitcoinworldwide.com/treasuries/.

The Block website, https://www.theblockcrypto.com/data/crypto-markets/public-companies.

CHAPTER 12

GLOBAL MAJOR BLOCKCHAIN INVESTORS AND USE CASES

Digital asset investment institutions worldwide are divided into four main categories: financial investors, eco-building investors, strategic M&A investors, and native community investors. Financial investors can be subdivided into two categories: traditional investors, including traditional VCs and university endowments, and blockchain investors, which refer to investment institutions specializing in blockchain investments, such as Polychain.

Eco-building investors refers to institutions that invest across the blockchain industry and run their own cryptoassets or blockchain-related businesses, such as Digital Currency Group, HashKey, and ConsenSys. Strategic M&A investors are those who invest through recapitalization activities, with the most active M&A buyers including Coinbase, Binance, and other digital currency exchanges. In addition to traditional investment institutions, the blockchain space has also seen other types of native investment organizations, DAOs – decentralized autonomous organizations – where members of the community will vote on whether to give financial support to new projects. DAOs represent a native and emerging investment method in the blockchain. Besides, with the vigorous development of the cryptoasset market in recent years, many companies in the blockchain and cryptoassets world have been recognized by the traditional financial world and entered the traditional capital markets. The listing ways include backdoor listing, IPO listing, direct listing, SPAC listing, etc. As a result, crypto enterprises have gradually been going to the mainstream market.

12.1 The typical blockchain investors and investment strategies

Investors in the blockchain and cryptoassets sectors have become very diversified, ranging from purely financial investment funds to strategic investors with a full strategic industry vision.

Table 12.1: Crypto investors	
Traditional VCs	Andreessen Horowitz, Union Square Ventures, Lightspeed, Danhua Capital, Greycroft, SVAngel, BEENEXT, Rubicon Venture Capital, etc.
Fund of funds	Digital Ventures, Bitbull Capital, CryptoLUX, Vision Hill, etc.
Asset management	Bitwise, Grayscale, JAFCO, FBG Capital, BitSpread, etc.
Hedge funds	Scalar Capital, Polychain, Ikigai, Pantera, Morgan Creek, Capital Management, etc.
Crypto VCs	Digital Currency Group, ZhenFund, Hashed, Blockchain Capital, Blockchange, Blue Yard, Fenbushi Capital, Node Capital, etc.
Companies	Bitman, Binance, Coinbase, Huobi Labs, EOS VC, etc.
Accelerators/ Incubators	Coinsilium, Techstars, Boost VC, ConsenSys, etc.

Source: The Block website

12.1.1 Financial investors

The below figure shows the top ten most active blockchain investors in 2020 summarized by The Block, a well-known blockchain media. Polychain Capital, Pantera, Dragonfly Capital and NGC Ventures are typical purely financial investors. Polychain and Pantera, two veteran blockchain funds in the United States, are the leaders in the first batch of blockchain funds, and most of their investment portfolios are European and American projects. Dragonfly Capital is a recent emerging fund with teams in North America and Asia. Such funds have the advantage of reducing the information asymmetry between Europe, America and Asia. NGC Ventures is an Asian fund with significantly more Asian projects than other institutions in its investment portfolio.

Table 12.2: Most active blockchain investors in 2020				
Polychain Capital	ConsenSys	Pantera	HashKey	Coinbase
Alameda Research	Digital Currency Group	CoinFund	Dragonfly Capital	NGC Ventrues

Source: The Block website

Financial investors can be subdivided into traditional investors and investment institutions specializing in blockchain investments.

(1) Traditional investors

A number of investment institutions have come from traditional investments into the blockchain space and crypto assets, such as investment funds in the internet business.

» Traditional VCs

Andreessen Horowitz, headquartered in Silicon Valley, abbreviated as a16z, in which 16 is the number of letters that the name Andreessen Horowitz has between A and Z. The firm is an icon in the investment circle, and its two founders Marc Andreessen and Ben Horowitz are also legendary investors in Silicon Valley.

Andreessen is one of the founders of Mosaic Communications (the predecessor of Netscape), whose Mosaic browser once dominated more than 80 percent of the internet. The company was eventually acquired by AOL (America Online), and its technologies, including JAVA, SSL, and cookie, have become the prevailing standards of the whole industry. After he left Netscape, Andreessen worked with Horowitz to create Loudcloud, a platform that provides internet infrastructure services, and then they got involved in the venture capital industry and founded a16z in 2009.

Relying on their entrepreneurial experience in the internet space and their insights into cutting-edge technologies, the two have successfully invested in a number of unicorns, such as Facebook, Twitter, Groupon, Skype, Zynga, Foursquare, Airbnb, and Oculus VR, and realized many high-return exits. Consequently, they have become legends in the internet investment community.

In 2013, this legendary VC began to engage in crypto assets and hung the full text of Bitcoin Whitepaper written by Satoshi Nakamoto on the wall of its office in Silicon Valley. The firm has investments in Bitcoin, Ripple, Coinbase and other leading crypto assets and companies, all of which in a very early stage. They follow the concept of "long-term investment" and "full-cycle investment" in the area of crypto assets, meaning that they are firmly optimistic about cryptocurrencies regardless of market conditions. Moreover, for high-quality projects, a16z is also willing to add investments along the way with its growth.

» Endowments

In addition to traditional institutional investors, university endowments have also participated in crypto asset investments.

For some universities or academic institutions, university endowments are pools of funds that are often contributed to support teaching and research and can be invested in various assets. Harvard University owns the most prominent university endowment in the world, with assets of more than US$40 billion. Yale University has over US$30 billion in assets, the University of Michigan has about US$12.5 billion, and Brown University has US$4.7 billion.

Different from ordinary VCs, university endowments are held in trust in perpetuity, and part of annual earnings is allocated to the daily activities of universities or academic institutions. Therefore, university endowments often need to allocate various types of assets to achieve risk diversification and make long-term, short- and medium-term investments to balance income and liquidity. So crypto assets, as an emerging type of asset, naturally attract the attention of university endowments, and the capital for asset allocation often comes from the venture capital or absolute return of the endowments.

Figure 12.1: Asset allocation of Yale University in the past 30 years

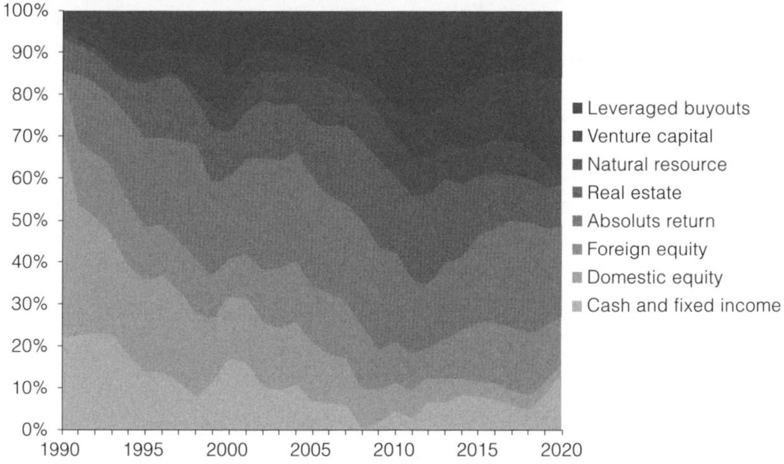

Source: Sina Finance website

At present, university endowments mainly invest in crypto assets in three ways.

Investing in blockchain funds: Early in 2018, David Swensen, the chief investment officer of Yale University, invested in two cryptocurrency funds, namely the first cryptocurrency venture fund of the well-known VC Andreessen Horowitz with a fund size of US$300 million and the cryptocurrency venture capital fund founded by Coinbase co-founder Fred Ehrsam and former Sequoia Capital partner Matt Huang. After that, many universities, including

Harvard University, Stanford University, Dartmouth College, MIT, the University of North Carolina, and the University of Michigan, also began to follow Yale's strategy of investing in cryptocurrency venture funds immediately in 2018, with each investing in at least one cryptocurrency venture capital fund.

Directly purchase cryptocurrencies: In the 2020 annual report of the regulatory compliance exchange, Coinbase, it is mentioned that some university endowments have directly purchased cryptocurrencies on the exchange for over a year. Some media speculate that these buyers are endowments of several Ivy League universities that invested in cryptocurrency funds in 2018, such as the endowments of Harvard University, Yale University, Business School of Brown University, and the University of Michigan.

Invest in blockchain projects: Some university endowments also choose direct equity investments that demand enough industry understanding, such as the Harvard Foundation and the University of Wyoming Foundation.

In 2020, Avanti, a compliant digital asset bank, completed its seed round of financing led by the University of Wyoming Foundation, with other investors including Morgan Creek Digital, Blockchain Capital, and Digital Currency Group. Avanti is a compliance bank founded by the Wall Street veteran Caitlin Long. It focuses on digital asset custody and payment services. Its services can also help to simplify the donation process, which makes it easier to raise more funds to support its blockchain work.

Earlier in 2019, the Harvard Foundation also directly participated in the public financing of Blockstack, which was completed directly in the form of a token sale.

Blockstack builds a distributed internet where users can have ownership of their identity. All the data is tied to their identity and stored on their own private devices, thus eliminating the dependence on third-party institutions. Developers can only access user data with user permission. In this way, the sovereignty of the data is returned to users.

The significance of the landmark project is that its token offering is the first one approved by the U.S. Securities and Exchange Commission (SEC) through Reg A+ exemption, with a total fundraising amount of US$28 million. Reg A+ allows companies to exempt issued tokens from registration as securities and raise up to US$50 million from public investors, which means that anyone has the opportunity to participate in their financing instead of only qualified investors.

According to the token sales documents submitted by Blockstack to the SEC, Harvard Management Company, a subsidiary of Harvard's endowment, and its related investors purchased 95,833,333 BlockStacks tokens corresponding to an investment of more than US$11.5 million.

In addition to university endowments, American pension funds with similar investment styles have also been involved. For example, two pension funds in Fairfax County of Virginia invested in cryptocurrency venture capital funds as early as 2019. The investment director said, "Bitcoin has the potential to save us from the current pension crisis." In addition, pension accounts such as IRAs and 401(k) s in the U.S. also allow holders to invest in Bitcoin through compliance trust products of Grayscale.

(2) Blockchain investors

Blockchain investors refer to those specializing in blockchain investments, such as VCs and hedge funds including Polychain

Capital, Multicoin Capital, Paradigm, Placeholder, Pantera Capital, Framework Ventures, and Fenbushi Capita.

» Polychain

Polychain Capital, one of the earliest native crypto hedge funds, was founded in 2016 by Olaf Carlson Wee, the first employee of Coinbase. The fund has always believed that with the development of the cryptocurrency ecosystem, there will be many different protocols to adapt to various application scenarios. Therefore, it is named "Polychain". Polychain Capital likes to invest in new technologies or unique business models generated by new technologies. It focuses on core technological breakthroughs and everything they brought about, as new technologies can make business models that were impossible in the past possible now.

Polychain Capital caught the cryptocurrency bull market in 2017 shortly after its establishment. It was reported that the total return of Polychain in 2017 was as high as 23 times. In Polychain's portfolio, it is not hard to see unicorns in various segments, such as the DeFi lending leaders MakerDAO and Compound, as well as Keep Network and NuCypher in the privacy space. Polychain also invested in infrastructure platforms like Tendermint, Parity Technology, and Protocol Labs, and exchange giants Coinbase and Coinlist.

» Pantera

Founded in 2003, Pantera is a California-based venture capital fund that focused on global macro investment and participated in the early investment in cryptocurrencies. In 2014, its CEO Dan Morehead decided to transform it into an institution focusing on cryptocurrency investment. In terms of assets under management, Pantera is currently one of the largest cryptocurrency funds in the world.

Morehead, who first learned about Bitcoin in 2011, was shaken by the idea of Bitcoin then, but he did not take any action. In 2013, when Bitcoin experienced its first bull market and saw about 200,000 users, he realized that Bitcoin could become a payment tool for large-scale uses, so he decided to make a strategic transformation. So far, Pantera has invested in some notable projects such as Wyre, Circle, Zcash, Ripple, 0X, Augur, and Omisego.

12.1.2　Ecosystem building investors

Typical ecosystem building investors in the blockchain and cryptocurrency industry include Digital Currency Group, HashKey, Coinbase, and ConsenSys. They invest in the whole industry chain and run their own crypto assets or blockchain-related businesses.

(1) DCG – A diversified digital group with a full ecosystem layout

Founded in 2015 by Barry Silbert, Digital Currency Group (DCG) is a diversified group of holdings and investments that started out by investment in the early days and is known for the breadth of its portfolio, touching almost all areas of crypto assets. According to its official website, DCG had made more than 220 investments or acquisitions and had done 39 successful exits by the end of 2020. Now it has 133 invested enterprises on six continents, covering every segment of the blockchain industry, including cryptocurrency trading platforms, blockchain infrastructure, identity authentication, payment, smart contracts, blockchain enterprise services, stablecoins, blockchain games, wallets, and custody. Among those companies, there are many well-known unicorns such as Coinbase, BitPay, BitGo, and Circle.

Although DCG relies mainly on investment, it is not a pure VC but rather a blockchain startup incubator. At the beginning of its establishment, it incorporated three major companies in the blockchain industry, namely Grayscale, Genesis and Coindesk, as subsidiaries, occupying three essential segments of the blockchain and crypto asset industry.

Grayscale was founded by Barry Silbert in 2013 and incorporated into DCG in 2015.

Today, Grayscale has become the world's largest crypto asset investment manager, whose assets under management reached nearly US$30 billion in early January 2021 as the price of assets, including Bitcoin and Ethereum multiplies. Its Bitcoin trust, the closest approximation to a Bitcoin index fund, allows the investment in and holding of Bitcoin in the form of the asset trust, and qualified investors can directly trade in trust shares in fiat currency in the OTC market through a broker, to be exposed to the appreciation of Bitcoin.

Table 12.3: Digital Currency Group's portfolio (incomplete)	
Trading and exchange	Radar, Genesis, BTCC, bitFlyer, ABRA, Coinbase, Grayscale, Circle, Unocoin, etc.
Supply chain	Fliament, Hijro, Skuchain, etc.
Compliance	Chainalysis, Elliptic, Norbloc, etc.
Custody	BitGo, Blockchain, Coinjar, Ledger, Vault, etc.
Information	Coindesk, JoyStream, Yours, Nickl, etc.
Media-Information-Data	Tradewave, TradeBlock, Nomics, Etherscan, Digital Assets Data, etc.
Enterprise	Axoni, Bigchain, Hedera, Hashgraph, etc.
Investing	BoostVC, Coinlist, Layer 1, etc.
Advertising	Brave, MadHive, etc.
Cryptocurrency	Ethereum Classic, Reserve, Carbon, Zcash, Filecoin, Bitcoin, etc.
NFT	Dapper, Decentraland, etc.
Data	Tierion, Dirt Protocol, Ocean, etc.
Infrastructure	Blockstream, Cobalt, OpenZeppelin, Protocol Labs, Parity, etc.

Rights management	Bitmark, Custos, Mediachain, Revelator, etc.
Identity	Blockstack, Cambridge Blockchain, Netki, Civic, etc.
Banking and payments	Wyre, Ripple, BitPesa, BitPay, Token, Ripio, Veem, etc.
Commerce	BitPremier, Gyft, OB1, Purse, etc.
Non-crypto	Congnito, Moni, Averon, Artie, etc.
Other	Mifiel, Stratumn, Decent, HashPlex, BTCjam, etc.

Source: Coinvigilance website

(2) HashKey

HashKey Group is a leading crypto asset services group in Asia. Its headquarter is in Hong Kong, China and has branches in Japan, Singapore, and other locations, with its business covering the whole Asia-Pacific region. Like DCG, HashKey is also a diversified asset services group with a whole ecosystem layout. Its business includes crypto assets trading platforms, asset management, venture capital, wallets, and mining pools.

Venture capital is an important business of the HaskKey and its tentacle in the blockchain and crypto assets space, gathering up-to-date information on industry dynamics. To date, HashKey and its ecosystem affiliates have invested in more than 200 companies in major cities of different countries on all continents. There are many large infrastructure projects such as Ethereum, Polkadot, Cosmos, Filecoin and Dfinity, as well as their corresponding ecosystem projects. As a crypto asset services group, HashKey has also made frequent investments in crypto-financial services and invested in unicorns, including BlockFi and Circle.

In addition, HashKey Group is also a sister company to Wanxiang Blockchain, which is based in Shanghai, China, and affiliated to China Wanxiang Holdings Co., Ltd. Wanxiang Holdings, a financial group in China, has subsidiaries in traditional financial areas such as banking, trusts, insurance, asset management, and financial leasing, with almost all the licenses in the financial sector. Besides, it also has subsidiaries in financial technology such as big data, AI, mobile payment and blockchain, and is one of the leading groups in financial innovation.

Wanxiang Blockchain is mainly engaged in blockchain technology R&D and enterprise-level technology solutions. In addition, it is the host of the Global Blockchain Summit in Shanghai every year, which is a global heavyweight event like Coindesk's Consensus and serves as an important channel for industrial exchanges between China and the West. The first summit, held in October 2015, was the first public blockchain event where the concept of "blockchain" was promoted in China for the first time, making it a landmark event for the development of blockchain in the country and making the year 2015 the first year of China's blockchain industry.

At the beginning of 2022, Hahskey Group also launched Asia's largest blockchain investment fund, which is expected to reach US$600 million, focusing on Web3, crypto finance, and metaverse investment.

12.1.3 Typical strategic M&A investors

As a fast-growing industry, blockchain and crypto assets are also quite active in capital restructuring. The public transaction data show that there have been over 130 M&A cases in the blockchain industry since 2013, with nearly S$3 billion in the transaction volume.

Exchanges are the most active M&A buyers. For example, Coinbase and Binance have made no less than ten M&A deals, respectively, and their average deal volume is substantially higher than that of other companies.

(1) Coinbase – The most active buyer

Founded in 2012, Coinbase is the world's largest compliant crypto asset trading platform and the first compliant exchange. It has over 45 million users in more than 100 countries worldwide, with over US$90 billion in assets deposited on it.

The company has become the most active in the blockchain and crypto assets spaces because its number of M&A deals ranks first. As an exchange with adequate capital, its M&A strategy focuses on the tuck-in of talent and technology. A tuck-in acquisition generally refers to a type of acquisition in which the acquired company is merged into a division of the acquirer to obtain relevant technologies and advantages at a cost lower than that of the acquirer's own implementation. For example, in April 2018, Coinbase announced its US$100 million acquisition of Earn.com and hired its CEO as Coinbase's first CTO. In 2019, Coinbase acquired the custody business of Xapo for US$55 million, and at that time, Xapo was already a top custody provider in the world. When the deal was done, crypto assets managed by Coinbase exceeded US$7 billion, ranking first in the world. In May 2020, Coinbase announced the acquisition of Tagomi, a prime broker of crypto assets. Prime brokers mainly provide liquidity, custody, lending, and other services for institutional clients. This acquisition coincided with the turning point of the blockchain industry, as the year 2020 can be regarded as the first year for institutions to engage in crypto assets, and prime brokers are the infrastructure that institutions need. In general, the mergers and acquisitions of Coinbase are fast with targeted and firm efforts, helping it develop faster to become a crypto asset giant.

Coinbase has always operated in a compliant manner. In the United States, it holds the Money Transmitter License (MTL) and e-money license of each state as well as the BitLicense issued in New York, where procedures are the most stringent. In terms of listing, it has strict coin listing policies, with no derivatives trading and only USD and USDC (a compliant stablecoin) trading. This is the foundation for Coinbase to become the largest exchange.

Coinbase is not a simple exchange. At present, its products have covered ten fields, including investment, trading, custody, and wallets.

Table 12.4: Coinbase's businesses			
For ordinary users		For institutions	
Coinbase	Virtual asset trade	Prime brokerage	Institutional virtual asset trading
Wallet	Virtual asset storage	Asset channel	Coin listing
USDC	Stablecoin	Business	Virtual asset payment
Income / learning	Courses / benefits	Custody	Institutional virtual asset custody
For senior traders		Venture capital	Early investment and fundraising
Pro	Complex virtual asset transactions		

Source: Coinbase website

Coinbase has gone through several rounds of financing, with a total amount of over US$500 million. Its valuation reached US$8 billion at the time of its final Series F funding round in 2018. In April 2021, Coinbase was directly listed on Nasdaq, which became a landmark in the blockchain industry and a milestone towards the mainstream.

Coinbase stock debut on Nasdaq reached US$328.28 per share, valuing the crypto exchange at US$85.8 billion. Coinbase's investors include a16z, Union Square Ventures (USV), Tiger Fund, Y Combinator, and others.

(2) Binance – The most generous buyer

In April 2020, Binance, the world's largest cryptocurrency trading platform, announced its US$400 million acquisition of CoinMarketCap (CMC), the world's most referenced website for cryptocurrency information, making it the largest acquisition of the crypto asset space. As CMC is the main data site used by crypto asset practitioners all over the world and has strong international influence and authority as well as great traffic value for exchanges, the acquisition enriches the blueprint for Binance's crypto financial services.

Binance's M&A strategy is in line with Coinbase's. In addition to data services, Binance is also actively pursuing mergers and acquisitions in the fields of fiat on/off ramp, derivatives trading, asset wallets, compliance licenses, and so on.

12.1.4   Native community investors

In addition to investment institutions in the traditional sense, the blockchain space and cryptocurrencies has also seen a number of native investment organizations, which become known as DAOs – decentralized autonomous organizations.

An investment DAO is similar to a venture capital fund led by its members, but it has no traditional management structure or board of directors like traditional VCs do. Instead, DAOs are stateless, borderless, and not controlled by one or a few members. When a good idea is generated in the community or a good start-up team enters the DAO community to seek financial help, all community members will vote to decide whether to offer support. The funds may come from the participants of the DAO community or from ordinary investors who entrust their funds to the DAO. In addition to financial support, the community may also provide some infrastructure, such as templates for project governance and community, or provide reward tools so that start-up projects can have additional help during their early stage. All investment-related actions of a DAO, including voting, signing investment agreements, transferring, receiving tokens purchased in the future, and so on, can be done through smart contracts on the chain. Through smart contracts, all participants can also automate the relevant operations of the organization and team, to reduce operating costs, improve internal management and enhance the overall transparency of the organization.

The concept of DAO investment was first proposed in 2016. In May 2016, some members of the Ethereum community announced the creation of The DAO, a platform that allows people with a project to pitch their ideas to the community in return for potential funding. Anyone with DAO tokens could vote on the proposal and get corresponding rewards when the project is profitable. The DAO achieved unexpected success in its inception phase that it raised 12.7 million Ether (then US$150 million), making it the highest-value crowdfunding project until 2016. Later, however, the platform was unable to continue due to a hacking incident, and the network forked into two, corresponding nowadays to Ethereum (where the hacking incident was reverted) and Ethereum Classic (which maintained the original chain).

The creation of The DAO has stimulated the thoughts and imagination of developers and crypto community around the world. Currently, many comprehensive DAO investment organizations such as the LAO, MetaCartel Ventures, DAO Square, and Flamingo DAO focusing on NFT asset investment, have emerged in the cryptocurrency space.

12.2 Going mainstream – The listing boom of blockchain projects starts

Many people think that blockchain and crypto assets have their own exit methods, such as issuing tokens, but it is difficult to enter the mainstream traditional financial market. In fact, many companies engaged in blockchain and crypto assets have been recognized by the traditional financial world and entered the traditional capital market. There are many ways of listing, including backdoor listing, IPO listing, direct listing, SPAC listing, and so on.

» Galaxy Digital – The first crypto asset company to go public in the traditional capital market through a backdoor listing

Galaxy Digital Holdings was founded in 2017 by Michael Novogratz, a well-known billionaire and hedge fund manager. Michael is a legendary Wall Street investor with several ups and downs. He worked for the Goldman Sachs Group for over ten years and was the most successful star hedge fund manager of the group. He was later rumored to leave in 2000 for personal reasons. However, he soon joined the private equity firm Fortress Investment as a partner and helped the firm expand its business to real estate, debt securities, hedge funds and other fields. Unfortunately, Michael had to leave Wall Street in 2015 due to his misjudgment of market conditions that led to the firm's huge investment losses. Before leaving, he had already started investing in Bitcoin, and after the fund storm, he got totally involved in the crypto asset investment market and founded Galaxy Digital.

Galaxy Digital is the first financial institution in the world that clearly proposes to provide all-round financial services for the crypto industry and aspires to the Goldman Sachs of Crypto. Its businesses include asset management, trading, principal investment, advisory, and so on, covering all merchant bank functions in the traditional financial world.

Galaxy Digital was officially listed on the TSX – Toronto Stock Exchange – Venture Exchange on August 1, 2018. The listing was made possible through the acquisition of a TSX-listed pharmaceutical company, which was renamed Galaxy Digital Holding Limited, and the reverse takeover of the actual operating entity of Galaxy Digital. It was the largest reverse takeover in the history of this exchange. The listing was delayed several times until August due to various difficulties.

As the crypto asset market entered a long-term downturn at the time of its listing, Galaxy Digital's businesses were also affected. According to its financial report, Galaxy Digital lost US$134 million in the first quarter of 2018, mainly due to the drop in cryptocurrency prices. Therefore, the share price after the IPO did not perform as everyone expected, dropping from an opening price of C$2.75 per share to only C$0.99 by the end of 2018. The founder, Mike, also said that if he had foreseen the long-term downturn of the cryptocurrency market, he might have chosen to go public a year later, but he did not think going public was wrong.

The performance of Galaxy Digital has been shown to slowly recover with the improvement in the market conditions. The short-term fluctuations in performance did not affect the company's long-term growth trend. In particular, its share price rose exponentially in 2020, from C$1 at the beginning of the year to over C$9 by the end of the year. In addition, Galaxy Digital joined the TSX sandbox program in July 2020. After 12 months of trading in the sandbox, Galaxy Digital left and opened trading on the TSX. As of December 2021, the stock price was C$22.

Following Galaxy Digital's successful backdoor listing, other companies, such as Huobi and OKX, have gone public in other markets through the same reverse takeover. In August 2018, Huobi acquired 66.26% of the shares of HKEX-listed Pantronics Holdings Limited which was renamed Huobi Technology Holdings Limited in September 2019. In January 2019, OKX acquired 60.49% of the equity of LEAP Holdings Group Limited which was renamed OKG Technology Holdings Limited on January 7, 2020. The two companies are still in the process of reverse acquisition of actual operating assets.

» Canaan Creative – The "first blockchain stock" to go public through IPO

In November 2019, Canaan Creative, the world's second-largest mining machine manufacturer in terms of computing power, successfully landed on Nasdaq and became the first blockchain enterprise to go public through an IPO.

As a high-profile "first blockchain stock", its road to IPO had some twists and turns. As early as June 2016, Canaan attempted to secure a backdoor listing by acquiring the A-share listed company Shandong Luyitong Intelligent Electric Co., Ltd. but failed. In August 2017, it failed to apply to be listed on the National Equities Exchange and Quotations (NEEQ, known as the New Third Board). These two failures may be related to the sensitive policy on "backdoor listing" and "blockchain" in mainland China at the time. Then it turned to Hong Kong stocks. In May 2018, the company planned to be listed on the main board of the HKEX as a red-chip company, but it was rejected six months later. In 2019, the market once thought that Canaan could be listed on the science and technology innovation board, but it finally chose to go public in the U.S. towards the end of 2019.

Following Canaan, China's mining machinery giant Ebang International Holdings was listed on Nasdaq on June 26, 2020, becoming the second Chinese mining giant that started trading on Nasdaq.

» Coinbase – The first cryptocurrency company to go public through a direct listing

On December 17, 2020, Coinbase announced that it had submitted a draft registration statement on Form S-1 to the SEC for a direct listing. The Form S-1 shows that the revenue of the exchange exceeded US$1.2 billion in 2020, with profits of US$322 million. On April 14, 2021, Coinbase was listed directly on Nasdaq. The reference price for its listing was US$250 per share, the opening price was US$381, the intraday high was US$429.54, and the final closing price was US$328, an increase of 31.31%. The market value reached US$85.8 billion.

Coinbase is the first large cryptocurrency exchange to go public, which was considered by its investors as an important milestone for cryptocurrencies to go mainstream.

Different from an IPO listing, a direct listing is more democratic. The traditional IPO process starts between listed companies and underwriters (large investment banks). Both parties will agree on the terms and structure of the offering, including the opening price, and then underwriters will provide these IPO shares for clients such as hedge funds and mutual funds, while individual investors cannot participate in pricing or buy low-priced stocks. In contrast, in a direct listing where no underwriter is involved, anyone can participate equally in the purchase of shares when they open, and their prices are determined by market supply and demand, which helps to reflect the real value.

Brian Armstrong, CEO of Coinbase, also said, "I hope there will be a real market to determine the price from the first day, not behind closed doors. I think it is more in line with the spirit of the crypto world." Coinbase's opening price of US$381 per share (a market value of approximately US$85.8 billion) also reflects the great enthusiasm of investors.

» SPAC opens a channel for blockchain companies to go public

SPAC, which is short for special purpose acquisition company, is special type company established to acquire a private company by issuing additional shares after the listing (de-SPAC transactions) so that the private company can be listed quickly and the sponsors and investors of SPAC can get the return on investment. SPAC is a shell company without any other business before the de-SPAC transaction completes. SPAC listing is different from traditional IPO listing and backdoor listing, and it is also one of the legal listing methods in the U.S. It has been preferred by many companies engaged in the internet, blockchain, and crypto assets in recent years because of its fast processing, low cost, simple process, and guaranteed financing. In 2020, the total funds raised by companies listed through SPAC had exceeded US$50 billion. We will likely see a number of blockchain companies go public in this way in 2021 and 2022. According to Bloomberg, at least eight companies related to blockchain and digital assets are planning to go public.

Bakkt, a digital asset exchange owned by the Intercontinental Exchange (ICE), announced its merger with the SPAC company VPC Impact Acquisition Holdings and its future listing on Nasdaq with an expected market valuation of US$2 billion. Bakkt is an exchange for cryptocurrency trading launched by the ICE and has many well-known investors, including Horizons Ventures, M12, and Tencent's major shareholder Naspers. ICE announced the Bakkt plan in August 2018, and Bakkt was officially launched in September 2019. Bakkt holds three U.S. licenses for trading (DCM), clearing (DCO), and custody (BitLicense). Its products are mainly Bitcoin futures contracts settled by physical delivery, including monthly contracts and intraday contracts, which are very different from CME cash-delivered futures. But Bakkt's trading volume is small, rarely exceeding US$100 million per day, while CME's daily turnover is at least US$500 million. Both Bakkt and CME operate only five days a week.

Similarly, BlockFi, the largest institutional cryptocurrency lending company in the U.S., will also choose the same way to go public. It is a strong crypto asset lender with lending as a key, which allows its users to mortgage cryptocurrencies, such as Bitcoin and Ethereum, for dollar loans. BlockFi connects the borrower and the lender and assesses the borrower's credit. In addition, ordinary cryptocurrency holders can also open a BlockFi Interest Account (BIA) to obtain certain yield denominated in cryptocurrencies, just like a bank in the crypto world. In addition to lending, users can also trade in digital assets on the BlockFi platform. On top of the services for retail investors, BlockFi has recently started OTC services for institutional investors. BlockFi was founded by Zac Prince in 2017 and it has many famous investors, including Winklevoss Capital, Valar Ventures, Morgan Creek Digital, CMT Digital Ventures, SoFi, and HashKey Capital. SoFi, a leading fintech company , also listed in Nasdaq through SPAC, with a market capitalization of US$12 billion.

References

"Mapping out investors in the crypto ecosystem", The Block, https://www.theblockcrypto.com/amp/genesis/17915/mapping-out-the-investors-in-the-crypto-ecosystem.

"Mapping out the 10 most active crypto funds' 2020 investments", The Block, https://www.theblockresearch.com/mapping-out-the-10-most-active-crypto-funds-2020-investments-87474.

"How legendary VC a16z plays cryptocurrencies: Its investments and strategies", ChainNews, https://www.chainnews.com/articles/603545490608.htm.

"David Swensen VS Warren Buffett: The real investment master", Sina Finance, https://finance.sina.com.cn/stock/usstock/c/2019-11-22/doc-iihnzahi2611382.shtml.

"Mapping out Pantera Capital's portfolio", The Block, https://www.theblockresearch.com/mapping-out-pantera-capitals-portfolio-13154.

"The investment territory of Polychain Capital", Sina, https://k.sina.cn/article_6465571420_18160ca5c01900ixtk.html?from=movie.

"Mapping out Digital Currency Group's portfolio", Coinvigilance, https://coinvigilance.com/mapping-out-digital-currency-groups-portfolio.

Coinbase website, https://www.coinbase.com/products.

CHAPTER 13

OUTLOOK ON BLOCKCHAIN INVESTMENT FOR THE NEXT DECADE

Ten years ago, it might not have been convincing to say that blockchain would grow such a prosperous ecosystem. But now, blockchain has more than 50 million users globally. From individual players, financial institutions, regulators, central banks to multinational organizations, players from various sectors were all taken into this decentralization storm that is sweeping the world, entering a stage where blockchain technology has to be taken seriously and cannot be ignored. The openness and inclusiveness of blockchain leave opportunities for every player to participate.

Bitcoin has been carrying an extraordinary mission since the day it was born. Starting as a new technology discussed in a small group of people, it has increased its influence and developed from a novel combination of ideas to an industry with continuous industrialization and increasing "going outside the box" use cases. Nowadays it is almost known to everyone. In the past ten years, countless people have entered the industry. Some has been flushed with success, some have exited disappointedly, still, most of them are full of ambition and plan to stay in the long term. The great charm of this industry lies in opening up unknown battlefields while realizing the ideas of the pioneers. The industry has been constantly exploring the development boundaries of organizations and the relations of production. It is the fruit of the integration of financial and technological development over the decades.

13.1   The next generation of blockchain comes from an iteration of technology and finance

Technologically speaking, blockchain is not an epoch-making technology compared to the other popular technologies of AI, cloud computing, and big data, but an organic combination of various technologies and the proper implementation of economic incentives. All the technologies used for Bitcoin are not a creation from Satoshi Nakamoto. The distributed ledger, peer-to-peer technology, and asymmetric encryption all originated in the last century. But Bitcoin is an excellent experimentation of a decentralized system with uncensored public participation in a real-world environment. So we believe that blockchain is on the right track in terms of technological innovation, trailblazing new opportunities that will bring a new paradigm to the upcoming generations. Every breakthrough in the blockchain space is not purely on the technological side, but also on improving productivity and optimizing the relations of production, that is, to achieve possibilities with technologies and to ensure feasibility with economic incentives. For example, the shift of consensus protocol from PoW to PoS is a change in the incentive model, while the underlying model has not changed much.

The path of blockchain development is not only outlined by technology but by institutions and economic models. The acceptance of Bitcoin's decentralized concept, with price and commercialization incentivizing each other, is the core path of Bitcoin's development to date, rather than technological innovation driving productivity progress.

Unlike other advanced technologies that are purely efficiency-oriented, blockchain has taken the needs of the general public into consideration by design to allow more people to participate openly and fairly. There might be other subsectors in terms of technology that can evolve into a large-scale industry, despite of being very niche with only big companies and institutions but few individuals involved. The most significant innovation of blockchain is that it allows economic incentives to be completed internally without an external monetary system, forming an excellent closed loop. That means everything, including the efforts made, costs, returns and incomes, is done through the incentives within the ecosystem, creating a new asset class.

Blockchain is inherently a combination of technology and industry. More essentially, blockchain creates two things, a technological industry consisting of distributed systems, consensus mechanisms, cryptography, and a new financial industry consisting of economic incentives plus alternative assets. We will see these two industries developing in parallel, and to some extent mutually reinforcing, but also often independent of each other.

13.1.1 Reinvention of financial applications

We believe that in the future, there will be a simple and easy-to-access version of the financial system on the blockchain, forming a parallel structure with the existing financial system.

(1) The financial system has achieved full digitization and credentialization in the recent 40 years

Every traditional financial organization has all its functions based on the central systems. The three primary functions of banks, i.e., deposits, loans, and remittances, can be realized by modifying the bookkeeping of the accounts of both sides of the business and do not require the transfer of physical assets. All the current financial transactions are based on contracts and bookkeeping that is legally recognized, such as bonds corresponding to deposits, the customer's right to withdraw corresponding to stocks which means that the customer does not directly hold any assets, but the credentials or vouchers (i.e., financial contracts) recognized by the law. A fully digitized and credentialed financial system is the basis for blockchain's reinvention of financial systems. These functions can be implemented through smart contracts on the blockchain, since blockchain has also an accounting system, i.e., identity management system, and is a payment system. Therefore, unlike any economic system tied to physical exchanges, the blockchain was born with the ability to transform the financial system.

DeFi has the potential to become a new financial system. The system's scalability, transaction volumes, and compliance levels are insufficient for large institutions to fully migrate their financial functions. Additionally, institutions not only need to upgrade their technology and processes, migrate, use and scale but also need to deal with the challenges related to legacy old systems. At the same time, no one can afford to give up the benefits of globalization from the current underlying financial infrastructure. In terms of pure economics, there is no incentive to migrate systems unless the new systems can offer effectiveness at least ten times higher than the ones currently used.

There is not just one way ahead for blockchain and traditional institutions are not the target users of decentralized finance. If you look at the potential market, traditional finance is focused on premium customers, while open/decentralized finance serves a long-tail of customers. As the Global Financial Inclusion Index points out, there are still 1.7 billion unbanked people in the world, but 2/3 of them have mobile phones, which can be potential users of decentralized finance. Traditional finance will clearly compete for this market. However, the problem is that traditional finance has certain customer acquisition costs, resulting in a market gap and bringing the need for decentralized finance.

(2) The reason blockchain can revamp the financial system is that it is an underlying layer for clearing and settlement

Clearing and settlement is an important function and the underlying infrastructure in the financial system. Unlike the upper layer of payment activities, clearing and settlement requires higher stability and processing capability. The payment systems in major developed economies around the world have an efficient clearing and settlement layer at the bottom, such as the real-time gross settlement

(RTGS) or the deferred net settlement (DNS), like TARGET2 in Europe, CHAPS in the U.K., FEDWIRE/CHIPS in the U.S., and China's large-value real-time payment system. The traditional settlement layer, which is considered as a tool and serves as an internal network, is supervised by central banks or industry associations and used by members who have the needs to settle in fiat currency.

The blockchain is an underlying clearing and settlement layer that is also in real-time and gross, except that a distributed system is used, and the settlement is made with open network token. At the same time, participation is also open to the general public. Payment, clearing, and settlement can be done at the same layer. The future public chain, that can be a global settlement network, needs to have the following features: 1) a consistent consensus; 2) a high value; 3) a fast-processing speed, which are the three factors of the "Impossible Triangle", i.e., security, decentralization, and scalability. The future public chain network (or its alternative) will have to give up one of the three parameters (a certain degree of decentralization generally) in exchange for being the underlying layer for clearing/settlement unless there is an epoch-making technology to break this architecture.

13.1.2 The underlying assets for multi-asset investments

Decentralized assets will officially become an important asset class.

It has been talked for years about institutions flowing into the industry, institutions holding crypto assets, and many others, but it is not that easy when we look at the path of institutions entering the industry: First, there should be a compliant platform, such as Bitcoin trusts and CME/Bakkt's Bitcoin futures. Second, there is a good opportunity. Behind the institutions is the demand of ordinary people, who must recognize the value of Bitcoin. Third, demand on hedge for unknown risks. The global central banks' easing policies followed the 2008 financial crisis have already caused a significant increase in asset prices, which was further exacerbated by the Covid-19 epidemic, with the Federal Reserve's balance sheet having more than doubled in size to that before. A large portion of this excess liquidity can be absorbed by the capital markets, while the other is to be translated into higher prices of consumer goods. Stocks and gold have already reached historically high in terms of prices. Therefore, there is a need for an alternative model that can hedge such risk in a completely different way. The answer is Bitcoin, something like gold, but better.

Still, if institutions accept only Bitcoin, then it will be an end for blockchain's development, meaning that the industry is no more valuable over the next ten years than it was in the past decade with that epoch-making technology. So, we think that in terms of overall asset attributes, blockchain will transition to another asset class that can be accepted by mainstream institutions, namely, incentive tokens for distributed systems.

We see the value discovery path for blockchain assets as below.

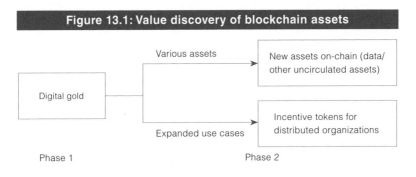

Figure 13.1: Value discovery of blockchain assets

Source: HashKey Capital

We have seen such a trend in the second generation of public chains represented by Ethereum and the third generation of public chains represented by Polkadot and Filecoin. The biggest difference between them and Bitcoin is that they are not just a means of payment but they also form a self-contained ecosystem that achieves particular utility. Despite being designed as a payment utility initially, Bitcoin has been moving closer to digital gold.

Utility tokens will also get a new meaning to be a substantial economic system that can solve typical problems, returning to the economy's essence. It can be understood as a new form of stakeholder or a new type of proof of stake. An organization, whether a company, a corporation or a government, has numerous stakeholders. When such an organization is a joint-stock company, the company's usufruct and voting rights will be turned into a form of stock to be listed publicly on the market for participation, which is a way to decentralize the value of the joint-stock company. However, it cannot be seen as fully decentralized of company equity in such a way. It represents only a part of the stakeholder, i.e., shareholders' interests, but there are other stakeholders, including employees, upstream and downstream suppliers, end-users. Some of them enjoy the benefits of the company's development to a certain extent, while some do not. An open distributed organization incentive token can satisfy the common good and become the emerging proof of stake for general stakeholders to participate.

13.1.3　New battlefield – Data as assets

(1) Lack of assets

As a value exchange network, Blockchain currently lacks tangible assets that are tradable. Bitcoin could be a kind of digital gold, but Bitcoin with digital gold as the only utility is not sustainable, which will lose value without blockchain as the solid medium of exchange. It will take a long time to phase in and adapt to the revamped financial system mentioned previously. There are too few valuable or consensus assets in the blockchain space compared to the physical world.

(2) Traditional assets also rely on consensus

The prices of most assets in the physical world, such as stocks, real estate and fixed income, are also produced by consensus, guaranteed by contracts, and supported by a set of pricing theories. It, however, took a century to be accepted by academia, business, investment institutions and even ordinary people. Think it over, the so-called guarantee of contracts and cash flow support are all based on trusts, which can change rather quickly. That is the reason that there are fluctuations in asset prices. It is just that the degree of trust is different, and the entities to be trusted do not exactly the same.

It is necessary to introduce real-world assets on chain in terms of value exchange, which has been going on for years and is trying to be compliant to be issued as securities, also known as STOs. Yet, there are challenges. Tools like asset securitization already exist, and most of the valuable and illiquid assets have already been found. The issuance of small assets with poor liquidity will not be welcomed by the market.

(3) Data as assets

What are the assets that have consensus off-chain and can run on the blockchain? We believe that these can be found in IoT, i.e., a completely new type of data in the real world. The amount of data generated expands with the increase of nodes and the communication between nodes. On the other hand, as the data transmission rate gets higher, the amount of data generated increases. IoT with 5G is an answer to solve problems of data source and transmission speed. The centralized processing model is not able to process the data generated by a large number of nodes and faster transmission speed, and that is where the help of distributed database is needed, which is to process related data locally. This kind of data, with a steady flow and continuous supply, can be an asset on the blockchain. The exchangeable, usable and computable data is the beginning of the future data assets being activated. In addition to the data created by 5G and IoT, legacy data can also be put on-chain.

(4) Legacy data: Discrete, to be leveraged

A large amount of data is generated globally every year and is controlled by internet companies. There is a large amount of data located in information silos. Many historical data are lying dormant and unexploited effectively in various SMEs, government departments, utilities, civil organizations, and many other entities. But the value of these data lies in their uniqueness and irreproducibility, such as consumer data on water supply, electricity, coal, transportation, medical care and insurance, which are completely different from the internet data.

Internet company tends to give the data back to the general public, which is a policy-oriented decision. For example, the EU and the United States have begun to regulate internet companies to prevent data misuse. In the future, the data will be controlled by the users. If it is not utilized, privacy will be protected, but the value of data will be hidden. When the data is returned to the public, and there is a need to monetize those data, a truly free, open and tradable market is needed for such exchange. Users can also choose to authorize the internet companies to take control of their data for value exchange in the lack of a marketplace. The exchange of data between customers and businesses will inevitably come with price suppression. Even if there is no price suppression or discrimination, such kind of exchange tends to be unfair in the end, with a variety of hidden costs added by internet companies.

The underlying network is provided by the blockchain, a peer-to-peer network that is truly open to the public. Blockchain can bring exchange value to data assets but does not protect the value of the assets. Secure multi-party computing based on cryptography can ensure that the ownership is separated from the right to use. Protecting data privacy is an important trend around the world. The secure multi-party computing based on cryptography enables the data to have computable and exchangeable value, with the underlying exchange and clearing network based on blockchain, providing a place and function for the exchange and circulation of data assets. Data assets can come from multiple sources such as the internet of Things, the activated data from information silos, or the redistributed data after being controlled by the users.

13.1.4 Community-driven investments are worth noting

How to invest in the blockchain industry is the central component of this book. Although investment is an old business practice, there is nothing special about investment in the blockchain industry compared with that in other fields of artificial intelligence, big data and cloud computing. However, according to our knowledge, blockchain investment will be different from traditional investment experience.

One exciting direction is that the investment can be community-driven. Traditionally, the main investment body is institutions and retail investors. But in the future, community-driven investment organizations may boom, such as the LAO, an investment organization launched by OpenLaw. Members of the LAO can participate in multiple decision-making processes such as voting, allocation of collected funds and investment by purchasing the LAO's equity tokens. Each member can contribute a certain amount of Ethereum to get a percentage of the voting rights and proceeds. The LAO will then allocate collected funds to projects built on

Ethereum and make investments through the Moloch smart contract. With the LAO, members can make investment decisions together through voting, which has already seen support to multiple projects such as decentralized asset management, trading derivatives, NFTs, development tools and infrastructure.

Looking at the DeFi boom in the summer of 2020, Twitter became the central battleground for KOLs to express their opinions and attract public attention. Projects were launching their products on Twitter with their founders (or anonymous teams) speaking out through KOLs to draw various types of funding. Project's progress has constantly been released on Twitter, attracting waves of followers. Some traditional funds also seemed to adapt quickly to such a situation and "shoutout" on Twitter. News from the community continued to spread on Twitter. The Chinese community also shifted from their original battleground to Twitter and soon got used to the new ways of getting information. The whole process of DeFi projects from their launch to fundraising is quite community-driven and much different from the previous financing process of crypto projects. Previously, crypto projects had to have a white paper when launching. However, it is no longer the case with the rise of DeFi. There was no white paper, and a project was launched with the founding team releasing an introduction on public platforms and the code on Github. The product and incentive (mining) mechanisms were similar to others, especially those that forked other projects. Nonetheless, such projects could still get hyped, receiving quite a lot of funding, sometimes not less than what they could get from a VC. KOLs analyze and make a guide on investing in the project, helping the project to gain traction.

Therefore, it is reasonable to believe that community-driven investment will be a type of blockchain investment in the future, for it is much closer to the ideology of the mass and more in line with the decentralized spirit of blockchain, which gives ordinary participants a feeling of contributing to the project. However, there are drawbacks to community-driven investment. When the overall market is bullish, the problems tend to be covered up due to the mindless flood in and the rising value of the project. Even though one project goes down, there will be other projects popped up.

However, investment is a professional sector that requires specific knowledge. Community participation will only form a closed loop of the capital flow but cannot identify the value, requiring professional screening skills. Community-driven investment raises the possibility that VC and community-driven investment could exist non-exclusively in the blockchain space, and there is even some overlap. For example, a partner of a VC can also be a leader or KOL in the community, who can help promote the project in the community with the advantages of different fields.

13.2   The direction of investment in the next decade

For future investments, the following areas will be our focus.

13.2.1   Exploring business value

The development of blockchain will go on along the four-stage path of technical development, extended application, community building and commercial realization. The value of blockchain in the future will be determined by two components: the community and consensus value achieved by the condensation of belief, and the actual business value, which is generated by the combination of technology and application.

The value of blockchain's early development lies in consensus, with Bitcoin being the best example. The consensus cannot be valued independently but depends on the business value. Even Ethereum, the so-called application-oriented chain, is quite weak in business value. That is why Bitcoin achieves such success by relying only on its value, while the application-oriented chain cannot go too far by consensus. The blockchain can be truly revitalized when a chain can be adopted commercially.

Consortium blockchains are the earliest blockchains that can be put into commercial use. Current consortium blockchains are constantly reducing costs for the sake of commercial use, which is more like polishing a business-to-business internet product. Consortium chains do not need to involve compliance and can be launch in production quickly. It is expected that the commercial booming of public chains will happen much later, which may be a platform that covers both businesses and customers. The business logic to be carried out is more complex. See the following chart we concluded that shows the value embodiment of the two types of chains.

Figure 13.2: Value distribution of public and alliance chains

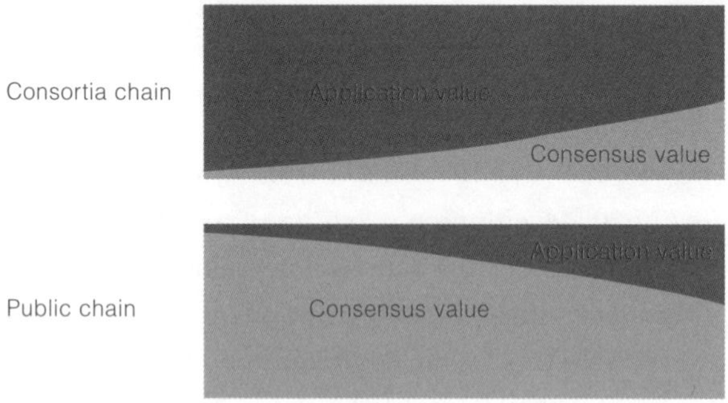

Consortia chain — Application value — Consensus value

Public chain — Consensus value — Application value

Source: HashKey Capital

Enterprise-level applications are the earliest use cases where consortium chain is adopted, such as R3, HyperLedger, Facebook's

Libra (renamed to Diem) that has shifted from a public chain to consortium chain, and JPM's Quorum. Major enterprises have also launched their blockchain platforms in China, such as Ant Financial, Tencent, JD and Baidu. The enterprise-level blockchain market is relatively small but growing at a faster pace.

IDC estimates that the overall spending level of the blockchain market in China will reach US$2.28 billion by 2024, with a CAGR of about 51%.

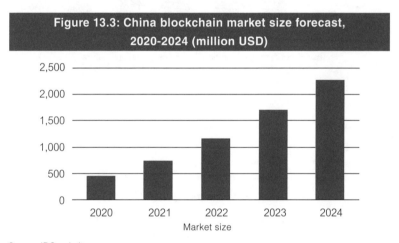

Figure 13.3: China blockchain market size forecast, 2020-2024 (million USD)

Source: IDC website

China is currently the second-largest blockchain market in the world. IDC estimates that China's total investment in blockchain technology solutions would reach US$470 million in 2020, with a CAGR of 60% from 2019 to 2023.

The global blockchain market spending is also expected to reach more than US$14 billion by 2023.

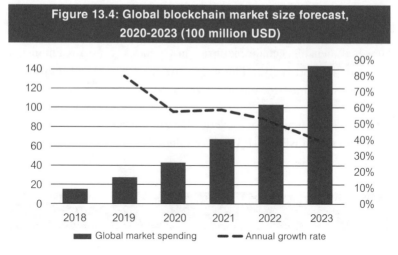

Figure 13.4: Global blockchain market size forecast, 2020-2023 (100 million USD)

Source: IDC website

IDC's top ten forecasts also provide ideas for blockchain commercialization, and we pick out a few that we think are of high likeliness:

- **Cross-border payments.** By 2023, 40% of China's top-tier financial institutions will use blockchain networks to process peer-to-peer cross-border payments.

- **Blockchain services.** By 2023, Chinese companies will spend 29% of their enterprise management service expenses on blockchain services.

- **AI and blockchain.** By 2024, more than 50% of regulated companies in China will apply blockchain to support AI applications.

- **Distributed supply chain.** By 2024, 85% of container shipments in China will be tracked by blockchain, half of which will use blockchain-powered cross-border payments.

- **Digital currency.** By 2023, 10% of cities in China will start using blockchain-based digital currencies to promote economic stability and e-commerce development.

China's industrial blockchain holds great promise. For example, the enterprise blockchain technology underlying infrastructure PlatONE, developed by Wanxiang Blockchain and MatrixElements, proposes an enterprise-level consortium infrastructure featuring privacy computing to meet the requirements of enterprise sharing and privacy. It provides a variety of innovative technologies and features, including secure multi-party computing, cryptography implantation such as homomorphic encryption, optimized and efficient consensus, high TPS, complete and easy-to-use enterprise toolchains and components, optimized user/permission model, and multiprogramming languages support, which are designed to solve the current dilemma in the development of consortium chains. Outside China, we have also found many companies committed to exploring opportunities in existing business systems to be supplemented with blockchain systems. Lightnet Group, for example, which we have been involved with, is supported by several leading Southeast Asian financial institutions, using a native blockchain network based on Stellar to increase the efficiency of cross-border remittances.

13.2.2   Combining investment and building

Although blockchain was born in the cypherpunk community, the development is closely related to the investment community. Investment in many cases is not only what is called traditional investment, but also in the form of donations, grants, and rewards. Many teams are launched to work on solving some protocol issues or new features. As more features are developed, the composability of those features becomes a product, which requires more workforce, resources, and sometimes even an organization to expand the product. That is where continuous financing is required. However, most projects stop before productization, resulting in many investments failing to achieve the desired outcome. While from another point of view, the industry needs trial and error, these can be counted as a contribution to the building of the industry. The trial-and-error costs still exist on a large scale. For example, the foundations of public chains like Ethereum and Polkadot are also sparing no effort to allocate money to projects in the form of grants.

13.2.3　Exploring compliant products

Blockchain has intrinsic financial attributes, which is one of the reasons that it has been sweeping the globe in the past 14 years. As a fact that cannot be ignored, finance will always be followed with hype, and if there is hype, there is a market. But what about the future? Blockchain as a technology does not have any concerns in terms of compliance, but on the other hand, its financial aspect is untenable without regulation. As the carrier of tokens, public chains are inseparable from their financial properties.

As an investment institution, one of the inevitable problems we face is how to build a compliant product framework so that blockchain, as a financial product, can be known by the public. One approach is to go for the appropriate license in areas with relative regulations in place, which depends mainly on the United States. The SEC's approval of the Bitcoin ETF is a big step forward in blockchain compliance and sets a precedent for other countries around the world. Blockchain companies have gone public so that the compliance of their operations has been transparently monitored.

The second approach is to actively engage in related business in some blockchain-friendly regions, such as Hong Kong, China, and Singapore. As far as investment products are concerned, these places, at one or more levels, have started to focus on the regulation of virtual assets, covering aspects of exchanges, investments, asset management, token issuance and security tokens. This can be done even under the current legal framework, just not as compliant and less accessible than traditional products. For example, they cannot be publicly offered and sold to retail investors.

The third approach is a long-term approach, which is to issue the fully compliant products after establishing the corresponding compliance system framework in one or several major capital markets. The issuance structure of current financial products is not complicated, but it needs to accept virtual assets as the future underlying assets. This approach has already started the compliance process in major countries and regions (the United States, Japan, Europe, Singapore and Hong Kong, China), but still requires global regulators to work together.

If regulations in Hong Kong, China and Singapore are fully completed, this compliant market will be even larger. Then the final step left for compliant investment products is to develop a product that is available for retail investors and crowdfunding.

13.2.4　Strong support to the ecosystem

The future ecosystem will also be made in an investment plus building mode. Our building model is also mainly ecosystem-oriented, i.e., relying on a large ecosystem like ours to empower projects, such as customers, communities, circles, and partners, including investors. We combine investment and project building with a pre-investment (funds support), plus an active post-investment management empowerment model. This process helps the European and American projects we invested to speed up the expansion into the Asian market and to open up the Asian market for projects through the way of cooperation. Even within Asia, information exchange between different regions can be interoperable. For example, the Bootcamp program initiated by Wanxiang Blockchain and Polkadot is a one-stop service for high-quality blockchain projects to connect with business resources and obtain technical support, helping projects accelerate their growth.

13.2.5 Cooperation between projects and academic research

Another model is the cooperation between projects. Our investment portfolio consists of over 100 projects, covering the technology infrastructure layers, middleware, upper-layer applications, financial services, and many other levels. The projects themselves have their own needs that correspond to each other. Therefore, through such an active model, the growth of these projects can be accelerated, the barriers between different projects can be broken down, and similar projects can get the opportunity to communicate, which is working well so far. Another progress is the direct funding of academic institutions. Funding research institutions on various technologies are helping to look for investment directions while building the ecosystem.

13.2.6 Finding out the real use cases

Another aspect of building an ecosystem lies in expanding our ecosystem and finding out real use cases for the commercialization of blockchain. As mentioned before, the business value of public chains will take a long time to emerge. At present, in addition to the use cases featuring cross-border remittance, or broad payment and asset reserve, there is still a long way to go for the further application of public chains, that is, from the asset/monetary properties to solving practical problems. The public chain has its own value positioning. For example, Ethereum is positioned as the "world computer", which is now shifting towards the bottom layer of financial asset clearing and settlement. That means, in the future, all financial assets and on-chain assets will use Ethereum as an underlying layer for exchange, and the security of the Ethereum blockchain will act as a global security guarantee. Dfinity – a nonprofit organization that develops the internet computer, a decentralized, open-source, general-purpose blockchain designed to host smart contracts – is beginning to redefine the term of world computer will position itself as part of the public internet, allowing for the widespread building of dApps and Apps, internal enterprise systems, and one-stop hosting of global software. The positioning and the future development of many public chains are mostly considered from the technical perspective, without considering the economic aspect. But just like the early development of the internet, it is only a protocol that has been established. It is not predictable as to what to run on it, how to run it, and what the effect is. The real leap of the internet occurred in the mobile internet era when there was a giant leap in infrastructure. If we draw an analogy with blockchain, the actual infrastructure construction has not yet arrived, and the large-scale commercial adoption is far behind.

13.2.7 Expanding the trend of digitalization

Digital migration is an inevitable trend for the entire humanity. Most of the traditional economy runs far away from users. While entering the internet era, users are directly facing the products of the largest internet companies, uploading their data to be used by internet companies. Our goal is to find opportunities along with such trends. IoT is a direction we are bullish on, and many industry insiders also believe that the combination of IoT, 5G and blockchain is a magnificent breakthrough. In a broader sense, IoT is a frame of relationships like the internet, but essentially a distributed, fragmented network that can be exchanged, which requires a blockchain network for bookkeeping and exchange to guarantee the authenticity of the data and provide a basis for exchanging value.

Another direction is digital finance, with open finance represented by DeFi making a prelude for the development of digital finance. A reliable digital asset exchange network will be born on the blockchain, and considering that they involve assets, it can be treated as finance. It is a logical development process. Optimistically, it is expected that the volume of digital assets will be about the same size as traditional assets in quite a long time.

Digitalization is a broader topic than blockchain. Being the underlying layer of trust and exchange of assets, it is an indispensable part of the blockchain. Only when all business logic is fully digitized, blockchain will show its great potential. In ten years, when we enter an immersive digital lifestyle, we will surely pay tribute to the contributions of the past pioneers with gratitude while looking back on the 20-year history of blockchain development. Our investment process is just a small footnote on the driving force for the unstoppable digitalization. The privilege to witness such an epoch-making revolution and find out opportunities that yet emerged in this great wave excites us every time we think about it.

References

"IDC: China's blockchain market size to grow at a CAGR of 51% over the next five years", IDC website, https://www.idc.com/getdoc.jsp?containerId=prCHC46978820.

"IDC forecasts slowing growth in China blockchain market spending size to reach $470 million by 2020", IDC website, https://www.idc.com/getdoc.jsp?containerId=prCHC46302420.

APPENDIX

GLOSSARY

Terminologies	Definition
Address	The transfer address on the blockchain, can be seen as a bank account number. Addresses typically derive from a public key.
Bitcoin	The world's first peer-to-peer, decentralized blockchain network. Bitcoin is the name of the network and the name of the native currency that runs on it.
Block	A type of data structure within the blockchain database, where transaction data is permanently recorded.
Blockchain	A distributed peer-to-peer network that links blocks together in a chain-like structure.
Cold wallet	A physical device that keeps the keys associated with a cryptocurrency wallet completely offline.
Consensus algorithm	A set of rules for different nodes in a distributed network to achieve agreement on a single data value among distributed processes or systems.
Cryptography	A branch of mathematics that can provide security in the form of mathematical verifications for activities such as encryption and decryption. Participants are permitted to hold secret keys.
DAO	A decentralized autonomous organization (DAO) is an organization represented by rules encoded as a computer program that is transparent, controlled by the organization members, and not influenced by a central government.
dApp	A dApp or decentralized application is an application that can operate autonomously, typically through the use of smart contracts, that runs on a decentralized computing blockchain system.
DeFi	DeFi or decentralized finance is a type of dApp that uses blockchain to remove third parties in otherwise centralized financial transactions.
Distributed ledger	A database that stores data geographically spread across a network of nodes.
Distributed network	A network that processes and stores data through a geographically spread network of nodes.

Terminologies	Definition
Ethereum	The world's first blockchain network with smart contract functions.
Fork	The creation of a new version from an existing blockchain network.
Hash	A hash is a cryptographic function that converts any input into an encrypted output of a fixed length.
Hash rate	The number of hash functions a computer can execute per second.
Hot wallet	A wallet that is connected to the internet.
Mining	The process of validating transactions on the blockchain through executing hash functions. Miners get rewarded for correctly validating transactions.
Mining pool	A business or company that pools miners' computing power and specializes in providing services such as hosting, operation, and maintenance of mining machines.
Peer to peer	A network where nodes interact directly with each other, without the need for a third party.
PoS	A type of consensus mechanism for the blockchain networks to reach consensus. With Proof-of-stake (POS), cryptocurrency owners validate block transactions based on the number of coins a validator stakes.
PoW	Proof of Work is a consensus mechanism and a form of cryptographic proof in the blockchain network, where one party (the prover) proves to others (the verifiers) that a certain amount of a specific computational effort has been expended.
Private key	A secret string that is used in the blockchain network, similar to a password. In cryptocurrency, private keys are used to sign transactions, prove ownership of a blockchain address and decrypt data in public-key cryptography.
Public key	A cryptographic string used to facilitate transactions between parties, allowing users to receive cryptocurrencies in their accounts. Every public key is associated with a private key and they are both part of public key cryptography.

Terminologies	Definition
Smart contract	A program consisting of functions that run on a blockchain network and automatically performs specific functions. Smart contracts were first proposed by computer scientist and cryptographer Nick Szabo in 1994.
Token	Also known as digital currency, digital asset and virtual asset. It refers to a payment currency running on a blockchain.